The shooting of my first man, face-to-face, was not covered by the Infantry School back at Ft. Benning, and I was deeply shaken. I'm glad I didn't kill him. The shock was bad enough. Going through the slam-bang tank duel beforehand hadn't helped. I was still trembling a few seconds later and would have been unable even to defend myself. My first hour in combat had been enough for my lifetime, and I was wondering if I'd last the day. . . .

IF YOU SURVIVE

George Wilson

PRESIDIO
PRESS

BALLANTINE BOOKS • NEW YORK

A Presidio Press Book
Published by The Random House Publishing Group
Copyright © 1987 by George D. Wilson

Published in the United States by Presidio Press, an imprint of The Random House Publishing Group, a division of Random House, Inc., New York, and simultaneously in Canada by Random House of Canada Limited, Toronto.

Presidio Press and colophon are trademarks of Random House, Inc.

ISBN 978-0-8041-0003-8

Printed in the United States of America

www.presidiopress.com

OPM   29   28   27   26   25

TO MY WIFE, FLORINE, AND OUR CHILDREN,
DAVID, STEPHEN, KEVIN, KRISTIN AND JONATHAN

Acknowledgment

I gratefully acknowledge the support and encouragement of Howard Thurlow, formerly of the Cannon Company of the 22nd Infantry, often attached to the 2nd Battalion. His help typing and editing from my longhand was invaluable.

CONTENTS

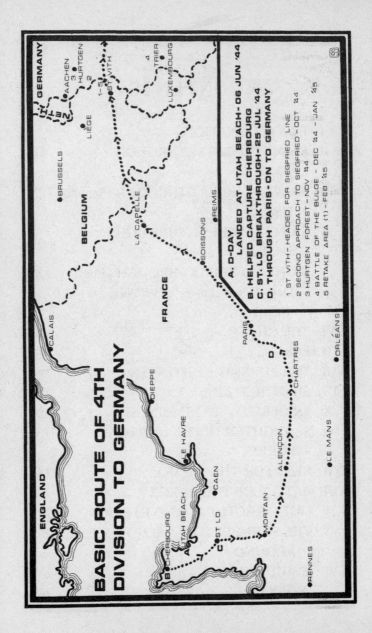

BASIC ROUTE OF 4TH
DIVISION TO GERMANY

A. D-DAY
   LANDED AT UTAH BEACH - 06 JUN '44
B. HELPED CAPTURE CHERBOURG
C. ST. LO BREAKTHROUGH - 25 JUL '44
D. THROUGH PARIS - ON TO GERMANY

1 ST VITH - HEADED FOR SIEGFRIED LINE
2 SECOND APPROACH TO SIEGFRIED - OCT '44
3 HURTGEN FOREST - NOV '44
4 BATTLE OF THE BULGE - DEC '44 - JAN '45
5 RETAKE AREA (1) - FEB '45

ENGLAND

GERMANY

NETH

BELGIUM

FRANCE

CALAIS
DIEPPE
LE HAVRE
BRUSSELS
LIÈGE
AACHEN
HURTGEN
ST VITH
TRIER
LUXEMBOURG
LA CAPELLE
SOISSONS
REIMS
CAEN
CHERBOURG
UTAH BEACH
ST LO
MORTAIN
ALENÇON
CHARTRES
PARIS
LE MANS
ORLÉANS
RENNES

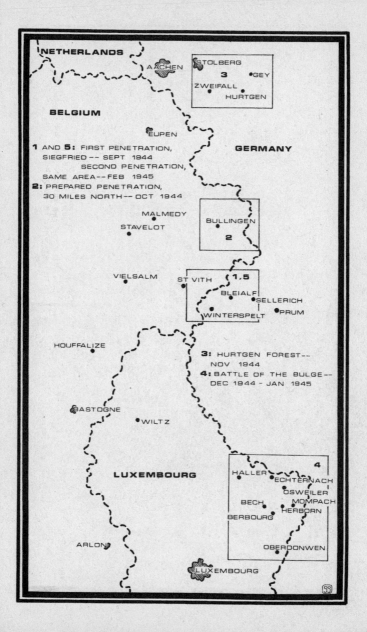

NETHERLANDS

AACHEN

STOLBERG
3
GEY
ZWEIFALL
HURTGEN

BELGIUM

EUPEN

GERMANY

1 AND 5: FIRST PENETRATION,
SIEGFRIED -- SEPT 1944
    SECOND PENETRATION,
SAME AREA--FEB 1945
2: PREPARED PENETRATION,
30 MILES NORTH-- OCT 1944

MALMEDY
STAVELOT

BULLINGEN
2

VIELSALM
ST VITH
1.5
BLEIALF
SELLERICH
PRUM
WINTERSPELT

HOUFFALIZE

3: HURTGEN FOREST--
NOV 1944
4: BATTLE OF THE BULGE--
DEC 1944 - JAN 1945

BASTOGNE
WILTZ

LUXEMBOURG

4
HALLER
ECHTERNACH
OSWEILER
BECH
MOMPACH
HERBORN
BERBOURG

ARLON

OBERDONWEN

LUXEMBOURG

I

INDOCTRINATION

Even though America was heavily engaged in World War II in the fall of 1942, I felt safe in enrolling in college because the Marines and the Navy had turned me down. I wore glasses. They were still being very selective, and anyone who wore glasses was an automatic reject. However, the Army was not the least bit disturbed by my slight visual impairment and on September 19, 1942, drafted me as a raw recruit—just a week before classes opened at Michigan State, where I had been awarded a football scholarship.

A group of us were inducted at Fort Custer, Michigan, where we were issued uniforms and long-needled shots, sat through films on venereal disease, and took a lengthy IQ test. Two days later we boarded a train with blinds drawn and were on our way to parts unknown. Rumors as to our destination quickly began, but no one guessed correctly. After two days, the train finally stopped, and some of us sneaked a peek through the blinds to discover we were in Macon, Georgia.

Camp Wheeler was to be my home for the next five months. The camp was a few miles outside Macon and, by a long coincidence, happened to be only about 135 miles from my birthplace in the hills of northern Georgia. We were immediately screened for assignment by sergeants who seemed to know all about us. I requested the Army Air Force but was denied. The sergeant informed me my basic training would be with a special battalion of men who were considered to have officer potential. At this point the Army really had very little knowledge of our abilities, except for whatever the IQ test was worth.

For the next seven weeks we struggled through a basic infantry course, with the usual KP and guard duties, with lectures on fundamentals such as military courtesy, some weapons training and actual firing on the rifle range, bayonet drill, and hand-to-hand combat. Everything was very strange and new to me. I had never been away from home for more than a week and was totally ignorant of the Army. At first I didn't know a corporal from a sergeant, and officers seemed like gods to me because everybody, including the sergeants, jumped to rigid attention when they appeared.

For reasons quite unknown to me, I was picked immediately as an acting squad leader over twelve men. Possibly this was because of my athletic background or maybe because, to them, I appeared eager to learn how to be a soldier.

The second half of basic was in communications. We were trained in the use of field phones, laying wire, using codes and code devices, and message center operation. The training was interesting and our lieutenant was an excellent instructor.

Near the end of basic we were told we could apply for Officer Candidate School (OCS), and seventy-eight of the men in my company signed up. Then we found it was not quite as simple to get accepted as it at first appeared. We were required to go before a board of six officers chaired by a colonel. They really gave us the third degree. We were asked all sorts of questions, some very personal. Our military bearing and quickness of response seemed as important as the correctness of our answers. It seemed as though they deliberately tried to get us confused, and apparently in many cases they succeeded in doing so, for they eliminated sixty-one and passed only seventeen for admittance to OCS.

At the end of basic training the seventeen of us from my company along with some others from the rest of the battalion were moved about a mile across camp to Non-Commissioned Officers School. This was the final step before OCS. It was a very tough, intensive four-week course, and only five of us passed and were promoted to corporal and made eligible for OCS.

At last we were sent across the state to the Infantry School at Fort Bennning. For the next three months the training was most concentrated and intense. We worked day and night in both classroom and field. It was a damn good, rough, tough, cram course on weapons, tactics, map reading, close order drill, field maneuvers, and basic infantry training.

Some of the men could not take the rugged physical program or the mental strain of the classes, and so they flunked out and were quietly transferred. Only two of my original group survived to get commissions. Somehow I made it, and on May 8, 1943, I was duly commissioned a second lieutenant in the Army of the United States. By Act of Congress we were now officers and gentlemen. Some called us "Ninety-Day Wonders."

My first assignment as an officer was to Camp Croft, South Carolina, as a basic training instructor. Then, only a month later, a group of us were picked out and dispatched to Camp Hood, Texas, to help start up a newly conceived seven-week crash course for the basic infantry training of college students. After this basic, they would be returned to college—and thus Uncle Sam would not call on the country's future brains as cannon fodder, short of dire emergency.

This experimental program never really got off the ground; only eight hundred men or so were trained in six whole months, by enough instructors to cadre an entire division of many thousands. Most of the time we instructors were bored silly and exhausted by the effort of trying to find something to occupy our time. Having no students, the instructors practiced instructing each other. After a while, even the brass gave up on the futile effort. So we played horseshoes, volleyball, and found similar pastimes for six months. My own training regiment did not receive a single college man to train. Finally, three days before Christmas in 1943, thirty of the officers from my regiment were sent to the Eighty-sixth Division, then on maneuvers in the swamps of Louisiana.

We struggled through the mud and rain and ice of the swamps until February 1944, and learned very little—other than how to exist in such terrible conditions. The weather was worse than any I had ever been through in Michigan.

Next we moved into nearby Camp Livingston, Louisiana, and resumed regular garrison training. The Army brass decided, however, that the Eighty-sixth Division was not fit for combat as a unit and began to break it up. Almost every day we received orders to ship out a few more men and officers as overseas replacements. It became quite a tough job choosing the men for the list, and each unit commander naturally tried to hang on to his best men. Finally, in April, 1944, my own turn came, and I was ordered to Camp Shanks, New York, with seven days leave at home en route.

At Camp Shanks we received all of our overseas shots, and a few days later we were on our way to England in a huge convoy of about one hundred ships, an awesome sight for this young man. After twelve days in the North Atlantic bucking through a tremendous storm that left most of us seasick—and a little jumpy from two submarine alerts during which our destroyer escorts dropped quite a few depth charges—we arrived safely at Liverpool, England, about April 20, 1944.

The first stop was Camp Warminster, a British Army base camp near Bristol. The base was overflowing with American infantry replacements, officers and men bound for combat divisions to replace battle casualties. We at once began some very limited training, mostly to keep us busy. Weapons were carefully cleaned and inspected daily. We also played a lot of ping-pong, and I had the fun of pitching a little baseball.

When D day—June 6, 1944—finally arrived, we watched its progress on a big operations map in the officers' quarters. From this very distant, very safe position, it was hard to imagine the real fighting. Then, late that evening, we began to get a few of the wounded paratroopers and some who had landed in the Channel. They were from the Eighty-second Airborne, and we crowded around to hear their excited on-the-scene stories of the fighting. Many of them were on the way back to their units the very next day.

Soon replacements were needed, and we were on our way to an assembly area near Plymouth. Security was very tight, and we could only learn that we would be leaving shortly for France. The next day as I looked into the anxious faces of the officers around me on board the Canadian Landing Craft Infantry (LCI) leaving the crowded harbor at Plymouth it struck me suddenly: *This is it*. We were headed directly into the war. Now, near the end of June 1944, our allies had slowly gained a foothold in Normandy, France.

Underway, each of the officers aboard seemed to be quietly facing his own personal battle with reality. It still seems a foolish mistake to have had the entire load on our LCI be all officers. The loss of a boatload of junior-grade combat officers would make very big problems for the people tasked with the manning of combat units.

Now the words of the port commander leapt back vividly. "You are going to Normandy as *replacements*." This could only mean that the position each of us was being sent to fill had become vacant because the other officer was killed in action (KIA), wounded in action (WIA), missing in action (MIA), or a nonbattle casualty (NBC). All sorts of dismal thoughts chased one another across my mind.

I wondered about my fiancée, Florine. How long before she would know I was at the front? Would I ever see her again and hold her in my arms? If I got wounded badly, would she still love me? Would I be able to support her? Somehow it seemed clear to me that I would make it.

I was brought back to the present by the drone of the duty officer calling the roll. As I listened and watched each respond it was obvious we were a mixed lot. I did not recognize anyone. It probably didn't matter, because we would all be sent to different units once ashore.

As hunger began to gnaw at my empty stomach, it occurred to me that none of us had rations. Somehow we had been sent aboard without chow. Someone took our problem to the Canadian naval captain, who came to our rescue with some cans of split pea soup from his emergency rations, one can each. Each can held about two cups and was heated by a cylinder in the center filled with some chemical that burned. Instructions told us to punch two holes in the top of the can before igniting the fuel, otherwise the can could explode. The soup was delicious, and I've loved pea soup ever since.

Someone was shouting, "Look at all the ships," and we jumped up to see a glorious sight. Ships by the hundreds were everywhere ahead as we approached Normandy. We strained to see the armada. Huge balloons were straining at cables. They were supposed to keep enemy aircraft from flying too low. The harbor was busy as a beehive. Cargo nets were being loaded in waiting amphibious trucks, called ducks. A steady stream came out for a load and then headed back to shore. Vehicles like ants seemed to crawl all over the beaches and inland roads.

We lurched forward as our LCI came to a grinding halt on the flat bottom. Gangplanks were lowered on each side of the bow, and we started single file down into the water. Holding our weapons high, we headed for shore. The water was up to my chin, and some of the shorter men had to be helped.

The fighting for Utah beach had been light compared with Omaha beach. Of course, those who were wounded and died there would never agree that it had been an easy battle. I understand most of the credit for the success goes to General Roosevelt, son of President Teddy Roosevelt. We sure were grateful the beach had been secured.

I'm sure much of the horrible results of that battle had been cleared away, and all the dead and wounded were gone. Still, the terrible scars of war seemed to shout at us. Burned-out vehicles, sunken landing craft, ships, tanks, guns, pillboxes lay twisted and still. It hardly seemed possible anyone could have survived, yet men had waded in and driven the Germans back, now some seven or eight miles inland in most places.

We marched quickly inland to a replacement center near Sainte Mère Église. Our first instructions were to pair off and set up pup tents in an apple orchard nearby. We would stay there until assigned to our units. It was impossible to find out where we would be going or when. Most of us took a good look at the situation map, and it appeared the front was about three miles from us. We could clearly hear our artillery all night as a constant shelling seemed to be taking place. The concussion was close enough to shake our tents, and sleep was difficult.

Sainte Mère Église was the small town made forever famous in the movie of D day. There the Eighty-second Airborne stubbornly fought its way back toward the coast to link up with the Fourth Infantry Division. Had I known the Fourth was to be my unit, perhaps I would have asked more about the battle there.

Since we were not confined to camp, several of us took the opportunity to see some of the battle area nearby. Our noses and grapevine information led us to a burial site about a quarter of a mile away. The ghastly stories we had heard about the fierceness of the fighting were true. German war prisoners were digging up the partially decomposed bodies of their own dead—buried in neat rows in mass graves about three feet deep—for movement to a new location. Working with shovels and bare hands, the prisoners stuffed the corpses into mattress covers and piled them on trucks in rows, like cordwood. Some of the bodies were badly mangled and very difficult to pick up. Stern-faced men turned white, and many had to turn away to vomit at the sight and smell.

The guard stated that several hundred American bodies had already been moved a few days before. Over three hundred Germans had been buried in the mass grave, but the two fields were being cleared to make way for a fighter plane airstrip.

Near the graves were the wrecks of many gliders, some still hung up in trees, others smashed into hedgerows, all riddled with bullet holes. It's a wonder to me that any of the glider troops survived or were able to fight once on the ground. I had tried to join the paratroops shortly after OCS. I was rejected because I wore glasses.

We walked through a field that had been shelled by the Navy, probably with rockets. The holes were about four feet deep and six feet across. They covered a pattern about twenty feet apart over a couple of acres. It seemed impossible that anyone could have survived such a bombardment.

We were pretty quiet as we made our way back to the tents. For me, the cruel realities of war came into vivid focus, and for the first of many times I felt the intestinal stirrings of fear.

Finally, on July 12, orders came through. I was assigned to the Twenty-second Infantry Regiment of the Fourth Infantry Division. About a dozen of us climbed onto a two-and-a-half-ton truck and were driven through Carenten on our way to Service Company of the Twenty-second Infantry. Our first taste of shelling occurred as we crossed a small bridge near Carenten, but it screamed overhead and exploded about one hundred yards beyond us.

Captain Hawkins, the commanding officer (CO) of Service Company, met us warmly. He took us directly to headquarters of the Twenty-second Infantry nearby, somewhere in the swamps near Carenten.

Colonel "Buck" Lanham was there to greet us. He was a small, wiry man who looked as tough as he was gruff. He wasted no time in scaring the hell out of us. He stated flatly that the German resistance was very stubborn, and our

losses were extremely high. He explained how tough it was
to cross a field with the Germans dug in behind every
hedgerow. Machine gun crossfire made advance very difficult. "We are only able to gain a few hundred yards each
day. As officers, I expect you to lead your men. Men will
follow a leader, and I expect my platoon leaders to be right
up front. Losses could be very high. Use every skill you
possess. If you survive your first battle, I'll promote you.
Good luck."

After our brief indoctrination by Colonel Lanham, we
were assigned at random to various battalions within the
regiment. Five of us were ordered to follow our guide to
Second Battalion Headquarters, then in regimental reserve
roughly a quarter mile behind the front lines.

Our guide was a corporal who was tired, hollow-eyed,
and jittery. He acted like a cornered animal. Just watching
his actions gave one the creeps as, bent low, he ducked and
ran from one piece of cover to the next. We ran with him
down farm lanes, between hedgerows. Some were sunken
below ground level. We passed many empty foxholes dug
along the banks. Some were partially covered with wood or
metal torn from some farm building. Bodies of dead Germans were strewn along the way. They lay as they had
fallen, in grotesque positions, glossy-eyed, cheeks sunken,
mouths open. The awful odor of death was increased by
the hot July sun. The guide said our dead had already been
moved, and we were grateful.

Second Battalion Headquarters was in a rather large
field with most of the battalion dug in nearby. Headquarters
was just a small ten-by-twelve tent set up under a tree near
a hedgerow. Lieutenant Colonel Lum Edwards was in
command. He greeted us briefly but made no speech. Captain Tom Harrison, the S-3, assigned us to companies.
Lieutenant Piszarak and I were assigned to E Company. We

became very good friends and served together from July until November, when he was killed in action. We had to go across the field to report to Captain Holcomb, commander of E Company.

Lieutenant Piszarak was assigned to the First Platoon and I was sent to the Second Platoon. Lieutenant Plume and Lieutenant Tawes had the Third and Fourth platoons.

One thing I felt important was learning the names of my men. So I made a real effort, and the men were pretty surprised to have me call all forty of them by name the very first day.

My first concern was my noncoms. Sergeant "Chick" Reid was the platoon sergeant. The assistant platoon sergeant was Otha Anders. These men had landed on D day and had about one month's combat experience. I was grateful they were both willing and able to give me a lot of useful pointers on what it was like at the front. At least four other officers had already been casualties in my platoon, and only five men of the original forty who landed on D day were still assigned.

I was lucky to have a few days with my new platoon before going into battle. Later, I saw many green lieutenants sent up to take over platoons in the thick of battle. They had no chance to meet any of their men or to find out who the noncoms were. I can't imagine a tougher, more demanding job being thrust upon any young man than that of a frontline infantry platoon leader.

My platoon was dug in behind a hedgerow directly across the field about two hundred yards in front of our battery of 105mm self-propelled artillery. At first this didn't concern me, but it proved to be quite disturbing as they began firing during the night. Not only was it very noisy, but the concussion caused the sides of my foxhole to cave in several times. Of course, sleep was almost impossible, even without the artillery, for my mind was filled with fears and questions about what it would be like to lead men in combat. How would I face my responsibilities? Perhaps tomorrow would tell.

One evening just before dark while standing in line for hot chow we got a real thrill. Four German fighter-bombers zoomed right over us at treetop level. We scattered instantly and dove for the nearest cover. But their targets seemed to be somewhere near the coast. In seconds just about every antiaircraft gun and machine gun within range opened fire, and we could easily follow the path of the planes by the red glow of the tracers. Every fifth machine gun bullet was glowing white phosphorus to help the gunners see where they were shooting. The display looked just like the fireworks back home on the Fourth of July, but the planes were so fast and so low that they were gone before anyone could take good aim, and none of them appeared to be hit.

About July sixteenth, our regiment moved northeast, close to Saint-Lô. Here we got the news that we were to become part of a special task force of tanks and infantry—with no other purpose than making a major breakthrough of the German lines. This was the first large-scale tank-infantry team action ever undertaken by the Allies. The enemy in our immediate front was to be carpet-bombed before our jump-off, and then a large army of tanks and infantry would drive through any hole created.

The crucial problem was the hedgerows. In Normandy, for generations the farmers had grown hedges to separate their fields, however small. They had started by digging small ditches around the edges of the fields. The earth was piled in rows between two fields, and over the years many of these dirt piles grew to become over two feet thick and three feet high. Hedges were planted on top, and their roots prevented erosion. Various bushes and trees also took root to form a barrier strong enough to fence in livestock.

The Germans, of course, seized upon hedgerows as the natural earthworks they were. They were excellent for the defense. Easy to hide behind, the thick dirt embankment served as a very good shield against our small arms. Usually the Germans put machine guns near the corners of each field, giving them a crossfire that made a frontal attack by infantry nearly suicidal. Sometimes the poor infantry would fight a whole day to gain a few hundred yards—and that only if they were lucky.

The special tactics that were developed called for the tanks to break out into a field and spray the next hedgerow with their machine guns while the infantry walked or ran behind the tanks, using them as shields. When the tanks got close enough to the hedgerow they'd raise their fire a little, and the infantry would run ahead, keeping as low as possible, throwing grenades over the hedge. The tanks would plow through the hedges and the infantry would follow closely, then fan out to either side to capture any remaining enemy.

Originally a tank could not handle a hedgerow very well, because the dirt mounds would tilt them up and expose their relatively vulnerable underbellies to the German panzerfaust—a lethal, armor-piercing rocket grenade similar to our bazooka, capable of knocking out a tank. After a while a sharp steel scythelike bumper, fashioned from old train rails and the scrap iron from German beach obstacles, was welded to the front of tanks about a foot above the ground. It sliced a chunk out of the hedge, which allowed the tank to keep low as it burst through and took the Germans by surprise.

If all went as planned, we would mop up the enemy and continue the attack across to the next hedgerow, and the one after. The tactic seemed practical enough, but even in dry runs it was utterly exhausting to carry all our gear while running behind tanks, bathed in their hot fumes and the churned-up dust.

After several days of grueling drill in the new tactics, we were ready to go. Every day we got our gear together and waited for orders to jump off. That went on for about a week, because the bombers that were to do the carpet bombing were grounded by the rotten weather. All the waiting didn't do our nerves any good.

Meanwhile, there were a few sidelights. One day I came upon one of my young soldiers who had his pistol in hand, apparently getting up the nerve to use it on himself. He was terribly depressed because he hadn't received any mail from home since his landing in France. I sat down and quietly talked with him alone for quite a spell until he was assured his family really did care, but that our mail was all messed up because of the fighting. The very next day he received a couple of letters, and that snapped him out of his depression.

One day our ever-resourceful cooks decided to treat us. They said that a nice young cow had wandered into enemy mortar fire, and that fortunately they had been nearby and so knew it was fresh meat. The steaks were a marvelous change from regular Army rations. A little later, however, Captain Holcomb was comewhat embarrassed when a French farmer came calling and excitedly demanded payment for his slaughtered cow. He was turned over to a major from Military Government, and I suppose something was worked out.

Another day Major General Barton, our Division Commander, held a regimental review to award medals for heroic actions since the invasion. As we marched by companies to the parade field some German fighter planes roared over at treetop level—and men and heroes scattered in every direction, with some diving right through dense hedgerows. The planes never fired on us, and may never have seen us, so we resumed our march to the review. We kept looking over our shoulders, but the planes never circled back.

One of the men had some barber tools, so we took turns sitting on a stump for a quick haircut. I don't remember getting my hair cut again during the next eight months.

II

SAINT-LÔ BREAKTHROUGH

(First Day)

It was probably very boring for most of the men to sit quietly and wait for the attack to begin. Especially since the jump-off dates were changed several times.

All of the officers were very busy. We spent hours studying maps of our objectives. Aerial photos were very accurate. With the use of special angles in glass, the photos showed orchards so close we actually could count the trees. Some of the photos were only a few days old. I was impressed with all the information at our disposal. I hoped the Germans didn't know as much about us but felt they could not because of our air superiority.

On July 25, 1944, the big attack finally got under way. The faraway drone of planes grew to a deep rumble as hundreds of huge bombers passed directly overhead, filling the sky. We were told there would be three thousand bombers and five hundred fighter-bombers in the raid.

Ours was a grandstand view just behind the front lines, and we watched in complete awe as wave after wave paraded over us. There seemed to be about two hundred

16

planes in each formation. What was splendidly inspiring for us must have been terrifying to the Germans.

The earth beneath us shook as strings of bombs began to explode just to the front of our infantry lines. The rush of air from the blasts gave us a good push, even though we were a half mile away.

Our orders were to jump off in attack immediately after the bombing to take advantage of a stunned, confused enemy. Staggering misfortune stepped in, however, with a cruel blow. One whole wing of bombers miscalculated and dropped its entire load on the front lines of one of our divisions. The losses in dead and wounded were over eight hundred, including the killing of Lieutenant General Leslie McNair, Army Ground Forces Commander. This tragedy and its confusion caused the postponement of the attack one more day.

The Germans, meanwhile, used the respite to bring up reserves to fill in much of the area the bombs had knocked out. The enemy we faced thus were a mixed lot of survivors of the bombing plus newly arrived paratroopers.

My personal "longest" day began as we jumped off— my first attack—the next morning, July 26, 1944. As soon as we crossed the Saint-Lô-Periers Road, just west of Saint-Lô, we came upon a dreadful sight. The destructive power of those thousands of five hundred-pound bombs overwhelmed the senses. The dead from both sides lay twisted and torn, some half buried by overturned earth. Bloated cows with stiff legs thrust skyward in death lay everywhere, as did burned-out vehicles and blasted equipment. I've never been able to erase it from my mind.

When the order to move out had first come, my muscles had been taut with fear. After a while I realized that somehow my body was moving forward behind the tanks as my platoon took the lead. It seemed to me like the first few moments of a football game. As we advanced I began to feel my mind and body working together again—still very scared, but functioning.

Our tank company was wonderfully aggressive, shooting up everything in sight. The tank commander's tactics were very sensible, it seemed to me. Since no Americans were ahead of him, his orders were to shoot and shoot. All that tank firepower blasting away kept the enemy pinned with his head down, unable to return fire, and allowed us to advance rapidly and capture many prisoners with very few losses.

Many of the Germans were still in shock from the bombing, and many had no desire at all to fight. Actually, I don't understand how any of them even survived. Bomb craters big enough to swallow a jeep were so close together in some areas it was difficult for our tank drivers to zigzag through.

Once, as we rounded the hedgerow at the corner of a big meadow, one of our tanks accidentally ran over a dead cow. It was bloated, and when it burst its entrails wound around the tank treads—and there was the terrible mouth-filling stench to add to the gore.

It was too much for me. I fell down on my hands and knees and was retching miserably when the sudden roar of a diving plane made me look up—just as one of our P-47s let go two bombs directly above me. I dove down flat in my own vomit—needlessly, for the bombs sailed on another two hundred yards ahead and knocked out a Jerry armored half-track I had not even known was there.

A few minutes later I lost my first man. He stood right up in an open spot and tried to match his rifle against an enemy half-track. They machine gunned him down and fled. I shuddered at his futile death, for a rifle was not much use against steel plate, and letting yourself get caught in the open by a machine gun is fatal. Better to take cover and fight again than to take foolhardy risks. If he'd armed himself with a rifle grenade or bazooka, it might have been a different story. I felt sick.

Our first village, Saint Gilles, now was close in front, and we approached with caution. It was just a small crossroads hamlet with about thirty buildings that seemed to go about a block in each direction from the one intersection. The buildings were close together, like stores, and built right up to the narrow street, with no sidewalk. The back yards were open country.

My platoon swung to the right across the fields and came into the village from the right, or west end, and headed toward the central crossroads. My men and I were walking on either side of the road following our lead tank into the little burg. As we approached I was on the left beside a high stone wall, and the first buildings were just ahead, not over ten yards beyond the end of the wall.

Suddenly a shell exploded inside the first building beyond the wall, and instantly I hit the dirt. When I looked up a few seconds later from my prone position in the brick gutter, a Jerry Mark IV medium tank was cutting around the corner only a short block away and heading directly toward me. Our Sherman tank and the Mark IV began to fire at each other at once from point-blank range. Our tank began to back up as it was firing, apparently looking for some kind of cover. And this left me in front, actually between the two tanks.

I looked around frantically, but the stone wall appeared impossible to climb, and the buildings ahead were too close to the oncoming Mark IV, so I stayed flat in the gutter and watched the tank battle. Each tank fired as rapidly as possible as the distance closed to less than one hundred yards. The muzzle blasts shattered windows in the houses and storefronts, and each explosion knocked my helmet halfway off my head. The narrow, walled-in street seemed to act like a sound tunnel, and the concussion smashed at my ears. (My wife tells me today I'm somewhat hard of hearing, and I'm not very surprised.)

The Mark IV kept firing as it came toward us. Both tanks somehow kept missing at this close range or their armor-piercing shells were bouncing off. Finally, after an exchange of about a half-dozen rounds each, the Jerry suddenly went up in flames. Two Krauts crawled out of the tank's belly escape hatch and ran back for the corner. Both were knocked down by machine gun fire from our tank.

The German tank commander, a sergeant, then jumped down from the turret—and charged right at me. I struggled to my feet but could not raise my M-1 rifle to my shoulder. As I shook with excitement and fright my rifle came up to my waist and fired three times—and was empty. Had I been more experienced, I would have reloaded my rifle before walking into the burg with a clip of eight bullets.

On the other hand, it was probably better for my peace of mind that I didn't have a full clip, for I probably would have killed him. After he had fallen, I did my best to reload but was all thumbs. I just couldn't get that damned clip to fit into the breech.

The Kraut sergeant had blood seeping from his ears and mouth due to the concussion of his tank being hit, and, with his eyes staring directly into mine, he grabbed his thigh where my bullet had struck and then hobbled across the street into a doorway—all before I managed to get my rifle reloaded.

Luckily, he never attempted to shoot me with the pistol he wore as a sidearm. He must have been in much greater shock than I and had every right to be unable to function. We didn't pause to search the buildings, so I don't know how badly he was hurt.

The shooting of my first man, face-to-face, was not covered by the infantry school back at Fort Benning, and I was deeply shaken. I'm glad I didn't kill him. The shock was bad enough. Going through the slam-bang tank duel beforehand hadn't helped. I was still trembling a few seconds later and would have been unable even to defend myself. My first hour in combat had been enough for my lifetime, and I was wondering if I'd last the day.

Because of the burning Mark IV in the middle of the street, another rifle company from our Second Battalion detoured around the buildings on our right. When this company came to the crossing road, they turned to their right and continued the attack toward Canisy. The artillery forward observer flying in a Piper Cub overhead mistook this company for Jerries retreating out of town and called down a very heavy barrage of 105mm artillery on them.

This blasting of our own men was stopped as soon as possible, but not in time to prevent many casualties. I'll never forget one GI lying in the road with a huge gash all the way through his shoulder, one leg badly mutilated near the ankle. A medic gave him a shot of morphine and slipped a cigarette into his mouth. The wounded man raised his good arm to us as we passed and yelled at us to go get the SOBs. Of course, he didn't know he was talking about our own artillery. Most of the time our flying forward observers were great, but identification from a maneuvering plane can be tricky, and mistakes resulted in a few tragedies.

Our progress was good, and we had taken quite a few prisoners as we approached the next town, Canisy. It was getting along into the late afternoon of a long, long day, and we were near exhaustion when one of the commanding officers gave us a chance to rest. He called for fighter-bombers to hit the town before we went in. We flopped down where we were in an apple orchard and sprawled out with our backs against a hedgerow, hoping we'd never again have to move.

During this delicious respite, one of my sergeants had a

premonition. He came to me and asked if I'd make sure his personal effects were sent home if he didn't make it. I tried to talk him out of his obvious depression but got nowhere.

A little while later, as we rested against the hedgerow facing the front, we heard one of our tanks making a big racket coming up to the hedgerow behind us. We got out of there fast, except for the sergeant. We yelled at him to get moving, but he just sat in a daze as the tank plowed through and buried him alive. A bunch of us dug him out at once, but it was too late.

Thus my second man was gone—and he as needlessly as the first. I knew then I'd never survive if I let myself get tied in with every case. It was vital for me to build some sort of protective shield within myself and concentrate only on what had to be done in the present and how to do it. I forced myself to suppress all thoughts of prior losses and gruesome mental pictures of the tragedy of war.

A little later the fighter-bombers hit Canisy, setting many fires and creating more rubble. We mounted our tanks and went on in. It was a bit larger than Saint Gilles, up to maybe seven or eight hundred people. The drifting smoke screened the fires a little and made an eerie glow in the oncoming darkness. It was all very spooky, and it seemed my eyes couldn't travel fast enough to find signs of a hidden enemy who might be watching us as we rode through town on the backs of tanks.

Fortunately, the Jerries had pulled out, and so we pushed right on through Canisy and into the night. Now we were in even more of a no-man's-land. The Germans were so unaware of our penetrations that in the darkness a German tank came up from the side and was moved right into our column by a smart MP, and then one of our tanks knocked him out from the rear.

As the Nazi tank burned and its shells began to explode, we were forced to detour in the field around it. When we returned to the road, a German colonel drove up with a staff car and was immediately captured.

At 2:00 A.M. we were still going strong and getting near our first day's objective—Le Mesnil Herman. My platoon was in the lead again as we approached town, and I was on the armored platoon leader's tank, which was third in line.

The point tank stopped about one hundred yards ahead, halting the whole column, and in the lull we immediately heard German voices jabbering away—apparently excited at seeing American tanks six miles behind what they thought were their front lines. Their chatter came in clearly, even above the noise of our idling tank motors.

I was now able to spot their voices at no more than ten feet from the right side of our tank, and I knew we had only a moment. I threw a hand grenade and at the same time yelled at Sergeant Williams, just behind me on the tank, to shoot his rifle grenade.

Just a second later the Germans let go with a panzer-faust, and I think our firing first may have upset their aim —for they missed the broad side of the tank where we were sitting and instead hit solid front armor about three feet to my left. The armor-piercing shell of the panzerfaust exploded, but the angle was wrong for penetrating the armor. Nevertheless, it left huge catlike claw marks across the front of the tank, some almost two inches deep and very jagged. My hand nearest the blast stung sharply and turned out to be burned.

I can't help believing that if we hadn't gotten off our grenades so quickly the German aim might have been truer and our tank would have blown up and taken the rest of us with it. But the tank commander inside our buttoned-up tank evidently wanted no more of that spot, for suddenly we took off at full speed, jerking ahead so fast that some of us nearly lost what were at best very precarious seats.

At that moment our fourth tank, just behind us, was hit

by a panzerfaust and burst into flames. I had no hope at all for any of the men—the five crew members inside, and all of my eight men riding the back. I really don't know their fate; I never saw any of them again.

Now we had a new problem. Previously the darkness had been some protection, but the flames of the burning tank lit up our road as brilliantly as a high school football field on a Friday night. We felt as though we were suddenly naked on Main Street.

Our three lead tanks now were bunched up about two hundred yards past the burning tank and some three hundred yards short of Le Mesnil Herman. My men and I piled off and took cover in the small ditches by the road. The hedges were not very close to the road there, and that was something of a good break because panzerfaust teams couldn't get quite so close.

The only way I could communicate with the tank platoon leader was through a field phone we'd rigged up on the back of his tank, and I used it now to talk over our awkward situation. We decided to radio the CO for instructions, since it didn't seem sensible to try to go on into Le Mesnil Herman with only three tanks and twenty-four riflemen. The tank lieutenant had been in the fighting in North Africa and Sicily, and, since it was my first day in combat, I asked his opinion on what to do with my men. He suggested I spread them out a little more to make sure the Germans didn't get too close with a panzerfaust.

Our radio instructions seemed slow coming in, and we waited nervously in the bright light for minutes that seemed to drag into hours. At last we got word simply to turn around and rejoin the main body of the task force, now in a field about a quarter mile back.

Great—but *how*? The tanks had to stick to the road, brightly lighted though it was, and that sure didn't look very attractive to me, but I couldn't see any other way out.

The tank lieutenant suggested I keep my men spread out while they turned the tanks around in the road. This done, I asked what next.

"Well," he said, "it looks like the only way out is to make a fast break for it."

"Then should I get my men mounted back on the tanks as fast as I can?" I asked.

"Hell, no," he snapped. "They'll shoot your men off like flies."

Without another word, all three tanks took off so fast the phone on the command tank was jerked from my hand and we were left standing in the road with our mouths open. I was furious, but I knew I couldn't waste time on anger. Something had to be done, and fast. Some of my men were on the edge of panic. One was crying, and I noticed a few others were trembling. I didn't particularly blame them; we were surrounded by Germans who could see us plainly and soon should move in on us. We couldn't even call for help, because our radioman had left his radio on one of the tanks. We were completely on our own.

As the tanks had charged away one of my men had run after it, trying to grab on from the rear. His feet bounced a couple of times in the road, and then he had to let go because of the extremely hot exhaust. So he was stuck with the rest of us.

The Germans shot panzerfausts at each tank as it passed the one still on fire, but they missed every time. The tanks thus had been lucky enough to get through; now it was our turn to run the gauntlet.

The instructors back at Fort Benning had never told me what to do in a situation like this, so I probably did everything wrong. I did remember one of their morsels of general advice, however: When in doubt, get off your butt and do *something*. It might take the enemy by surprise.

I quickly got the sergeants together and told them that

my simple plan was to make a break right down the road past the burning tank, fighting all the way. One thing in our favor was that I'd made each man carry four hand grenades instead of the usual two (my first hunch).

My orders were to move out in single files on either side of the road with the men ten yards apart and no two abreast, to avoid bunching. Each man was to have a grenade in hand to be thrown over the hedgerow on my command. After getting rid of the first grenade, they were to run like hell. While they ran they were to keep throwing grenades as often as possible, but to be sure to keep on running. When they were out of grenades they were to fire their rifles at the top of the hedges while they ran. When rifles were empty, the orders were to keep on running without stopping to reload.

Grimly, and without a word, the sergeants moved off and quietly lined up the men. In a few moments we headed for the burning tank. Platoon Sergeant Reid took the lead on the right, and I took it on the left, since I already knew where the German panzerfaust team was on that side. The other sergeants brought up the rear.

On my side of the road there was no hedgerow for some seventy-five yards, until we came to the corner of a field. As we walked toward this hedge I carefully pulled the pin from my grenade, just in case it was needed quickly.

When I had walked only a few yards (which seemed miles) beyond the hedgerow corner in the glaring light, I heard German voices just over the hedge. Evidently they were excited about seeing American infantry walking openly down their road. I instantly threw my grenade.

The Germans yelled, "Grenade! Grenade!" and I could hear them scrambling for cover. I then yelled, "Let's go!" at my men—and we broke the world's record for the 440.

Somehow I threw my other grenades and emptied my rifle as we tore along the road. The Jerries fired machine guns and tossed grenades into the road. One grenade landed about three feet from me, but I was long gone when it went off.

When we passed our burning tank, we were too scared of enemy action to worry about any of its shells going off. It was very hot and bright, almost incandescent, and smelled of burned flesh. A couple of dead GIs lay by the road, but we couldn't help them, so we kept on pounding down the road like a bunch of berserk Indians, firing all the while.

Suddenly we came upon the poor GI on guard in the road for our main body, and he just stood there transfixed, as though he'd seen a ghost. He couldn't even open his mouth to challenge us.

I checked my twenty-four men and all had made it, though two were slightly wounded. We had been miraculously lucky.

It was now about 3:00 A.M., and my longest day finally was over. We dug slit trenches just deep enough to get our bodies below the surface of the ground, then tried to get some sleep. Though I was totally exhausted, my mind was much too wound up to relax in sleep. The tragedies and excitement of the day kept racing through my mind over and over. Also, the Germans were famous for counterattacks, and I didn't know at what moment they might come.

I knew two of my men had been killed and two others wounded, and I could only assume the eight riding the blazing tank had been killed. I hoped some of them might have escaped, but I didn't see how.

I certainly did not consider myself any sort of hero in any of this action, but my men thought otherwise. They wrote me up for a Silver Star, for gallantry in action above and beyond the call of duty. It was duly approved and later presented to me in person by our division commander, Major General Barton.

Thoughts of a medal had never occurred to me, though I did appreciate it once it was awarded. My thoughts during the action were very rudimentary: *How in hell do we get out of this mess?* As it turned out, all we needed was speedy action—and a tremendous amount of good luck. Speaking of luck—I had indeed been very lucky to survive my first day of combat. In the tank shootout at Saint Gillis, if the Germans had knocked out our tank, I'm sure they would have turned machine guns on me and at thirty to forty yards would have mowed me down. Again, when the Germans hit our tank with the panzerfaust, just a foot to the left would have knocked out the tank and me with it. My rabbit's foot worked great that day!

III

SAINT-LÔ BREAKTHROUGH

(Second Day)

The few remaining hours of darkness passed uneventfully in the task force bivouac, a large field a half mile north of Le Mesnil Herman. Few of us settled our nerves enough to sleep, and the cold damp earth of our slit trenches had not eased our muscles.

At first light we were told to get ready to move out again. The orders were inevitable, but the part that galled me was that my platoon was to lead the attack again. Customarily, each of the three rifle platoons in the company took turns up front, which was only fair. Captain Holcomb explained it was the battalion commander himself who insisted my platoon lead again, since we had been the last ones in contact with the enemy and therefore knew his location better than anyone else. I still felt misused but didn't trust myself to say anything.

We struggled off in the attack after hastily jamming down a cold K ration breakfast. This time, as we headed for Le Mesnil Herman, we at least could see where we were going and didn't have to stick to the road. The tanks cut straight across the hedgerows behind which the Germans had been the night before.

Rifles and machine guns opened up on us at once with an angry clatter. My men ran over the rough field as fast as they could to get behind the tanks, and they fired their rifles back at the hedgerows whenever possible. They panted for breath, and their faces were flushed.

Each tank had two machine guns and one 75mm cannon, and they let go with all weapons blasting away as they drove ahead. The enemy were so well pinned down they didn't even lift up enough to fire their panzerfausts at our tanks. Soon our combined firepower was too much for them, and they began to wave white handkerchiefs. I learned later that over two hundred prisoners had been taken in this attack, and I'm sure glad I hadn't known there were that many of them around. Some of them, I think, must have come from beyond the small fields we fought in.

The Germans usually were very good at taking care of their dead and wounded. After burials they stuck a bayonet on the man's rifle and jammed the rifle in the ground at the head of the grave, with the soldier's dog tags hanging on the stock and his helmet on top of the butt.

We did pass about ten new graves, obviously dug during the night, and this must have been the toll of our grenades. There was no way of knowing, of course, how many additional might have been wounded.

As we continued forward a frightful, almost inhuman scream came from the hedgerow close by on my left. I jumped through and found a wounded German bellowing in terror. He lay in the cart trail that ran down the middle of the hedgerow, and he was right in the path of one of our tanks. The tank was buttoned up, and the driver probably couldn't even look down to the road through his vision slits.

I instinctively jumped in front of the tank, waved it to a

halt, and dragged the wounded man to the side. His eyes showed me gratitude far better than words—for I wouldn't have understood words anyway. I couldn't help wondering whether a German would have helped me the same way, but somehow a helpless wounded man didn't seem like an enemy.

As we finally came to the first buildings on the edge of Le Mesnil Herman we began to pick up some sniper fire and had to hit the ground and then run from cover to cover. We moved quickly from house to house and found that most of the enemy had fled.

As we crossed one street my radioman was shot by a sniper hiding in the upper floor over a store. I had crossed the road myself running hard, with the radioman following. It seems he had dropped a K-ration box, roughly the size of a carton of cigarettes, in the street and stupidly went back to pick it up. When he bent down to pick it up, the sniper got him.

Our platoon medic rushed out to pull the radioman back, but he was already dead. Before the medic could run back, the sniper shot him in the side—even though he wore on chest and back the big red cross on white background that is supposed to give immunity. The medic was able to drag himself back to shelter, where he calmly dressed his own wound and stayed in action. He would have evacuated a rifleman with a similar wound, but he knew how badly he himself was needed.

To my mind, the medics were the unsung heroes of the war. Their duty was so routinely hazardous that it was hard to tell when they went beyond its call. Most important was their deep effect on morale; we just knew that if we ever got hit, a medic would come out to get us, no matter where or when.

Later, when we were able to reach the radioman, we found he had stuffed his pockets, his shirt, and even his oversized leggings with boxes of K rations. He had lost his life over a box of barely palatable survival food.

Now we had three men definitely killed, and each was unnecessary—the man who stood up in the open and fired at an armored half-track, the one buried by our tank, and the chowhound.

Sergeant Williams also was wounded in this action, but he was a very unusual case. A mortar shell had exploded near him, and even though the medic could not find a scratch on him, he was paralyzed from the neck down. He could move nothing but his eyes.

This same Sergeant Williams had taken a bullet through the neck around D day and returned to the front in six weeks. He had a very heavy, bull-like neck, but, it seemed to me, he had returned too quickly after such a severe wound. He was an exceedingly stubborn individual, for he recovered from his second injury and returned to action in September. Then he was too close to a German grenade and was paralyzed a second time. After his subsequent recovery, he again applied for frontline action, but was finally turned down. Some guys really did take a lot of punishment and had the starch to come back willingly for more.

After going through the few remaining buildings in Le Mesnil Herman, I was ordered to take my platoon around to the left side of town and clear out a pocket of Jerries in an apple orchard.

Along with some tanks, we made our way to the first hedgerow on the edge of the apple orchard, about two hundred yards beyond the northeast corner of town. These tanks were from the Sixty-sixth Regiment of the Second Armored Division, and we had trained together as a team for breaking through hedgerows.

Our practice was for the tanks to fire all out at the hedgerow as they advanced, and when they got close enough they would raise their fire and my platoon would duck under, rush in, and toss grenades over the hedge at any Krauts waiting to ambush the tank. This was the way our attack on the apple orchard began, but for some unknown reason the lead tank did not wait for our grenades but plowed right on through the hedgerow.

As the tank tilted upward on a small crest of dirt it had plowed ahead the waiting Germans hit it with a panzerfaust in the underbelly. The tank immediately burst into flames but continued to roll on for about thirty yards until it stopped against an apple tree. It was the second of our seventeen tanks to be knocked out by panzerfaust near Le Mesnil Herman.

The sergeant in command of the tank climbed out of the turret and, with .45 pistol in hand and bleeding from his nose and ears, he charged back at the hole his tank had made in the hedge, and captured the six Germans who had ambushed him and who were by then waiting for the rest of us to come through.

Without pause, the sergeant then asked for help to get his wounded crew out of the tank. Several of us rushed right out and got two of the crew out, but it was now too hot to go in for the driver and assistant driver. They both were dead anyway, the sergeant said.

After dragging the two wounded tankers back to our side of the hedge, we yelled for a medic—and the wounded medic himself came up to help. He immediately asked for an ambulance, and so the tank captain got on his radio. One of his half-track ambulances soon arrived and drove right out to the hedge where the wounded lay.

At this point the rest of us were ordered to fall back one hundred yards to another orchard and take cover with the remaining tanks. The captain thought we were too much of a target and would attract shelling up where we were.

So we watched from a distance as the ambulance driver

and the crippled medic tried to load the wounded tank men onto stretchers and then into the ambulance. The painful wound in the side prevented our heroic medic from bending much or lifting; he couldn't help the driver, and so they had to call out for aid. The tank captain asked for volunteers, and four of my riflemen went right out.

The four of them worked as a team and quickly loaded the first wounded man into the ambulance. They were grouped around the next man, about to lift his stretcher, when a mortar shell—which came down vertically without a sound—exploded with a bright flash and sharp crack right on the stretcher. The wounded man was blown to bits; he never knew a thing. Our four volunteers were all hit badly, though they did manage to struggle aboard the ambulance with the driver's help. Our medic was killed.

Later, when I got the chance, I wrote up the tank sergeant for a Silver Star and requested a posthumous one for the valiant medic. My four wounded volunteers were each put in for a Bronze Star. It seemed so terribly little to do for them.

I happened to exchange glances with the tank captain, a really huge man, and then quickly looked away. He was crying. My own emotions weren't any too strong. It sure was tough to lose good men, and you never can get used to it.

After the ambulance pulled away, we went right on through the apple orchard and by this time found no more enemy troops. On the way back we heard a moan coming from one of the farmhouses near the edge of town and found a badly wounded young German soldier lying on a pile of blood-soaked bedding in the middle of the bare floor. It seems one of our planes had strafed his unit the day before, and a fifty-caliber machine gun bullet had entered the top of his right shoulder and gone out under his arm after puncturing a lung.

Air sucked through a large hole in his side each time he took a breath. Judging from the amount of blood caked on the bedding and on him, I didn't see how he could still be alive. I covered his wounds to try to stop the air from sucking in too much dirt, and our ambulance team took him to the rear. They thought he would pull through, but I never heard any more about him. We hoped our wounded might get the same kind of humane treatment from the Germans.

With Le Mesnil Herman secure, we dug in for the night along the road on the southeast side of town. The Germans were watching us, of course, the whole time, and we soon received some very concentrated shelling. This was my personal introduction to the famous German 88mm artillery piece. The shells traveled faster than sound, hitting the ground all around us before we heard their incoming whistle.

This time we were very lucky, simply because a great many shells did not explode. Later we learned the French Resistance had been sabotaging 88mm shells. I counted eight duds sticking in the ground within thirty yards of my foxhole. So thank you, Mr. Frenchman.

That night, as usual, I went around a couple of times to check my men and found one asleep on guard. When on the actual front we always kept half the men on guard at all time, following the buddy system—one man on guard while his buddy slept. I really gave the soldier hell, trying my best to scare the life out of him. He assured and reassured me it never would happen again, so I let him off. Perhaps some may say I should have court-martialed him, but we all were on our last legs, and I felt he deserved another chance. As it turned out, he later proved himself a good soldier, a man I could always count upon.

As my second day of combat came to a close I found my casualty list very high. Of my original forty men, three had been killed in my presence and fifteen others were wounded, although this last was optimistic in that it included the eight men on the burning tank.

Totally exhausted by two endless days of fighting, I quickly fell asleep in the shallow foxhole I had managed to scoop out. It was about eighteen inches deep and barely wide enough and long enough to lie in. The ground was hard and damp, and we didn't have a blanket, so we just lay down with our clothes on and used our helmets for pillows. Only a man completely done in could manage to sleep like that.

Our combat fatigues were chemically impregnated to keep out enemy gas, but they also kept in all the July heat and body odors. Fortunately, we were in the open air and rather busy, for we were becoming a bit fragrant. It was a good thirty days before we got a change of clothes, and what a relief! The Army Engineers set up hot showers in the open fields, and they were really great, but they never had them very close to the front.

Now, at the end of the second day of a great drive, we were a solid six miles deep into enemy territory. We had no idea what units behind us might be doing, but our great hope was that General Patton's army might have started through the gap we had opened.

IV

SAINT-LÔ BREAKTHROUGH

(Third Day)

After an unexpectedly quiet night at Le Mesnil Herman, we climbed aboard the tanks again and moved toward the rear over the very same road we had fought along coming into town the day before. At the first crossroad we turned eastward toward some high ground. This maneuver puzzled me, as did most of our other movements during the day, but frontline junior officers rarely knew the picture beyond their own necessarily small operations maps.

We came to some farm buildings off to our left, and my platoon was ordered to go out there and search them. We found no Germans but did come across something interesting. We heard a wireless operator sending a message. The *dit-dot* of his signals carried loud and clear all over the farmyard. In the middle of the yard was a huge old dry well, and we easily traced the sound to there. I carefully peeked in but could see nothing in the dark depths, even though the sound now almost jumped at me.

I was not about to go blindly down that well or send

anyone else, and since we had to move on quickly we sent a message of our own. We dropped a grenade down the shaft. That ended all transmissions, though we had to rejoin our unit and never got a chance to check out the wireless gear.

A short time later, as we got closer to the ridgeline ahead, we got off the tanks and went into positions along a hedgerow on the right side of the road. We waited there until the rest of the company caught up to us. I don't know what happened to Captain Holcomb, but Lieutenant Tawes appeared to be in command of the company.

My platoon went through the first hedgerow and into an open field beyond, with our tanks all around us. One of the tank captains was standing up in his turret looking to our right front through his field glasses when a German high-explosive (HE) shell whipped in and exploded just below the turret. The captain was killed instantly, and all of the tanks pulled back through the hedgerow to reorganize.

The situation was now thoroughly confused, so we also went back to the hedge and awaited orders. During this interlude we had our first psychiatric case, when one of my men lost control completely. His body began to shake violently, and he broke into loud sobs.

This was a genuine medical emergency and I just did not know how to cope with it, but realizing its frightening effect on the rest of the men, I had to do something quickly. So I simply turned the man over to the medic and told him to evacuate him immediately.

It was too late, however, to keep the fear from spreading. My men looked sick, and they wouldn't look me in the eye. In a little while we were ordered to try to cross the field again but this time without the use of tanks. Not one of the men would volunteer to go out in front as the lead scout.

I had to do something at once to get my men moving, so I stood in front of Private Phearson, a soldier I had noted before, and told him I'd promote him to sergeant on the spot if he'd lead one half of the platoon while I led the other. At this point we were down to half strength, nineteen out of the original forty, with no sergeants at all. I don't know why Sergeant Reid was gone. He was back with us a few days later, and was wounded at Saint Pois. Sergeant Anders was on special patrol duty at Battalion. He also rejoined the platoon before Saint Pois.

The private had no desire to take the lead, and he certainly didn't care about being a sergeant, but he finally agreed. So my new Sergeant Phearson took the lead on the left, close to a neighboring unit, and I took the right flank, which was completely open.

We ventured out across the field in two columns about one hundred yards apart, with no man directly behind another and with ten yards between men. As we crossed the open field and I came to within ten yards of the next hedgerow a German popped his head up, took a quick look, and ducked.

I instantly hit the ground, quickly threw a grenade over the hedge, and then got up and ran forward to dive behind the base of the hedge for cover. My men quickly joined me on each side, and we all threw a few more grenades for good measure. Then I took a very cautious peek through the hedge and saw an apple orchard about fifty yards wide and three hundred yards long. There were several pieces of German equipment on the ground nearby and in among the apple trees, but no other sign of enemy soldiers.

At this time Lieutenant Tawes came running up and, without knowing the situation before me, told me to get my men over the hedge and get on with the attack. I couldn't understand the great hurry; we had been there only a few

minutes, and since we knew the Germans were close, I
wanted to check around a little. I just didn't feel safe going
into that orchard. About thirty yards to my left was a gate
through the hedge into the field just to the left of the orchard, and I asked if we could try that way. He agreed,
saying, "Get moving right away."

So we went quickly through the gate and moved ahead,
staying close to the hedge that bordered the left side of the
orchard. It was a good thing we did, because the Germans
had moved to the parallel hedge opposite us across the
orchard and would have hit us from the side had we gone
right on through from where we'd thrown the grenades.

They fired at us with rifles and threw some potato
masher grenades (grenades with handles about eight inches
long to give leverage to the throw). The small depression
behind the hedge gave us cover from the rifle fire, and
most of their grenades fell in the orchard or struck tree
limbs and never reached us. Of course, we would have
been easy targets if we had gone into the orchard.

No one was hurt, so we kept on moving along the hedge
toward the next cross hedgerow in front. When I looked
through this next hedge I could see some farm buildings
about three hundred yards ahead and, about a mile farther,
another small town—probably Moyen.

At this far point in our advance, we were pulled back
abruptly. I never did understand why, since the few enemy
I could detect ahead did not seem capable of stopping us.

We mounted the tanks and went back along the same
road we'd advanced along earlier, but when we reached Le
Mesnil Herman we kept right on going a good four miles to
the ruins of the small village Villebaudon, which had been
torn apart by a savage battle. Knocked-out tanks, German
and American, lay all over the place, and some were still
burning. Houses had walls knocked down, and furniture

spilled out. Many homes were totally destroyed.

Perhaps we had been intended for reinforcements, but by the time we arrived the battle was over. I can't say I was disappointed.

It was getting late in the day, so we were ordered to set up our defensive positions on the edge of town and spent the next few hours digging our two-man foxholes. Mine was next to a knocked-out Sherman tank. The night was blessedly quiet, without any action in our sector.

As I lay in my foxhole the unexpected calm gave me time to mull over some impressions of combat. At first glance the Army's infantry training had been very thorough and practical, yet now that I had some actual battle experience I had come across some serious gaps in the training. Three incidents during the day had caught me without warning or preparation.

First was the fact that while training was based on leading a full-strength unit, in actual combat I found myself at about half strength, or less, much of the time. This makes a big difference in tactics, and I was forced to experiment as I went along—and this could have been tragic. Even a little training in understrength deployment would have helped.

Two other items I would have liked to have been at least introduced to in advance were how to recognize the onset of mental breakdown and what to do about it and how to replace leaders. My on-the-spot lessons showed me that seeing it happen is much different than simply hearing about it. I was convinced that all soldiers have a physical and emotional limit. The private who stepped in at once as sergeant made me wonder how many others might be able to handle a leader's job if they got the chance or were forced into it.

My third day was now over, and I found we still had

nineteen men left of the original forty, the combat fatigue case being my only loss of the day. Nothing in this world could induce me to go through even a small part of it again, but I think I learned something about myself and about other people.

V

SAINT-LÔ BREAKTHROUGH

(Fourth Day: *The Massacre of Villebaudon Ridge*)

Our battalion was ordered to clear the Germans off a high ridge several miles long running parallel to the Villebaudon–Tessy sur Vire road. Other units attached to us, and thus making a combat force, were a company of seventeen Sherman tanks, each with two .30-caliber machine guns and a 75mm (or three-inch) gun. Supporting us were a platoon of tank destroyers with .50-caliber machine gun and 90mm gun, plus artillery and mortars, and a cannon company with four 105mm howitzers.

Fortunately for our peace of mind, we had no inkling this routine assignment would turn out to be one of the most disastrous of the entire war. By nightfall, nine of our seventeen tanks would be demolished, and the infantry would be almost wiped out.

Our ruination was the famous German 88, the incredible 88mm artillery piece. Its power was awesome. A direct hit did not bounce off the sloping four-inch solid steel armor plate front of a Sherman tank; *it went clear through and out the back*. I saw smoking tanks ripped through from

43

front to back by a single armor-piercing 88. Rarely did any of the crew survive, for along with the shell itself were the ricocheting chunks of tank metal it tore off, not to mention the inevitable concussion and internal bleeding. Fires also made it difficult to rescue the wounded as shells inside exploded from the heat. Tanks were often deathtraps for the crew.

Rifle companies F and G led off to the right of the road, probing cautiously toward the top of the ridge. The road had a gradual upward slope for about five hundred yards. E Company, minus my platoon, and H Company followed the two lead companies. My platoon trailed the two lead companies, holding about one hundred yards to their right rear as protection against a possible flank attack.

Suddenly the Germans opened up on the forward rifle companies with rifles, machine guns, mortars, and artillery. The exposed infantry instantly hit the ground and dove for any cover available, returning the fire as soon as they got into position. Our artillery was getting in quite a few rounds also as we could hear it going out over our heads.

The calm hillside exploded into a full-scale battle. Quick pinpoint flashes of small-arms fire blinked along the bottom of the hedges. The sudden bright flash of bursting shells flowered among the dark green helmeted shapes of the infantry. Worst of all on the nerves was the endless pounding of the noise, the thundering blasts of artillery, and the angry staccato of machine guns.

The Germans were close on our right flank, and they were firing just as hard as those on the battalion front. Apparently they had been pushed aside by the battalion's advance, and they stayed out there and let us parade across their front as though it were a shooting gallery.

I moved my platoon out to the right behind a thick

hedge, along with five tanks and two tank destroyers spaced out alongside my men. We opened fire on the Germans some two hundred yards away across the flat top of the ridge. They did not let up, but at least we were giving them plenty to keep them busy. Our concentrated fire should have been enough to drive them off the ridge, but one of those sorry accidents of fate turned the tide against us, almost wiping us out. Suddenly we were caught between two fires—the Germans to our front and our own efficient artillery to the rear.

It seems one of the prearranged signals with our artillery backfired. Red smoke was a signal for our artillery to open fire on the smoke. As luck would have it, someone dropped red smoke right on our position. Before we could move we began to catch hell from our artillery as well as the Germans.

Artillery and mortar shells were dropping on us from all sides, and we had no choice but to dive for cover. Some crawled under the nearest hedge, while others tried to get close to or under tanks to use them as shields.

Few things are as terrifying as the target area of an artillery barrage. You cannot think, cannot talk, and there is no place to go. You must fight your instincts to get up and run. All you can do is hang on and hope the shells will miss you or the barrage will end.

Tanks and tank destroyers were the exception. They *had* to move out of there. The tanks' overhead hatches had to be closed against the artillery, and that practically blinded the drivers. All they could see through the driver's slits was a narrow horizontal strip directly to the front. There was no view at all of the ground close in front of the tank.

The withdrawing tanks thus could not see some of the men on the ground, and the men, because of the overpowering din of the explosions, could not hear the tanks coming. Two of my men were crushed by the maneuvering tanks. I told myself they were already dead from the shelling.

Another of the men on the ground next to me was killed instantly by a mortar shell that landed on his back. His buddy and I were splattered with flesh and blood but were not touched by shrapnel. His body must have absorbed the shell.

The survivor broke in panic and ran wildly past me. I tackled him instinctively, but he was a big man, and he dragged me along for a few yards. I managed to hold on and kept talking to him quietly. He quickly regained control, and just about then the barrage ended.

While our single medic manfully attended the wounded, I collected the few men still able to stand, and we resumed our positions along the flank. This was typical hedgerow country, with many small hills and gullies and occasional gaps in the hedge. The Germans were on the ridgeline along our course, and they were able to follow our every move. We advanced as carefully as possible while taking cover behind the hedges, hoping they might not spot us; then we rushed across the gaps.

Our tanks kept out of sight below us, coming up to help us only when the hedges were high enough to hide them.

At one time, while I was lying on the ground beside one of our tanks waiting for the men to get into position, I suddenly got the urge to move—and did crawl ahead some ten feet closer to the hedge. There was no purpose in this move, just a compulsion. The next moment, a machine gun cut up the very ground I had just left. What impelled me to move I'll never know. This lifesaving hunch might have had the same source as the one I had received just three days before when, for no particular reason, I ordered the already overloaded men to carry extra grenades—those grenades that served us well while we ran the gauntlet the night the blazing tank lit up the road. Perhaps there is some unknown sense we call upon subconsciously.

The main body of the battalion had been forced to stop, and during the breather I got a chance to take stock. I found I now had six of the original forty men, two of the original five tanks, and both of the tank destroyers. The rest of the battalion was also in rough shape and was almost stripped of officers; I was the only officer left of the original six in E Company.

A tank destroyer, incidentally, has tracks and armored sides like a tank but is completely open at the top. This gives the crew a clear view of the enemy targets, but, of course, no overhead protection. The great thing about the TD was its 90-mm gun, the only one we had capable of knocking out the big German Tiger tank and its six inches of armor plate. Our Shermans and their 75s could handle the Mark IV medium German tank but was no match for the Tiger. The TD was a must on our team.

At one time during a lull I happened to be standing beside a TD, studying the enemy position through my field glasses. The TD captain was doing the same thing from his open turret above me. Suddenly he yelled, "Hit the dirt!" Instantly my men and I dove for the hedge; an 88 high explosive (HE) shell burst on the front of the TD, and its shrapnel flew everywhere.

The captain had seen the quick flash of the German gun, and he reacted at once. His shout gave us a split second that probably saved our lives, for the 88 travels faster than sound, and we never would have ducked if he had not yelled.

As it was, the shell had exploded only five or six feet from where we lay in the dirt. None of my men was hurt, and I got off with only a splitting headache—and I couldn't hear too well for a few hours.

The captain immediately moved his TD back down the

hill out of sight, and the other TD and tanks also moved. He was almost in shock from the concussion, but he refused to be evacuated. His TD was not damaged, for it had shed the HE shell. If the 88 had been loaded with armor piercing (AP), the TD would have been ripped apart.

A few minutes later a battalion of infantry from another division came up to relieve what was left of our battered battalion. A captain from this new unit came over to me and asked me to fill him in.

I pointed across the small open gully ahead to where the frontline riflemen were taking cover behind a hedge and told him the enemy were directly in front of them. I also showed him the hedge on the ridge two hundred yards to our right where the Krauts could observe our every move and had plenty of machine guns, mortars, artillery, and 88s, and I told him they hit us hard whenever we crossed an open space.

Finally, I suggested that, everything considered, the best route for his men to take up to the frontline riflemen would be a short detour to the left behind a small rise that avoided the open gully. Possibly the captain was preoccupied with other problems, or he didn't completely understand my suggestion; or he might not have seen enough combat to appreciate what the Germans could do. He thanked me politely—then led his men, followed by another company, into the exposed area across the gully.

To my astonishment, the Germans did not fire on them, and I began to wonder if they might have pulled out. I quickly found that I, too, had underestimated their shrewdness. They had been watching the new battalion, and they guessed their mission. So as soon as the new rifle companies were mixed in with the companies they were relieving and both were somewhat confused and exposed, the Krauts commenced shelling the entire area with very heavy artillery and mortar fire. They knew the exact range, having just withdrawn from that location, and they opened up with all available weapons in a very fierce barrage, right on target. Exploding shells flashed everywhere and raised much dust and smoke. In wild panic, the men dodged about, screaming, and headed for the rear. Their eyes were wild with fright, and tears streamed down their contorted faces. They were in complete panic.

We stayed in our position on the flank and watched helplessly, our stomachs churning. We watched the desperate officers of the new battalion as they tried frantically to regain control. They stood at gaps in the hedgerow behind us and intercepted their men as they rushed by. We could hear them shouting out where they wanted each company to collect. About half an hour passed, the men milling around in the rear, sorting themselves into companies. During this time they were very vulnerable to further attack, but they were fortunate. In a short time the shelling tapered off enough to allow vehicles to move. All available ambulances and medical teams moved up to get the wounded taken care of quickly. Every vehicle able to carry a stretcher was used. For over an hour we watched ambulances, jeeps, light tanks, and half-tracks hauling out those wounded unable to walk. The Germans also must have been watching but did not fire again. I found out why later.

During all this blasting by the Germans I saw no return fire at all from our cannon or artillery. Probably all the forward observers, or their radios, had been knocked out. Our Air Force wasn't around either, but they probably were busy helping Patton's tanks in the breakout.

When things began to quiet down and seemed under control, a captain from the battalion staff of this new unit came over and cautioned me that we might be in for a heavy counterattack soon. I agreed, for I had anticipated this very thing. He went on to say that if my men would stay to help, he'd see that we all got hot chow. We then had a total of about thirty men, including the crews of the tanks and TDs and some stragglers from the company.

At this point food of any sort held little interest for us, but since we had no orders to fall back, I told him we would stay until ordered to move. Shortly afterward a major in a sharp, clean uniform with the Fourth Division patch on his shoulder came walking up to me from the rear all alone. He informed me that he was Major Walker, our new battalion commander.* He told me briefly and simply that Major Drake had been a casualty in the last barrage. I had never met Major Drake and did not know how or if Lieutenant Colonel Lum Edwards, the commander when I joined the battalion, had become a casualty.

Major Walker asked me several questions about the recent action and the enemy location and potential, and I held back nothing—including the warnings about going straight out into the gully. He nodded his understanding, told me to stay in position until further orders, and took off for the front along the route that detoured the gully.

I don't know what he found at the front, beyond complete demoralization and no great desire to go get the SOBs, but he quickly gained control. Soon I received orders to follow when he jumped off in the attack and to continue protecting the right flank. My first thought was "What the hell with?" The tanks had been moved up to support the attack at the front. There were only the two TDs, plus about a dozen riflemen—six from my original forty and a few stragglers.

I have often wondered if the new battalion CO knew the enemy had withdrawn and, if he did, just how he knew.

*This same Major Walker many years later rose to command the entire fourth Division in Vietnam, eventually retiring a Lieutenant General. When I talked to him in July 1986, after he had read this book, he told me that the sharp, clean uniform had been his first change of clothes in 30 days. He had landed on D. Day with the regiment.

Was it simply luck? Anyway, it worked, and I was impressed.

Later on we stopped for the night in some fields not far from Tessy sur Ville, digging in along the hedges where we placed our TDs and tanks and other vehicles under the trees to hide them from aerial view.

As full darkness settled over us about 11 P.M. we heard occasional German planes overhead. By now we could distinguish the characteristic sound of enemy planes. Our planes had a steady drone; theirs was more of a hesitant *put-put*.

As the enemy up there floated around looking for a target one of our trigger-happy gunners on a .50-caliber quad (four machine guns mounted to fire together from the back of a half-track) opened up. Soon other quads in his unit joined in, with the tracers streaming up into the night sky in a huge arch of ribbons. This cone of tracers didn't touch the planes at all but did pinpoint our location very neatly. A few minutes later a solitary pathfinder plane drifted over us and dropped two brilliant parachute flares, lighting us up brightly, like a football field, so that the night bombers could see us easily.

As we looked up nervously through the flares to the sky above we clearly made out the dark shapes of the bombers, now directly overhead. Our gunners again opened up, shooting through the shredded tin foil the bombers were dropping to mess up our radar. The tracers looked to be way off target, and certainly no planes were hit.

It seemed those little parachute flares never would reach the ground, and we were nakedly helpless in their eerie glare. We were down on our hands and knees pressing against the earth, with mouths open—to reduce the effects of concussion—and fingers in our ears as the bombs whistled down.

As the whistling shriek of the free-falling bombs ended

just over the hedge we were utterly defenseless. We were in the bottom of an elevator shaft awaiting the crash of a runaway elevator cage. There was nowhere we could go.

A couple of five hundred-pound bombs hit just over the hedge, about thirty yards away, and I was knocked flat in the dirt. For an instant I was in the eye of a tornado with the air crushed from my lungs. My head was whirling and pounding, and I gasped for breath. I tried to stand up, but my legs sagged, and I collapsed. Suddenly it was over. After a short while most of my senses returned and I checked my men. They were shaken and frightened, as I had been, but no one was wounded.

A medical unit had the rotten luck to be in the field next to us, and they lost several ambulances and many of their men.

The rest of the night passed quietly, and for this we were immensely grateful.

Around noon the next day we were pulled out of the line. Our part in the Saint-Lô breakthrough was over. E Company was down to about twenty-seven men out of the original one hundred sixty-eight; only six of us survived from the original forty of our platoon. I was very lucky to have survived my first major battle.

We were told, officially, that we had accomplished our mission. Later the Twenty-second Infantry received the Presidential Unit Citation for its part in the Saint-Lô breakthrough. General Patton had been able to swing through the gate we had opened in the German line at Saint-Lô and began a big circling drive to capture a whole German army. Combat team A—made up of the Twenty-second Infantry and the Sixty-sixth Regiment of the Second Armored, also known as "Task Force Rose" after General Rose of the Second Armored Division—has done its job well.

Now a new phase of war was possible. Our troops

were no longer confined to the small beachhead, stymied by crisscrossing walls of hedgerows. Now every unit was needed for a new role—pursuit of the Germans across France. We were ordered to rejoin the other two regiments of the Fourth Infantry Divison on the road to Saint Pois.

Somewhere en route we stopped for the night. I fell asleep, so exhausted that I was not aware of the heavy rain falling. It was close to dawn when I awoke, stiff and cold and wet, with about five inches of water in my foxhole.

Somehow our young bodies were able to endure such punishment.

VI

THE CHASE

The Saint-Lô breakthrough was completed by August Second and the enemy was occupied with Patton's tanks, so we had time to stop and take on new officers and men.

Lieutenant Toles was our new commanding officer in E Company. Lieutenant Piszarak had returned after a head wound and resumed command of the first platoon. I had the second platoon, and Lieutenant Blume had the third platoon. A Lieutenant Lloyd was brought up to lead the weapons platoon.

Platoon Sergeant Reid was back with me, although I don't know where he had been, and Sergeant Anders was returned from special patrol work. The newly minted Sergeant Phearson had survived and was still with us. We received enough replacements to bring the platoon back up to forty men. With the sergeants and about four other men, plus myself, we now had eight experienced men. All the rest were green recruits.

Meanwhile, Patton's Third Army stormed through the gap and raced wildly in three different directions: westward toward the great port city of Brest; in a northerly circle to help trap two German armies; and straight east to the Seine near Paris.

Our rest and replacement period was a short two days. We were moved along the route toward Saint Pois and assigned to clear up some pockets of German resistance and defend against possible penetration by the enemy.

One night, as we took up defensive positions along a ridge facing east toward no-man's-land, I felt very vulnerable because our men had to dig in so far apart. I checked my platoon area several times during the night and found several errors the new men were making. One stands out as a major error to this day. I found one man sitting on top of a hedgerow with no cover around him. He stood out vividly long before I got near him. I showed him how to take advantage of a big tree and its shadow, which was only ten feet from his exposed position. I told him to think and thus avoid giving a Jerry an easy opportunity to kill him.

Our next objective was the village of Saint Pois. As we approached along the road, in an attempt to make the Jerries take cover and thus lose some of their advantage, our artillery began to lay down a barrage on both the village of Saint Pois and the ridge behind it. The infantry then started to move up. Our company was not in the lead this time, so we missed the fighting, but we did catch some incoming artillery. Also, one of our jeeps ran over a big antitank mine and was destroyed.

When we got into Saint Pois our company was ordered to go house-to-house on the right side of the road. We took only a few prisoners, for most of the Germans had withdrawn.

Much to the delight of our men, we did find quite a bit of hard cider. Because of impurities in the drinking water, native Frenchmen do not drink water unless it is boiled. Instead, they settle for wine or cider. After two weeks of steady fighting, our men were glad enough to have a taste of it. The cider barrels we came across were used as reservoirs, lying on their sides. They measured eight feet in height and twelve feet in length and almost filled the small barn that stored them.

My platoon had one casualty in Saint Pois, Sergeant James "Chick" Reid, who was hit in the upper thigh by a rifle bullet. Sergeant Otha Anders moved up to platoon sergeant.

We continued our advance in the wake of Patton's Third Army. Near Mortain, the Germans were making a desperate attempt to break our line behind Patton's tanks and cut his supply lines. Here they ran into the Thirtieth Infantry Division, which at one point was using its artillery like rifles, firing low-level point-blank shots at German tanks and infantry.

Artillery fired in a direct line instead of a long arc is very effective. When the enemy is close enough to fire in this manner the gunners can usually see the targets, and this allows them to fire directly into the mass or at tanks. All that shrapnel really tears up the enemy. Of course, it also gives the Germans a good chance to knock out your guns—and their crews as well, if they can get in close enough. The enemy can see the artillery and direct all kinds of fire on the guns. It takes a lot of guts for the artillery crew to man their pieces when in such exposed positions. The exposure often requires the men to fight like infantry. They are better suited for long-range action, but that time it worked for us. The combined infantry and artillery fire was too much for the Germans, and they withdrew with many casualties.

During the German attacks on the Thirtieth Division, my platoon was sent out to support a couple of antitank guns at a road block. The officer who came out to relay the order, told me very little. As we were in enemy territory, I thought I should know more about the road block, such as its exact location, how long we might be gone, and how much food and ammunition to take along. He refused to tell me anything except to get moving. I obeyed reluctantly. I could smell alcohol on the officer's breath, and I resented having to take orders from someone even slightly drunk.

The roadblock assignment turned out to be an easy one, for no enemy appeared. The desperate German counterattack at Mortain had failed, but we were held in the area a few more days before we began a series of shuttle movements by truck toward the Seine River. With our new orders—"Keep your eyes open, but keep moving"—the chase was in full swing. Our infantry rode trucks through Alençon and Chartres, stopping only to refuel or to clear out pockets of the enemy.

The trucks were from service companies, and each had two black drivers. As though we didn't have enough problems on our hands, yet another one, albeit minor enough, cropped up. The drivers' orders were for both of them to ride in the cab; our orders were for either an officer or a sergeant to ride up front to make sure the trucks did not get lost. The drivers were very upset by our orders, and some refused to obey. Some officers had to pull a gun to settle the conflict in orders. I had no problem with my drivers, though they did grumble.

By now the bulk of the German armies was trapped by the combined Allied armies. British and Canadian armies were crushing down from the north to meet two American armies driving up from the south. This maneuver became known as the Falaise Gap. Worst of all for the Germans caught in this pocket must have been the annihilating bombing and strafing by Allied planes, then in complete control of the skies. Thousands of Germans nonetheless made their escape toward the Seine. The dead Germans

were literally stacked by the hundreds—in some places
two and three feet deep. It was a real massacre. All of the
roads for miles were strewn with German corpses and littered with hundreds of smoking or burning tanks, trucks,
and wagons. The debris of the fleeing Germans was everywhere. Hulks of burned-out tanks, trucks, half-tracks, and
self-propelled and towed guns were dramatic proof of the
devastating power of airplanes. My feeling of utter helplessness during the brief bombing a few nights earlier made
me realize what must have been absolute terror and total
panic for the German soldier under the deluge of destruction from our Air Force.

Large foxholes had been dug by the enemy all along the
road, ready for instant use. The strafing and bombing
planes gave the retreating Germans no rest. The ability of
German supply forces to get food and ammunition to their
armies had been obliterated. I imagine the German truck
drivers were always looking for the next foxhole they
might dive into if strafed.

The combination of our devastating ground tactics and
our superior air forces had almost totally destroyed two of
Germany's best armies in less than a month.

I wonder if the Air Force ever received enough credit
for its awesomely effective job. One can only speculate
how many infantry lives the Air Force saved. For all that, I
am willing to admit that I always resented the extra pay
and comfortable living of the Air Force boys. I am now
prepared to declare my deepest, most profound apprecia-
tion for the work they did and for the incredible risks they
took every time they were in the air. We were in a war that
was coming at us from all sides, from the front, from the
rear, from the flank—from the ground up, if we happened
to step on a mine. Or from the air from bombs, strafing,
and artillery of all sorts. Our rest was in a foxhole with a
helmet for a pillow. The foxhole was considered our fur-

nished quarters, so the Army did not allow us our forty dollars a month quarters allowance. Such is the life of the infantry.

We rode big six-by-six trucks day and night. After dark the truck column was blacked out except for cat's-eye slits in their lights, which were so dim the weary drivers could hardly make out the truck ahead. Combat military police were at some of the road junctions directing traffic.

On one of the quick turns my driver's reactions were too slow, and we careened into the ditch, breaking the front left spring and tearing the front axle loose. When the last of the convoy wheeled past, we found ourselves all alone in a private no-man's-land. I posted guards, and the rest of us tried to get some sleep. The driver crawled under the truck, but he was too scared sleep.

Around sunup a big maintenance truck hooked onto us and dragged us to an orchard where a maintenance crew began repairs. We were ready to roll again at noon, and the crew captain let me study his map for the route the Fourth Infantry Division had taken. I made some notes, and we headed out by ourselves. I told our driver we had to catch the division before dark or we'd be camping out again by ourselves.

I never knew a two-and-half ton truck could move so fast. That driver, with tires screeching, wheeled us around curves and bounced us through village after village. We ripped across open country until, just before dark, we caught the division. It had stopped to gas up, and some of the trucks were already moving out as we arrived. We quickly tanked up, grabbed some rations and water, and found our place back in the column.

Rumors began to come alive. The most exciting was that we were going to bypass Paris. None of the junior officers really knew what was going on. We could only listen to our seniors and use our imaginations.

One morning about the third week of August we were ordered up to west bank of the Seine some twenty miles from Paris. We were in the Arpajon-Corbeil area. It seems that one of our other battalions had tried to cross the river in twelve-man pontoon boats under the screen of fog, and about two thirds of the way across, the fog had lifted and left the battalion helpless. Most of the boats had been sunk, and many of the men lost, hit by direct fire from 20mm-antiaircraft guns that were based on the other bank. Rapid-fire antiaircraft artillery makes a very effective weapon for sinking small boats on a swift river. It was a disaster. Very few of the men made it back to shore. The men had carried a lot of heavy equipment, and the current was swift, so only those able to shed their equipment quickly had been able to escape.

With a precedent like that we were not too crazy about our assignment, as it was now our turn. We gladly waited for the engineers to bring up more boats, and meanwhile our mortars and artillery blasted away at the other bank. We could clearly see the German gunners abandon their guns and run back over the hill.

The Seine at that point was still very large and deep enough to allow oceangoing freighters, which meant it was a least twenty feet deep. The current was frightening, much too fast for our flat, square-nosed boats. We were told the current was nine miles per hour, good jogging speed, but to us it looked much, much faster.

Soon my platoon was loaded, twelve to a boat, and we took off, paddling like mad for the east bank. The wild current swept us a couple hundred yards downstream, and every moment we braced for some kind of enemy fire as we paddled hard for shore. This time all the luck in the world was with us, for there was no opposition from the Krauts. Our artillery and mortars had completely routed the German AA gunners. We hit the east bank without a loss.

We quickly pushed straight ahead inland to the high ground a half mile ahead. As soon as that position was denied to enemy observation our engineers began to build a pontoon bridge, a frustrating, if not impossible, job. As soon as they set up a section it was swept away by the powerful current. Soon they were running out of pontoons, and something had to be done.

It seems an older Frenchman, a retired World War I naval captain, had been watching interestedly, and he now came forward and told me he probably could help if I could lend him about twenty men. His idea involved three ships that happened to be moored on the east bank directly across from the pontoon bridge. The plan was to release the huge ropes on the downstream ship's stern, letting it swing out across the river as a kind of gate to slow down the river enough to get the pontoons assembled across it. Carefully following the old captain's able directions in English, my men wound the big ropes around the dock snubbers and a few trees. The swift current eased the ship's stern out until it was straight across the river, slowing the current just enough.

The engineers' sectional spans began to settle in place, and soon the bridge was complete the first tank rumbled across. I was sure those engineers would not soon forget that French naval captain and his ingeniously simple strategy.

Now that the bridge was in place and the east bank secured, we were no longer needed there. So we walked back on the bridge to the west bank. We did not know it at the moment, but our next stop would be Paris.

VII

PARIS

Paris, the City of Light, the flower of Europe, was about to fall again. This time some of the troops headed for the city were, indeed, Frenchmen, being part of the French Second Armored Division. Our Fourth Infantry Division was held back, for political reasons, to let the native division go in ahead.

We were, nonetheless, the first American troops to enter Paris on August 25, 1944, an incredible, indelible day! It was exactly one month after my first day in combat.

Within the city itself, all was confusion and wild celebration. The population had gone insane with jubilation.

We stayed in our vehicles and slowly moved through the crowded streets on our way toward the Eiffel Tower. Small cars with FFI—French Forces of the Interior—painted in bold white letters on their sides sped around corners. Young, wild-looking French men and women hung from every window of the cars. They waved hysterically and brandished weapons as they passed. We were afraid we might become their targets. I guess they were all right, but somehow we did not trust them very much.

It was little chilling to watch some of our Sherman tanks, now in the hands of this French Second Armored Division, wander all over the road. The drivers were either too drunk or too excited to keep in line. What a nightmare for a traffic cop, a drunken driver in a Sherman tank! We really didn't blame them, after their four years in exile or underground.

Then we were on the Champs Élysées, and it was packed with insanely joyous Parisians. Men, women, and children hung precariously from every window and jammed every doorway. The streets were almost a solid wall of humanity, and our trucks could barely crawl through them.

These people shouted and cheered at the top of their voices in sheer ecstasy. In a desperate attempt to thank us for freeing their lovely city, they tossed us flowers, candy, cookies, bottles of wine, and other things they really could not spare.

They just could not find enough good things to shower upon us. The young French girls threw kisses, and many were able to climb aboard our trucks and give the GIs the real thing. Our boys hated to let them go. I shook so many outstretched hands that my arm ached.

One French blonde clambered into the cab of one of our trucks and settled onto the lap of a sergeant and kissed him. The sergeant must have figured that was unmilitary behavior, for he promptly pushed her back into the crowd. It was many, many weeks before the men let him forget it.

We pushed right on through the center of the city to the northeast corner, which was much calmer. There we were assigned areas for bivouac and cautioned not to wander, since there were still Germans about. I had my men pitch tents in some backyards and told them to stay put. Less than an hour later, you might know, two men from another platoon wandered off in search of wine and women. They immediately ran into Germans instead. One of them was shot in the exchange of fire, and the other fled back to the company.

He ran into an officer on the street and excitedly told him what had happened. The officer at once grabbed all the men he could load onto a jeep and took off up the road after the Germans. Very quickly he ran into the Germans and found himself in a small-arms fight that was too big for his small group. Without telling the men, the officer jumped in the jeep and tore back to our lines for more support. My company was then ordered to attack.

We marched up the road about a half mile, passing our dead GI, who was sprawled by the side of the road where he had fallen. As we approached a railroad yard and roundhouse where the Germans seemed to be holed up I was ordered to take my platoon on a right flanking move and attack on signal to take the roundhouse.

We maneuvered behind houses and through backyards until we were in position, and I radioed that we were ready. Instead of being ordered to attack, I was told to withdraw back to the company area. I was told only that there had been a change in plans.

We learned later that we had been led into another regiment's combat zone. This neighboring regiment had almost let us have it with their artillery. Fortunately for us, their artillery forward observer was on the ball and recognized us as friendlies.

The next day I witnessed one of the emotion-ridden French kangaroo courts. There were several defendants, mostly women, on trial for collaboration with the Germans. As each was convicted in about five minutes she was led out onto the porch of a large house, and a local barber shaved her head. At the end of the trial, the convicted were lined up and forced to march through the streets.

Their shaven heads made them stand out, and the mob jeered and poked at them and pelted them with rotten eggs, tomatoes, and even paper bags of excrement.

Many such trials were going on around us, we heard. The retribution was beastly. With their bare scalps, these people were marked for a long time. They had to struggle and beg for the essentials of life. If guilty, perhaps they were lucky. Some of these luckless people might have been trying to make the best of a desperate situation. Some of the women had two and three children fathered by Germans. Others believed their husbands had been killed and so had fallen in love with their captors. For those, on the other hand, who had suffered without collaborating through four years of privation and hunger, the sudden release was emotionally explosive. To them it was not a time to grant mercy they themselves had been denied.

It reminded me of an occasion back in Normandy when we actually had to shoot a Frenchwoman because she was firing at us. It seems the father of her children was a German soldier, and he had been killed right in the yard of their farmhouse.

Near the end of the war, I saw the long trains of 40 & 8 boxcars. The capacity of each was stenciled on its side: "40 hommes, 8 chevaux"—forty men or eight horses. Each was loaded with Frenchmen heading for home after four years in Germany as slave labor. I wondered if they had any idea what awaited them. They all were riotously happy.

After only a day or two on the northeast side of Paris, we again took up the pursuit of the Germans. We started out on foot in two columns on either side of the road, with my platoon in the lead. At the far edge of town we came upon a large villa enclosed by a stone wall. The huge house had a nice stand of tall pines in front, and the Germans had not failed to build platforms close to the treetops so that they could observe our actions. East of the villa stretched a huge sugar beet field, and beyond that a hayfield.

Artillery shells began to land among the trees where we stood, and we spotted some Germans out in the beet field about a quarter mile away. Lieutenant Colonel Walker ordered my platoon right out into the open field to clear it out. I sure didn't like being that sort of sacrificial offering, so I asked him to shell the Germans as we went out.

In a few minutes our shells began to land among the Germans, and I led the platoon out into the sugar beet field. Our artillery soon became too much for the enemy, and they began waving white flags. I had my men hold their fire, and we waved to the Germans to come on in and surrender as soon as we could stop our artillery from firing on them.

About thirty of them got up and came toward us with their hands on their heads. We covered them until they reached us and then passed them on to the rear as prisoners. For them the war was over.

We continued our advance across the open field. It was a very tense business; we were so completely exposed. At one point I just missed stepping on a terrible antipersonnel mine we called a Bouncing Betty. Three tiny prongs showed through the earth about three inches from my foot.

I instantly yelled "*Mines!*" and told my men to watch where they walked. Those things really scared hell out of me. They were completely hidden, very deadly. They work in two stages. Stepping on one of those prongs or touching a trip wire with five pounds of pressure sets off the first stage. The mine shoots up like a small rocket, and when it's about ten to twenty feet high it explodes again. The second explosion scatters hundreds of ball bearings in every direction, like a shotgun. No one is safe within forty yards of the device. The second explosion is so close to the first you hardly have time to move. Falling down, which is the natural reflex, just exposes more of the body.

Somehow we made it all the way across the sugar beet field and then far into some hayfields where we stopped for the night. At least we were able to make comfortable beds among the haystacks.

About this time a solitary Frenchman wandered by. It seemed he owned a small fleet of buses, and the Germans had taken them all in their escape from Paris. He knew they were short on gas, and he hoped to find them abandoned and unharmed along the road. We wished him luck.

Paris was now safely in Allied hands, and the rest of the pursuit was ahead. I hoped our luck would hold out. My platoon actually had not lost a man since Saint Pois.

VIII

THE PURSUIT CONTINUES

With Paris behind us and the German armies in full retreat, we tossed all caution to the wind. Combat teams were thrown together by mixing a few tanks with each infantry battalion. The infantry rode on the back of the tanks or followed in two-and-a-half ton trucks.

A wild, mad, exciting race seemed to be on to see which army could gain the most ground in a single day. We were in the First Army under General Hodges. The headline hailed the colorful, flamboyant Patton as the hero of the day, boldly announcing, "Patton's tanks roll fifty miles." While our First Army usually made about the same distance, we were not mentioned; or, if anything was said, it was usually hidden on a second or third page of *Stars and Stripes*, the Army newspaper. Back home, too, the bold headlines were all about Patton. He did deserve a lot of credit, but we resented the neglect of the First Army and the efficient General Hodges. He never received near the credit he deserved.

Resistance continued to be very light, and we were able to gain fifty or sixty miles each day. The German rear echelon blew up a few bridges and toppled some trees across the roads at points difficult to detour. Places with a hill on one side and a ravine on the other were ideal for that type of roadblock. Usually the Germans did not defend those roadblocks, but you had to assume they were mined or an antitank gun was hidden somewhere, or you might get caught in a trap and lose some men or equipment.

Sometimes we traveled all day without any action. Ironically enough, we now crossed some old World War I battlegrounds that we recognized from historical markers or statues.

One city I remember was Soissons. Many of our men had fought and died in its vicinity some twenty-five years earlier. Somehow, being on the scene, it all seemed so unreal. Theirs was the war dedicated to end all wars, yet here we were on the very same scene again. Perhaps members of Congress should serve automatically as front-line troops. Surely such top-notch, intelligent men could find a way to stop wars much sooner if they were directly involved. It seems the young men are destined to carry out, mostly without question, the plans and orders of their seniors.

It was near Soissons, after dark, that we heard our first buzz bombs fly overhead. We had been reading about their hitting London, and now we heard them roar over and saw the afterglow of their rocket motors. It was spooky.

Our advance continued toward Belgium and Germany, retracing the paths of the Allies of World War I. Near the French-Belgian border a German regiment came out to stop us. In this particular action my outfit enjoyed the luxury of being spectators. We stayed right in our trucks and watched our fighter planes dive at the enemy ahead with all eight

50-caliber machine guns blazing away from each plane with a fearful, deafening clatter. We also heard our tanks joining in with their cannon and machine guns. The terrifying noises pressed upon our senses, and I think we would have been almost paralyzed had we been on the receiving end.

The battle was over in what seemed only a few minutes, and soon a babbling mixture of local civilians and wounded Germans streamed toward us in carts and wagons. Everyone was confused and excited, and there seemed to be no order. Some women wearing Red Cross armbands and aprons hurried out of a nearby village to help the wounded. Some of the litter cases were carried into houses, and the walking wounded cluttered around outside awaiting their turns. At the height of the turmoil our truck column began to move ahead through the village, and this only stirred up the weltering mess.

The German regiment that met up with our Air Force and tanks had been in the woods north of the village, and as we came among the trees I could hardly believe my eyes. Dead German soldiers and dead and wounded horses and wrecked wagons were scattered all along the road. The equipment for this unit must have been left over from World War I. Everything was horse-drawn.

The equipment may have been dated, but it was beautiful, and this I appreciated, for I had been partly raised on a farm. I was amazed at such superb draft horses and accouterments. The harness work was by far the finest I had ever seen. The leather was high polished, and all the brass rivets and hardware shone brightly. The horses had been groomed, with tails bobbed, as though for a parade.

Some of the horses were still alive, though crippled, and our men mercifully shot them as we drove by. This was one of the worst massacres I ever witnessed. I'm sure even the fighter pilots had no idea of their awesome destructive power. We were lucky our own columns had not been attacked by German planes, though the closer we got to the Fatherland the more we expected it to happen.

Many of the Germans had run deep into the woods to escape our planes, and our regiment now had the job of surrounding the huge area. Our company had to cover a wide stretch of meadow farmland along one perimeter of the forest, and we dug foxholes for the night. Fences divided the pastures, ending at the edge of the woods.

We placed machine guns to cover the fences, because they were partly overgrown by small bushes. In this way we could defend the only escape route for the enemy, straight through our lines.

A herd of beautiful Holstein cows was grazing peacefully along the edge of the woods. Toward evening the Belgian farmer, his wife, and a hired man came out into the pasture dragging carts loaded with ten-gallon milk cans, and they began to milk the cows right out there in the open field.

One of our GIs grabbed his canteen cup and ran over and asked for a cup of fresh milk. He mixed in some K ration chocolate powder, took a sip, and broke out into a big grin. More GI Joes decided this was good deal, and soon a line formed from the cows back across the whole platoon area.

Men from neighboring platoons also got the idea, and before long the farmer had given away all his milk. He seemed pretty philosophical about it, however, as he headed back to the farmhouse with his empty milk cans.

Before he left, I had my interpreter suggest to him it would be better if he moved his cows elsewhere for the night. I told him we expected the trapped Germans to try to break through us during the night, and that some of his cows might get shot. He expressed his thanks but added that he didn't have any other place to put them.

During the night a few Germans actually did try to escape. One even got all the way through our lines, and the last I saw of him he was running like a deer, clearing the fences in stride as rifle bullets whizzed all around him. I don't know where he was headed, but it was in the wrong direction to get home.

I was up repeatedly during the night to check on the gunfire by my men. The machine guns pointed down the fence row were very busy. The guys were trigger-happy, nervously firing at any sound to their front. Most of the time I could not find anything they thought they were firing at, and I cautioned them to be careful of the cows.

At daybreak we found we had killed two cows and wounded two others. I sent the interpreter back to break the news to the farmer, with the suggestion that he bring the equipment to butcher them and thus save most of the meat. Our medic took a look at the wounded animals, a change of pace for him. His professional opinion was that one cow would have to be put way, but that the other would recover from a small flesh wound.

We were very distressed about this nice farmer's losses, for he had been kind to us. Some our men helped him butcher the cows, and he was able to save most of the meat. There was nothing more we could do.

Just about then I was ordered to lead a patrol into the woods to see what could be stirred up. We didn't find any more Germans, but we did find out why they had thrown up so much resistance. Deep in the woods a series of tremendous log warehouses had been dug in the ground. They were filled with all kinds of supplies, plus a lot of ammo. The spiffy horse and wagon unit must have been attached there. With some difficulty we discovered a small network of very cleverly camouflaged roads and a rail spur that serviced the huge arsenal.

I reported the storage depot to the CO, but no one seemed interested, and soon we were back on the trucks again, headed generally northeastward across Belgium.

At one small town in Belgium we arrived just a few minutes too late.

The Germans had rounded up a dozen or so people, mostly teenaged boys, and shot them down in cold blood. It seems the victims were suspected of being in an underground group, and their fate was intended as a lesson to the community.

It was getting dark by then, so we stayed in the little town overnight. I slept in one of the homes as a guest. Much to my dismay, I heard later that it was a house in which one of the dead boys had lived. They had not mentioned their loss when we asked to stay. You could tell there was some grief, but I assumed it was for all of the poor kids slain. They did not mourn as you would expect a family who had just lost a son to do. They tried very hard to make us welcome. When I learned of their loss the next morning, I expressed my regrets as best I could.

After a K-ration breakfast, we moved on. I did not know then that we were very close to where the Battle of Waterloo had been fought between Napoleon and Wellington. Much blood had been spilled there in three wars in little more than a hundred years.

Our orders were suddenly changed shortly after we crossed into Belgium but before we reached Bastogne. Perhaps we were getting closer to Germany and a stronger defense, or maybe our trucks were getting low on gas. Regardless of the reason, most of our regiment now had to move on foot. My platoon was not so lucky, as we were given a new job.

The new assignment required me and my men to get out in front of the rest of the infantry and clear out any pockets of resistance we found as quickly as possible. To add to our punch we were given a platoon of five Sherman tanks and four tank destroyers, plus enough jeeps for my forty-man rifle platoon to ride in. Most of the jeeps had .30-caliber machine guns mounted on the hood, but one had a pedestal-mounted .50-caliber machine gun. Thus, all of a sudden, I found myself the rifle platoon leader of a miniature task force under the command of Lieutenant Toles.

We moved out on a winding easterly course toward the Siegfried Line from near Saint Vith, Belgium. I had no idea how far we had to go or how soon we might get some action. I was also not aware of the overall situation and so did not know at the time that we were the point of the right column of our regiment, and that another unit was in a similar position a few miles to our left, north of us.

Our column went through one small village after another. The people there, as in much of Europe, seemed to draw their houses together in small clusters two or three miles apart. They would farm the outreaching fields around them. Most of the population of the villages stood by the side of the road and waved as we went by. In this area of Belgium we were most welcome, and the faces of the men and women showed their warmth. It was interesting to see the changes in expression as we moved closer to the German border—the faces by the side of the road grew much tighter, and smiles became rare. Then nervous uncertainty appeared in their expressions, and a hint of fear. At first the fright was evident in only a few, then it showed in about half the expressions, and finally nearly everyone stared straight ahead with frozen faces, too afraid to look us in the eye, fearful of more fighting in their village. The Germans had overrun the same area in World War I.

After a while we came to the tiny village of Auel on the banks of a branch of the Our River meandering through a valley in the village. As we approached its small bridge there was suddenly a quick flash, and a ripping explosion, and the bridge disappeared in a cloud of debris.

As soon as the sounds of the blast died away we heard the roar of a heavy motor speeding away. At that moment I was standing near the front of one of our tank destroyers staring at the road ahead, and I was almost knocked flat by the concussion when its 90mm gun started rapid fire. Windowpanes in the houses were shattered all around. I staggered to the rear of the TD to get away from all that noise.

The blasting stopped in a few seconds, but it was some time before my hearing returned and I could understand the TD commander's report. It seems they had picked off an enemy half-track speeding away up a winding road. The range was sixteen hundred yards, nearly a mile, and the target must have been tearing along about forty miles per hour. To me it was incredible marksmanship, better than a rifleman might have done at four hundred yards. I really didn't believe the claim until I saw the smoking half-track.

After we forded the small river, we became very cautious indeed as we pushed ahead. It seemed highly questionable to me to be leading the column with defenseless jeeps, but the tankers and TD men argued that jeeps were faster, more maneuverable, and more expendable. This did make sense, though I didn't like the word expendable. I put the jeep with the .50-caliber machine gun in the lead with Crocker, my best scout. My jeep was next in line, followed by the other jeeps and then the armor. Crocker stayed about two hundred yards ahead of me, and the other vehicles followed at thirty-yard intervals.

Our pace was now a discreet twenty miles per hour with frequent stops to check out potential enemy positions.

Once, when we came around a curve in the road, we spotted a few Germans in the woods to our left. The men piled out of the jeeps and started shooting. At the same time someone swung the .30-caliber machine gun on my jeep to the left and opened up without looking. This stream of bullets knocked the rifle out of the hands of one of the other men, scaring the devil out of him but not touching him otherwise. He lost all his color, and I thought he was going to faint, but instead he quickly snapped out of it and got really mad. Then someone laughed, and the tension was broken. Meanwhile, the enemy took off back over a hill, and we resumed our advance.

Having seen enemy soldiers at Auel and again on the ridge beyond, we now approached the next town, Winterspelt, with extreme caution. This was fairly open country —easy for long-range enemy fire, I was thinking—so I decided to hold up the column about a half mile out and sent Crocker in alone in the lead jeep.

As Crocker's jeep got close to the edge of town it stopped, and everyone scrambled out and ran up to a small orchard on their right. A moment later one of the men ran back to the jeep and radioed for us to come on in. He said they had just caught a German antitank gun crew asleep and captured all of them.

I couldn't help wondering how many men we might have lost if that gun crew had stayed awake. Our luck was still with us. An antitank gun would disintegrate a jeep with one shot.

The rest of the unit moved into the town immediately, and the men began a house-to-house search for enemy soldiers. There was no sign of civilians, and there were no white flags showing, as there would have been had the military left. We could all feel the enemy's presence, and the eerie sensation built up as we nervously awaited the first shot.

The spell was partially broken by a crusty old German-Belgian farmer who issued from a house on our left and began to saunter across the road in front of us, clanking a couple of empty milk cans. We stopped this character, and our interpreter asked him where the Kraut soldiers were. He spat on the ground, shuffled his feet, and said that they had all left the day before. This old rascal was a pretty good actor and wasn't about to give us any info, so we let him go.

I still felt that there were Germans close by, and I began to examine the road ahead through my binoculars. A building stood about two hundreds yards ahead, and against its side were some German bicycles with the usual gas mask canisters on their rear fenders. German soldiers did not usually leave their bicycles behind.

We continued to work down the road, searching each building along the way. All we came across were pitifully scared civilians, usually huddled together in a back room or cellar. They had no way of knowing we wouldn't harm them. I wondered how many times the war had passed their front doors.

Quite a bit of small-arms ammunition turned up, plus some antitank shells, gasoline, and food rations. And in one shed we came upon the half-track that had towed the antitank gun we'd captured at the edge of town.

Once Private First Class Crocker and another man, who was always very aggressive, spotted a couple of Germans running from a barn into the house with the bicycles parked alongside. Crocker quickly emptied his rifle through the door, reloaded, and then—without waiting for help—jerked the door open. He stepped over a dead German soldier by the door, glanced at the terrified old civilian couple cringing in a corner of the room, and unhesitatingly followed a track of blood up the stairs. There he found two unarmed Kraut soldiers hiding under a bed, and he ordered them to come out with their hands up or he'd toss in a grenade. They may not have understood his poor German, but they did understand his manner, and they quickly surrendered.

When next I saw Crocker, he was coming down the road with his prisoners in tow. One of the prisoners had blood running down his arm and was begging to lower his arm, but Crocker just prodded him with his rifle and made him keep moving. Winterspelt was a border town, and the prisoners told us they were home on furlough. Later, when I had time, I recommended Crocker for a Bronze Star for his bold actions.

The men were ready to go into action again across the road because they'd heard movement in the basement and couldn't get anyone to come out, but I restrained them because I suspected scared civilians. I had the interpreter yell down that if they didn't come up, we'd throw down a grenade. Sure enough, five pitifully frightened old men and women came crawling up the stairs.

They had been told the American soldiers would kill the men and rape the women. We tried as best we could to assure them they had nothing to fear from us. I was grateful my own parents and grandparents would not have to go through this sort of terror.

Just as we were ready to leave town, a tank sergeant yelled at me from his open turret. He told me to take a quick look at the ox team near a farmhouse a half mile ahead. My binoculars showed a team of oxen plodding along with a two-wheeled cart loaded with household goods. Their route passed along across my front from left to right. A careful study revealed signs of another vehicle on the far side of the oxcart, hiding behind it.

I asked the sergeant if he had any idea what the hidden vehicle was, and he said, "Yes, sir. It must be the half-track we saw going behind a building when we first came up here. We didn't have time to get a shot off then."

"Well, you've got time now. Go to it," I told him. The sergeant just grinned. His first round blew up the oxcart, and his second got the half-track, which was trying to streak away. It seemed a shame to blow up the oxcart, but the war was not a game, and the oxcart was not being put to innocent use.

When I radioed in my position at the next road junction I was ordered to hold up and await further instructions. I supposed they were trying to decide which direction we should take. The equipment was pulled over to the edge of the road, and the men had all taken cover in the tall grass on the right shoulder of the road.

Suddenly a German motorcycle with a sidecar appeared on the road coming in our direction. I waited until he was almost on top of us before ordering the men nearest me to jump up and stop him. The motorcycle came to an abrupt halt. Both Germans quickly threw up their hands in surrender. I ordered them to dismount. The driver stood up and came forward immediately.

The corporal in the sidecar rose slowly, stepped up on the seat of the bike, and then fell astride the bike and gunned its motor full speed and headed down the road toward Germany.

He only made it some twenty feet down the road. The sharp, deadly crack of several rifles broke through the roar of the motorcycle, and the corporal slumped over dead. His back was riddled with bullets. The other German just shook his head in dismay and wonderment at the daring but stupid attempt to escape. In any event, the war was over for both of them.

Our next town was Grossbangenfeld, a pleasant little hamlet. We did not find any German soldiers there but did come across an English-speaking woman with a two-way radio. She got very indignant—in fact, she cussed me out splendidly—when, for obvious military reasons I ordered her radio destroyed.

Meanwhile, our Private Crocker was having difficulty with the .50-caliber machine gun. It jammed too easily and apparently needed head-space adjustments. I tried my hand at the repair and told Crocker to go out to the edge of town and fire it a few times to try it out. Soon we could hear the .50-caliber machine gun in rapid fire, as expected, but there came some rather insistent rifle fire as well.

It seems that two Kraut soldiers had just rounded a small bend in the road headed for town when the .50-caliber machine gun opened its practice fire. Both of them dumped their bicycles and rolled into the ditch with their hands raised. The one farther back suddenly decided to make a break. He jumped a small fence and ran like hell down through a little orchard. The riflemen opened fire, but the German was too evasive and got away. He probably would have been better off as a prisoner.

The captured man was so frightened he shook convulsively and his forehead was beaded with sweat. Then he began to jabber in a foreign language and gesticulate, as though he were begging for his life. When one of the men began speaking to him in Polish, the prisoner quieted down.

Once the prisoner was convinced he was not going to be harmed, he began to talk. He was a Russian forced into the German Army after his capture. He was told the Americans would shoot him as a spy if he surrendered, and he was threatened constantly by the German who always rode behind him with orders to shoot him if he failed to do his job. He told us he was the lead scout of a bicycle company coming up the road to fight us, and he said they were only a few hundred yards behind. The poor guy was frantic, almost berserk with fear.

I quickly moved men and tanks into defensive positions, hoping the Germans would blunder over the little hill to our front. When they didn't appear after a few minutes, I sent a few jeeps with machine guns to explore the road up to the next curve.

In a few minutes they radioed back that they had found a lot of bicycle tire tracks in the road where the Germans had turned around and headed for home. Apparently they had been warned by the clatter of the .50-caliber machine gun and rifle fire. When their scouts disappeared, they knew their bicycles and rifles were no match against us. Especially if they had spotted our tanks and TDs. We could hardly blame them for leaving.

By now we had the feeling that the Siegfried Line couldn't be too far ahead. We came down a long slope and passed what appeared to be a railroad freight yard with a small station that bore the sign BLEIALF. We could see the town buildings about a half mile to the northeast.

The rail tracks led northward into a tunnel, and we discovered the tunnel had been widened for machine shops and appeared safe from bombing. The machinery, plus any war material, evidently had been moved very recently. You could see where machines had been positioned before the wires had been cut so that they could be moved.

Some of us went into the beer hall across the road from the tunnel, and as we entered something made a noise behind the counter. My Browning Automatic rifleman began shooting without questioning. He ripped off his entire twenty-round clip into the bar, but, to his regret, all he hit was bottles. *C'est la guerre*.

When our eyes got accustomed to the dim lighting, we spotted a young woman and an old man, both very frightened by the shooting, hiding in a corner. They were father and daughter, slave labor from Poland. She had been a teacher, and she spoke several languages, including English and German. Her father was ill, and she had hidden him when the Germans had moved out all of the machines and other people a few days before.

She also told us we were getting very close to the Siegfried Line, which was not much more than a mile away. She had been there several times with German officers. She was sure the line was occupied, and she volunteered that the bicycle outfit had come from there.

We passed all this information back to the rear and then were told to go on into Bleialf with extreme caution. We stayed on the road and went past a rather large butter factory and right on into the center of town, marked by a church and a cobblestone square. I was greatly surprised that we had no trouble, for there were several excellent defensive positions.

The road eastward toward Sellerich was a long, winding incline, and halfway up the hill I stopped the column and very gingerly walked the rest of the way up, taking one man with me. There was considerable cover from underbrush and scrub pine along the way. We had to go a bit beyond the crest before we could get a clear view of our road winding down the hill and across a small valley, only to disappear into the thick pine forest beyond.

I lay on the ground and used my field glasses to very carefully study every inch of the little valley and the edge of the thick woods. At first I saw nothing at all; then a slight movement caught my eye. A couple of German soldiers were cutting wood with an axe partway up the slope, right in the edge of the woods. One guy picked up an armload and disappeared behind a door that seemed to open into the side of the hill.

I fixed my eye on the spot and saw the door open again,

and the man came out for more wood. Now I could clearly make out a mound of earth and the outline of gun emplacements. This fortification was just across the valley and only about one hundred yards from the road. Suddenly my stomach turned a little, and I got a slight chill as I realized I might well be the first American to set eyes on a pillbox in the famous Siegfried Line.

The earthen mounds looked like piles of dirt with tufts of grass and bushes on top. Darker spots apparently were doors or windows cut into the earth. I could not see any cement or guns, but we found out later they were very much there under that pile of earth—cement walls eight feet thick with roofs ten to twelve feet thick.

I was able to spot several more mounds that might have been pillboxes covered with earth and grass. Huge iron doors were slightly ajar, and there was no longer any question in my mind that this was indeed the Siegfried Line.

Using my compass, I took azimuth readings for each pillbox, marking them on my map. Then we crawled back over the hill to our vehicles and radioed headquarters of my find. I was told to wait there for further orders.

Luckily for us, from what I heard later, Colonel Lanham's original orders never reached us. I never found out if he changed his mind or whether the orders somehow went astray. Friends told me he had originally wanted me to go right over the hill and attack the pillboxes, to find out how well they were defended. I suppose I was flattered he thought my small combat team could do this, but I don't see how we could have attempted it alone and come out alive.

Finally, around dusk, I received orders to pull back and rejoin E Company south of Bleialf.

Some other unit in our regiment got credit for being first to cross the German border, but I am sure we had to have been the first to see the Siegfried Line. At least our regiment, the Twenty Second Infantry, got credit for being the first on German soil, on September 12. Unit pride was important in those days.

We did not know how much or how often we would have to fight there in the next few months.

IX

SIEGFRIED LINE

During the night of September 12–13, while I rested from the tense days on point, Colonel Lanham was busy planning to attack the Siegfried Line the next morning. He had maps, aerial photos, and the reports from his two point leaders on the positions of pillboxes, and he would assume the line was fully manned from the information he had received.

Colonel Lanham also had an uncompromisingly aggressive nature. He believed the best way to end the war quickly and save lives was to attack and attack. He also believed wholeheartedly that the boys of the Twenty Second Infantry Regiment shared his spirit, that they could do the job if anyone could. The Siegfried Line was, to him, more an opportunity than an obstacle. He wanted his regiment to be the first Americans through the line, as they'd already been first across the border into Germany. Plans were to attack east from the vicinity of Buchet.

The attack plan was starkly simple. The Third Battalion, led by veteran Lieutenant Colonel Teague, was to jump off in column of companies—that is, with one company leading the attack as point and the others following one by one in its path. After the penetration, the two other battalions were to follow through the same gap and then turn left and right to attack the neighboring pillboxes from the rear.

It was important to cut a wide swath through the lines because each pillbox was close enough to its neighbors that they had overlapping fields of fire. An attack thus drew fire from the pillbox it faced directly, plus crossfire from the pillboxes on each side.

The vulnerable part of the pillbox was its rear. The crossfire support did not reach back there, and all they had was some barbed wire and whatever rifles and machine guns could be transferred to the rear trenches. The trick was to get behind a pillbox quickly.

The lead attack company faced the worst beating, but it was not simply going to walk into the "jaws of death." The open ground close to the pillboxes did have some small depressions into which the infantry could duck, and a scattering of small pines and scrub brush offered some cover.

The tanks and TDs also were to come up to within two hundred to five hundred yards of the pillboxes and plaster them with direct cannon fire against their firing apertures and steel doors. Artillery would fire hundreds of rounds onto the same targets. Many of the Germans thus would be pinned down and occupied with their own safety, and thus —it was hoped—would not be very effective against us.

For close support, right up beside a pillbox, the infantry had two deadly weapons, flamethrowers and satchel charges. The flamethrower was operated by one man with a tank strapped to his back, The flame from the hose was huge, but the man had to get within ten to twenty yards of his target. If he could get close enough to an aperture, he could blind or suffocate those inside the pillbox. Some of the enemy might also be set on fire.

The satchel charge had a long fuse attached to twelve pounds of TNT, six pounds in each side of a saddlelike bag. If it could be set off in one of the pillbox openings, it would kill or stun anyone inside. With both weapons, a man had to get in very close. Dangerous work, but it really paid off. Either close-in weapon could finish off a pillbox —providing the attacker could stay alive long enough to use them.

Our splendid Third Battalion (Companies I, K, L, and M) was the one Colonel Lanham seemed to use in crucial situations, and they did not fail him this time. They absorbed their casualties and drove a small hole right through the Siegfried, and then they widened it into a wedge. The First Battalion followed close behind and then turned to the left to wipe out the pillboxes on the north from the rear. The bulk of the Third Battalion then turned right toward Brandscheid, a fortified town astride the Siegfried almost a mile to the south. Meanwhile, the Second Battalion, which included my E Company, kept straight ahead through the gap for over a half mile, then fanned out in two-company width, facing southeast across some open fields.

The First Battalion found it rather easy to take pillboxes from the rear, and they took many prisoners as they headed northward. They advanced as far as reasonable, perhaps a thousand yards, and then consolidated their position.

Our job in the Second Battalion was even easier. We simply set up a good defense and waited for the enemy to attack, which he failed to do, and that was a break for us.

The Third Battalion moved smoothly southward until they hit the heavily defended village of Brandscheid and a very tough Kraut battalion. The battle raged on for the next two weeks, and Brandscheid never did fall. This little burg was circled by pillboxes, and it just wasn't worth the cost of storming it, so Colonel Teague's men kept plunking away at it to keep it contained.

Meanwhile, the First Battalion was hit by a very heavy counterattack and had to fight desperately for a couple of days to keep from being overrun.

We in the Second Battalion were alerted for a probable counterattack, but none ever materialized. We did detect a convoy of Germans moving eastward on the Sellerich road, and I led a patrol to within thirty yards of the road to confirm that they were, indeed, Jerries, but nothing was ever done to try and stop them. I found out later that we were really handicapped by lack of supplies, having only enough gas to move each vehicle in the division five miles, and we had only one day's supply of ammunition.

Colonel Lanham had asked division headquarters to permit him to continue the attack right on through to the Rhine, but Division did not have the supplies to support him, and we lacked support from other units for the same reason. Colonel Lanham claimed, and history proved, that no German unit was strong enough to stop us short of the Rhine. It's hard to imagine how many lives might have been saved if our troops had reached the Rhine in September, instead of six months later in March. This assumes, of course, that neighboring divisions would have kept up with us so that we would not have been cut off. I feel sure they could have if we had all been given the supplies we needed.

Eisenhower himself made the decision, allowing only what he called "pencillike" thrusts through the Siegfried. We can only hope this was not a major error.

We really did not fault the quartermaster people for our supply shortages, because their lines stretched clear back to Cherbourg and they were just beginning to open up Le Havre. There were ugly rumors, however, that Patton's Third Army was getting more than its share, sometimes even through pirating. It was also believed that the High Command favored Patton, not expecting that Patton would be stopped cold in the Metz-Nancy region, nor that Hodges's First Army would make such tremendous progress. Too bad hindsight always seems to beat foresight.

Meanwhile, we were still in defensive positions deep behind the Siegfried with our E Company on the extreme right. We were about a half mile east of the Siegfried, at the edge of some woods which overlooked a valley just below Sellerich. As the sun came up we had a clear view of the rolling farmland generally to our southeast. In a little while we found ourselves with what amounted to grandstand seats for a remarkable panorama of war.

Another battalion, perhaps from the Ninetieth Division, moved into the woods about a quarter mile to our right, east of Brandscheid. Soon they began an attack eastward, directly toward Sellerich. They jumped off with two companies abreast and headed down through the valley that led to the hills around Sellerich. The rifle companies were leading, supported by tanks along each side of the Sellerich road.

At first everything went exactly by the book as tank-infantry teams performed beautifully, wiping out pockets of Germans in their path. We could see every move and hear the continual clatter of the tanks' machine guns and the crack of rifles. We could even hear the excited shouts of men in combat.

Maybe it was because we were not used to being spectators, but somehow all the action seemed unreal, almost as though it were a training film. Each unit performed smoothly; they were in full control as the enemy melted away.

Then unexpectedly German mortars and artillery, which had not been evident up to that point, suddenly came down hard on the infantry and tanks as they reached a small exposed area at a crossroad. There was no cover from the terrible barrage; the Germans knew the exact range and obviously had been waiting for the Americans to reach that point.

The American tanks turned and raced back toward the woods to escape the slaughter, panicking the riflemen, who chased after the tanks in confusion. The retreat was an uncontrolled stampede, and a great many casualties were left where they fell. Even at our safe distance we all felt sick. It could so easily have been us.

It had taken about forty-five minutes for the tank-infantry teams to reach the crossroads in the low ground west of Honthiem, and the entire gain had been wiped out in less than five minutes. Dead and wounded lay all over the fields, and the officers were fighting desperately to regain control of the survivors. They were now all back in the woods where the attack had begun almost an hour before. Perhaps the Germans were short on ammo, too, since they did not follow up their victory by dropping more artillery in the woods.

The whole disheartening episode was at least a lesson in the naked power of artillery and its effective use. The Germans had destroyed an attack without committing any of their tanks or infantry. The results could have been much worse if they had followed up with more artillery.

Our company abruptly had some major changes in officer personnel. Our executive officer was transferred out, and the company commander, First Lieutenant Toles, who had not fully recovered from earlier wounds, stepped down to the executive position. We received a new company commander, Captain Arthur Newcomb, who had been on the battalion staff since before I had joined the outfit in July of 1944. He was one of the officers who landed with the regiment on D day. We felt lucky to get him.

During the rest of the day our artillery forward observer (FO) managed to fire some rounds at the German positions we could see in the hills around Sellerich. He timed the shells to explode just over the heads of his targets, and the airbursts looked to be very effective. It was the first time I had seen them in use. Later in the day we watched a long line of German ambulances pick up wounded in that area. Our forward observer had to cease firing after a while, however, because he ran out of ammunition, and he was pretty disgusted.

During the evening of the day on which we witnessed the slaughter of the other battalion in the low ground between Honthiem and Sellerich, we were alerted for an attack in that area the next morning. Then we were all told to get a good night's rest because we would be jumping off in the attack early in the morning! How do you forget such carnage while trying to rest up to repeat it?

At the first sign of dawn I ate a hurried K-ration breakfast, which I warmed over the wax-paper carton it came in, and then joined Captain Newcomb and the other officers for a briefing. The attack plan was for E Company to lead the way, with the other companies following in column behind us. We were to swing wide to the left and hit the Germans from the flank. At least we didn't have to follow the same route those people had taken the day before, and we wouldn't be surprised by Kraut artillery.

I called my sergeants together, brought them up-to-date, and had them get their men ready to move out. Then one of my most experienced men crawled out of his foxhole, got to his feet, and fell in a heap. His body shook with convulsions; he was a total wreck and had to be evacuated. Apparently the stress and worry in anticipation of our attack, after witnessing the terrifying slaughter the day before, was too much for him.

Captain Newcomb apologized because he had only one map for the entire company, and it was a 1914 edition. He warned us to be cautious because he was sure the roads and trails in the wooded area and other landmarks had changed since 1914. He then told me to lead off with my platoon and said that he would be in close contact by radio.

The company moved out in column of platoons. We picked our way cautiously through the thick stand of pines on the right side of the road. These pines had probably been planted shortly after World War I and were about thirty feet tall. The underbrush was thick and tangled, and it was enough trouble to struggle through without worrying about the enemy. What had been a dreary mist turned into a drizzle and soon became a downpour as we slapped and pushed our way through the wet branches.

We had worked our way ahead for about a mile when Captain Newcomb radioed us to hold in place because there was some confusion over our route. So we stopped where we were and sat down to rest with our backs against trees. In about ten minutes Captain Newcomb plowed his way up through the brush, looked at his map, and told us to continue on again in the same direction.

I got the men on their feet and signaled the two scouts to move out ahead. Private First Class Crocker acknowledged with a wave. He and his partner stood up and immediately opened fire across the road to their left. The second scout emptied the eight-round clip in his M-1 so fast it seemed almost like a machine gun. Then he turned and ran like the devil for the rear while steady old Crocker crouched in place, watching the road.

The second scout told me they had spotted several Germans in the road not ten feet ahead of them when they stood up. The Germans had not returned the fire, so they had been killed or had taken off.

The rest of us moved very cautiously and found three dead enemy soldiers in the road. Crocker was sure one or two others had gotten away. It looked as though we had been lucky enough to spot a German patrol just before they saw us.

But as soon as we got up to move we were flattened by vicious machine gun fire. I was pinned down behind a small mound of earth while bullets whipped into the dirt in front of and just over my head. My knapsack got torn up, and the canteen on my hip took a direct hit and leaked water all over my back and legs. It was difficult to just lie there and not try to get up and run for cover.

My radio was not touched, so I called our mortar squad to set up and fire a few rounds. I couldn't see the Kraut machine guns, so we had to guess about where they were from the sound. It took a bit of adjusting, but after a few rounds we heard the wild screams of German wounded, and the machine gun was silent. Apparently we had achieved a lucky hit.

After throwing in a few extra rounds to make sure, we were able to get up and continue our advance. I judged this to have been a small forward outpost, and I wondered just how far out the Germans were from their lines.

We had made about another half mile into the woods without opposition when Captain Newcomb again ordered us to halt. This time he came running up with the map in his hand and told me we were about a half mile off course, and he said that he wanted us to make a sharp left and head up the hill through the woods to the next road and then turn right. According to the old map, the next road was much better than the present one, which was not much more than a fire trail.

The left turn led us up a long hill deep into woods thick with tall white pines. We moved as quietly as we could, and our steps were muffled by the wet pine needles that were matted on the ground. They even seemed to absorb the downpour of cold rain. Crocker was the single lead scout, since the other man had had enough for one day. He worked his way up the hill about thirty yards ahead of me, with the platoon following close behind. Suddenly he dropped to the ground and waved me forward cautiously. I crawled up to him over the wet ground, and he pointed a few yards ahead to a collection of German rifles, machine guns, and other gear leaning up against trees.

We lay quietly and could neither see nor hear any other sign of the Germans, who had apparently abandoned their weapons. The trees had thinned out there, and through the murky light I was able to make out a clearing about one hundred yards ahead. I told Crocker to keep low and go take a look. Some of the men had moved up close behind me, and we covered Crocker as he crawled forward through the rain.

Crocker soon reached the edge of the woods and motioned me to crawl up beside him. Then he carefully pointed to a clutch of Germans standing around a shelter that was tied to a wide, bushy pine tree. They were only about forty yards in front of us across the road. We could see several groups of them all huddled up, trying to take shelter from the pouring rain.

I couldn't conceive how blockheaded or green those troops might be, leaving their weapons a good hundred yards away. They were sitting ducks on a pond in the rain, with no idea we were near. Maybe the rain had blotted out the sound of gunfire less than a hour before, yet only a half mile from them. Perhaps they thought the downpour had canceled the war for the day.

My ever-aggressive, impulsive Crocker wanted to open fire, but I was able to restrain him. The closer I looked, the more Germans I saw. There seemed to be a whole platoon of them scattered along the edge of the road for about one hundred yards to my right. I signaled my platoon forward and carefully positioned them along the edge of the woods parallel to the road.

About this time Captain Newcomb came up to find out the reason for the delay. I showed him the situation and told him I planned to attack in a few minutes. He asked if we needed any help and quickly agreed to my request for another platoon to assemble to the right of mine and for a third platoon to protect the right flank. Captain Newcomb said he would send up Lieutenant Mason with his Third Platoon and told me that I should tell Mason where he should place his men. He said, "Go ahead whenever you're ready, and I'll take care of everything else."

While we waited in the rain for the Third Platoon to come up, we had a brief scare. A German corporal stood up and stretched, threw a rain cape around his shoulders, and walked out into the middle of the road. I froze in step between two pines as he looked out our way. One of my men lying on the ground near me wanted to shoot, but I whispered, "No." I was proud of the control of my men, for not one of them moved, and the corporal was lucky he walked away.

A few minutes later Lieutenant Mason signaled he was ready, and our two platoons, eighty men on line, opened up on those poor Jerries who were stupidly lolling under the trees only forty yards across the road. All those M-1 rifles, plus six Browning Automatic rifles, blasted away at once into a continuous crackling din. They were throwing almost one hundred rounds a second into the screaming, bellowing, scrambling Germans. Not a single shot was fired in return. After a few minutes, I led the men in a wild charge across the road to the stricken enemy.

Our attack was so sudden and such a brutal surprise that not one of our men was touched. We did not know how many weapons the Jerries might have had with them, and of course we couldn't take a chance. Most of the fifty or so Germans were dead, and we found only one man among them who was not wounded or dead. He was about eighteen and so scared he couldn't talk. I took his new Luger pistol as a souvenir and sent him to the rear. He and the corporal who had walked down the road were the only lucky ones.

We had very little time to exult. In fact, even before I had time to report to Captain Newcomb or confer with Lieutenant Mason, the Germans hit us with a full-platoon counterattack. They seemed to come from the woods directly across the field from us.

I instantly ordered my men back across the road and into the ditch where they had some protection. The Jerries would fire at us as they ran toward us and every few seconds they would hit the ground and fire some more. We tried to pick them off every time they got up to rush us, but the rain continued steadily and the visibility was poor.

Some of them made it up behind the pines and fired rapidly enough to pin us down. I yelled at my men to throw grenades and return the fire. Then Captain Newcomb ordered me to withdraw into the woods and rejoin the rest of Company E, so I moved along the line and got each squad to pull back two men at a time.

Between the woods and the road was a strip of a hayfield about thirty yards wide. The hay was two feet high, and most of our men crawled back safely, though the last squad lost two men. Sergeant Williams, the same man who had been shot through the neck around D day and who returned to action only to get paralyzed at Le Mesnil Herman back in July, had a grenade land by him, and he became paralyzed again. Apparently his old neck wound could not stand the shock. So we had to drag him back into the woods.

I yelled at one of the sergeants to hurry and get his men out of there. The sergeant thereupon stood right up in the open, for no reason at all that I could figure—and immediately was cut down by a German burp gun, a small machine pistol that fired so fast it sounded like *b-r-r-r-ip*.

To my mind, the sergeant's girlfriend was responsible

for the naked carelessness that caused his death. Just the day before he had shown me a Dear John letter he'd received from her. It was the most wickedly cruel letter I had ever read, and it morbidly depressed the sergeant. He was from the south, and this little wench told him, among similar tidbits, that she had been sleeping with a Negro and that he was twice the man Sergeant Hester was.

The rain still came down in torrents, and the Germans made no attempt to follow us into the woods. We had seen enough action for one day, so we dug in for the night among the tall pines. Each foxhole had to be big enough for two men, with one being on guard while the other slept, taking turns every two hours all night. The tree roots gave us plenty of trouble, but we managed with a few axes.

The rain finally stopped sometime during the night. Shortly after daybreak the next morning I was shocked at the actions of a lieutenant from Captain Clang's F Company, which had moved in on our left. This lieutenant walked right out onto the road we had been shooting over the night before. His .45 automatic was still in its holster, and he stood all alone waving his arms in the air as he harangued the Germans in their own language.

My interpreter told me in hushed whispers that the adventurous lieutenant was urging the Germans to surrender, saying that the war was almost over, that the situation was utterly hopeless for them, that they were about to be killed or captured anyway.

I watched spellbound as several Jerries put their hands up and came forward to surrender. He searched each one, relieved them of a few souvenirs, which he stuffed in his jacket pockets, and then sent them to the rear. He continued the spectacle for over an hour, inducing at least a dozen Germans to surrender.

At this point I asked Captain Clang why he didn't haul

the lieutenant back in, and he said, "Let the nut go on. It looks easier than fighting them."

We looked up when some of our men let out cries of warning and alarm, and we found the lieutenant now crossing the road and walking right into the hayfield amid the enemy. He had been there for almost two hours, and perhaps had become a little intoxicated with his own prowess and good fortune. He managed to entice three or four more Germans to cross over, and then suddenly it was all over.

He finally hit one of the more vicious Krauts, and this one simply cut him down point-blank. We heard the *b-r-r-r-r-ip* and saw the lieutenant topple over, dead before he hit the ground.

The Germans all withdrew the next day, and we recovered the lieutenant's body. His chest and stomach were full of holes; his jacket pockets were crammed with pocket watches, German money, penknives, and photos of German soldiers and their families. Someone asked if we should send this junk home to his wife. No one bothered to answer.

Most German units were composed of excellent troops —tough, well trained, and with good discipline. Luckily for us, this outfit was an exception. Some of the prisoners later told us they had not been trained for the infantry, and only a few of the officers and noncoms had seen combat. Most of the soldiers were emergency transfers from service companies, antiaircraft, and the air forces. They had been thrown together into an outfit and tossed out in front in the hopes that they could delay us long enough for the regular infantry to regroup from the cataclysm of Normandy and Saint-Lô.

By this time our own forces had lost some of their thunderbolt punch. We were, in fact, too thin and spread out for a solid breakthrough. Our wild, thrilling rampage through

France, Belgium, and into the Siegfried had been too fast and far for our supply lines. We were lucky to have enough ammunition and food for the day.

We had no orders to move ahead, so we began to improve our defenses where we were, widening our foxholes, collecting logs for their tops and pine boughs for mattresses. Some of our boys, had they known this was to be their home for the next few weeks, might have built chalets. The Germans, meanwhile, pulled back some three hundred yards behind the hayfield and also dug in.

The Graves Registration people were slow in coming to collect the body of Sergeant Hester, and its presence was demoralizing; we had never actually had to bury one of our own, but I felt the time had come. We got the proper instructions from Graves Registration and went ahead quickly to get the job over with, marking the grave with his upright rifle bearing his helmet and dog tags.

After a few days, our platoon was ordered into new positions about three hundred yards to the right rear. Captain Newcomb was adjusting the company defenses, and we were to be the reserve platoon. It was a very simple, quick move, but when I was assigning each squad its new area I was surprised to find that Sergeant Hood and some of his squad, the last ones in line, were missing. We had heard some incoming artillery a few minutes earlier, but it didn't sound too close to our area.

I walked back toward our old positions very puzzled. I was badly shocked to find several of my men on the ground. Sergeant Hood didn't look hurt at all, but he was dead. A small fragment had severed his windpipe. Our medic, Grazcyck, had a hole in the back of his head; he looked gone.

Another man, a big, burly former boxer, was in his foxhole screaming for a medic. I ran over there and found him frantically gripping what was left of one arm with his remaining good hand. The arm was gone, almost to the shoulder. I quickly put a tourniquet on the stump and helped him out of the foxhole. As he lay on the ground I sprinkled sulfa powder on his open wound and tried to cover it. It was a terrible, grisly mess, and I didn't have enough bandages.

Then our wounded medic, Grazcyck, somehow got up and came over to help me. He gave me some of his first aid equipment, including an ample supply of morphine, which he told me how to use on the wounded man. He also guided me on how to truss up the gory stump. Then both men fainted. I didn't feel too well myself and certainly was grateful for the little bit of first aid training I had received at OCS. Both injured men were quickly evacuated by stretcher to an ambulance waiting below the hill.

Grazcyck was recommended for the Bronze Star for actions beyond the call of duty, and I hope he received it; he certainly earned it.

After our wounded had been cared for and our dead removed, we began to settle into our new area. Everyone dug foxholes, rushing to get them done before nightfall. The light was blocked out early in the woods, and the darkness was total blackness.

While checking around I found that Sergeant Anders was not putting one of his men on guard duty because the man was too jittery. I told Sergeant Anders that the man, whom we'll call "Hill," would have to pull guard, at least in a rear area like this. We were over three hundred yards from the enemy and even had some of our own troops in front of us. That far back we posted only a few guards during the night, and I suggested that Hill be put on an early shift at the outpost only thirty yards beyond our foxhole.

Soon Hill was carefully stringing #110 field telephone wire along the trees from the guard post back to his foxhole. The men were teasing him about it, though it wasn't a bad idea, since it can be difficult to find your way in absolute blackness.

"Hey, Hill, how are you going to get back to your foxhole if someone cuts your wire?" someone called out.

"They better not, godammit!" Everyone laughed.

Sergeant Anders and I shared a foxhole, and around 10 P.M. we heard someone stumbling along Hill's wire, which passed about six feet from our foxhole. The footsteps came along in total darkness to almost opposite our foxhole, and then they suddenly stopped, and we heard Hill's harsh, frightened whisper: "Who's that?"

We could almost feel the fear in Hill's voice, and I was startled for a moment because I didn't know what had alarmed Hill. Then a few yards away in the night came the dry response: "It's Bill, goddammit. Don't shoot!"

The drama was so intense that neither Sergeant Anders nor I could take it. We burst out laughing.

Meanwhile, Bill came up along the wire and told Hill that he had been trying to find his own foxhole for the hour since Hill had relieved him. Visibility was less than a foot, and Bill was thoroughly lost. Fortunately, I had noticed Bill's foxhole and was able to direct him to it.

It seemed almost natural for seasoned veterans to form a mental picture of where everyone was dug in. I don't remember any training on that subject; however, I do know that many of the veterans were keenly aware of everything near them. Perhaps that's why they lived to be veterans.

Sergeant Anders then asked Hill if he thought he could find his own foxhole. "Yes, if somebody hasn't changed the goddamn wire!" He groped his way off, muttering to himself. His foxhole was only about twenty yards away.

After about twenty minutes we heard some shuffling back along the wire, and Sergeant Anders called out, "Is that you, Hill?"

"Somebody changed the goddamn wire, and I can't find my foxhole," complained Hill.

Sergeant Anders then told him that no one could have touched the wire and that he should go back to the very end of the wire, make a sharp left, and take one big step, and he'd fall right into his foxhole.

Hill retraced his steps, grumbling all the way. Shortly we heard a sharp crack and then a wild yell from Hill; he had been afraid to let go of the wire when he came to the end of the line. Rifle slung over his shoulder, he held on to one end of the wire with one hand and groped for his foxhole with the other. He reached too far, the pine bough holding his wire snapped, and Hill plummeted headfirst into his foxhole.

Nothing but his feelings were hurt, and Hill eased them by letting out a torrent of purple cusses. Sergeant Anders went out to check, but Hill was so mad he wouldn't talk. I don't think I ever laughed so hilariously in my life. We all were a little close to hysteria at times, and the episode was a great release.

During the night a German walked in alone and surrendered to the outpost. Some of the men hung the German's coat and helmet on the bushes in front of Hill's foxhole. When he saw them he wouldn't come out of his foxhole all day. In fact, he just dug it deeper.

This had gone far enough and probably would get worse, so I had Hill transferred to the rear with regimental headquarters, where he should have been in the first place. In his new assignment he managed to survive the war.

Meanwhile our penetration of the Siegfried was not exploited. We stayed put for over a week with neither the ammunition nor the gas to continue.

In early February 1945, we had to retake the exact same ground.

We stayed in the defensive positions for another week with nothing much happening. The shelling continued, but it all went over our heads and on to the rear. The only things that really scared us were the German "Screaming Meemies," or *Nebelwerfer*, six-barreled 150mm rocket launchers that seemed to crank up with a high-pitched metallic scream. The sound was so intense and nerve-shattering we couldn't tell where the rockets were going to hit.

After about a week we were pulled back through the hard-won Siegfried territory and moved northward a few miles, still in the Schnee Eifel forest. A change in position is always stimulating, and this time we had a wonderful bonus; the kitchen trucks were able to join us. We had hot food for the first time in over a month. It was an almost-forgotten luxury. No one griped to the cooks.

Once again we had the Siegfried in front of us, and this time there were many acres of thick woods between us and the enemy. The neutral zone could not be neglected; in fact, it was made to order for one of the most hated and dangerous chores of the foot soldier, a chore which requires exceptional skill—patrolling.

A patrol is a moving outpost without an outpost's defenses. Its only real defense is luck. Of course, the men can move from tree to tree, from cover to cover, but they do have to keep moving, and that means that sooner or later they will come upon the enemy—and may allow him the first shot.

Each patrol had a mission, usually to find the enemy and determine his strength. To find out anything about the enemy, one had to approach him. You might run into total ambush and get wiped out, and you might only draw a single shot. Ideally you would see the enemy and gather information without being detected.

If you kept spread out, you had a better chance of avoiding ambush. And you also had a better chance of losing track of your men, and of losing control. In the end, you varied your methods according to terrain and visibility. Night work hid you from the enemy; it also hid the enemy.

Patrolling required the utmost teamwork. Each man knew he might be the first to spot the enemy, and each knew he depended on the others for help. Visual and vocal signals were essential to keep us in touch, and at the same time the signals could not give us away to the enemy.

There was very little chance of surprising the enemy because he expected us to be out there and because he had patrols of his own.

I usually had the men move in a staggered line, with a man on each flank and one in the lead. I would be close behind the lead scout. Actually, all of us were scouts— playing Indian for real.

Night patrols had hazards of their own. In all patrols we were shown on the map where we were and where we were supposed to go. We quickly learned to distrust the maps, to use them only as a guide. Enemy positions are not always marked accurately on the map, and of course the enemy may move.

We relied heavily on our compasses to give us the right direction at night. Sometimes we found the landmarks shown on the map; sometimes we had no way of knowing distance and had to pace it off ourselves.

It would have been very easy to goof off on patrol, because you were out there all by yourself and no one could check on you. In fact, at times all you could think of was how nice and safe and comfortable the rest of the people were back in their foxholes, not to mention those in rear headquarters.

So it took extra discipline and extra-steady nerves while

you waited for that first shot or your first glimpse of the enemy.

Sometimes we were sent out with the general mission of trying to locate the enemy and learn what he was doing. At other times my patrols were supposed to find out if a certain bridge was still intact, the exact location of a German gun, the location of German outposts and their frontline positions, the strength of their units, the location of pillboxes, the accuracy of a certain aerial photo.

Apparently our work was satisfactory, because we seemed to be getting most of the new patrol work.

My platoon had three squads of a dozen men each. Each squad had ten men plus a sergeant and corporal. I seldom employed more than a squad of men on patrol, and to keep the risks fair I rotated the squads. The only thing that didn't rotate was the leader of the patrol. The platoon leader led every patrol. That was one time when none of the men envied the officers' privileges.

There were times when I led one patrol during the day and another at night. In one stretch I had patrols of one kind or another for eight consecutive days. It was a great relief when another company finally took over the patrol work. I admit I was close to exhaustion.

Way back in the swamps before Saint Lô, Colonel Lanham had promised us promotions if we survived our first major engagement, and my promotion to first lieutenant finally came through while we were in the Schnee Eifel. Lieutenant Piszarak also was promoted at this time.

Captain Newcomb made something of a ceremony out of presenting us with shiny new silver bars to replace the gold ones of second lieutenant. The date was September 29, 1944, which also happened to be my twenty-third birthday.

I was proud of the promotion but was careful to conceal the new silver bars under my collar, since the Germans liked to pick off officers and I didn't want to advertise. All of my men recognized me by then, bars or no bars.

It seems I was now considered a true veteran, having survived both the Saint Lô and Siegfried Line campaigns. At about this time the division historian came up to interview me and took a lot of notes about our combat experiences, but I never saw any of it in print.

My platoon had lost four sergeants, a medic, and two privates during our month in the Siegfried, the only men lost since Saint Pois. Replacements again brought us back up to forty men.

We didn't know where we're going. The next day we were due to be relieved.

X

SIEGFRIED....AND MINES!

A new phase of the war began when the GI's met stiffened enemy resistance at the Siegfried Line and at the same time ran perilously low on gas, ammunition, food, and other necessities. The rugged terrain of the Schnee Eifel forest, with its dense woods, steep slopes and ravines, poor roads, and strategically placed pillboxes, gave the Germans a telling tactical advantage. From behind these natural and manmade defenses, a very few Germans could pin down a great many attackers.

While we had indeed made some 'pencillike' penetrations, we did not have the backing to expand them, and we were forced into a holding operation. Both sides used the time and circumstances to bring up fresh troops and supplies and to redeploy units along the line.

About October 10 our regiment was trucked thirty miles north of Brandscheid to the vicinity of Bullingen. Here we were told that our mission was to break through the Siegfried once again. This time, however, we had plenty of materiel.

Our trucks had barely stopped and had just gotten our

feet on the ground when I was ordered to take my platoon out on a combination reconnaissance and combat patrol. Somehow I was neither elated nor flattered to be hand-picked for such a challenging assignment.

My recon job was to approach the Siegfried and check the roads and bridges to ensure our tanks' safe passage. The combat assignment was to seek out the enemy, engage him in a fight, and try to estimate his strength, and then make it back alive to report the information. At times I couldn't help thinking it would be nice to work in some headquarters thinking up that sort of assignment for someone else. A sign of fatigue, I suppose.

We moved out from town in an open column about 10 A.M. on a sunny day and took the road eastward. Wide-open stretches of farmland on all sides gave the enemy a clear field of view and made us nervous, and so we were grateful for the row of pines that bordered the road and gave us some cover. After about a mile of semiexposure, the road entered a dense pine forest, and we were able to get off the road itself and keep to the woods alongside.

After about another half mile we slowed down and made our way from tree to tree with extreme caution because we were getting close to a crossroad that showed on our map. Suddenly Crocker, as always the lead scout, opened up on some Germans he spotted at the intersection.

The Germans promptly returned fire with heavy machine guns and a fusillade of rifle. We took cover behind trees, bushes, and small depressions and fired a few rounds back. The crackling exchange kept up for a few minutes, but the woods were too thick to allow much accuracy. We never got a good look at the Germans, but they seemed to have at least two machine guns, a few squads of infantry, and what was probably an antitank gun emplacement.

I decided the roadblock was much too difficult and

costly to attack with only one platoon, so I brought my men back and reported to Captain Newcomb. I told him that all bridges and roads looked safe but that it would probably take at least a rifle company to knock out the roadblock.

When I returned to the platoon I was met by a very grim-looking Sergeant Anders who, as staff sergeant, was my second-in-command. Sergeant Anders said that one of the privates was missing. None of the men could remember having seen him since we had left the roadblock.

The only thing to do was go back and look for him, so Sergeant Anders and I and five volunteers took off again. We spread out and crawled all over the area but found no sign of the missing man. If he had been wounded, he might still be alive if we found him in time. In the back of our minds we also knew he could have been killed or captured. After a while we gave up and returned to camp. We had been careful, but the Germans should have seen some sign of our search, and I was surprised they hadn't fired on us.

Staff Sergeant Anders was quite upset about losing a man needlessly. Anders was a very tough, raw boned man from the hills of Arkansas. He reminded me of what I had read of the rugged Army scouts in the days of the Indian wars out west. He often volunteered for patrols and other hazardous ventures not expected of him as a platoon sergeant. He and Crocker were of the same genus; they both really enjoyed a fight, and they both knew how to win.

All of the men respected Anders. I know he could have led the platoon in any kind of combat.

As we walked back to the company area I did my best to assure him that the soldier's loss was not at all his fault. But when we arrived home, there was the man, who said he had run into a problem faced by all frontline troops, the sudden call of nature; while the patrol was firing at the roadblock, he dropped back into the woods to relieve himself.

We were gone by the time he tried to rejoin us, so he made his way back to the company alone. He must have gotten lost for a while because he reached town just after the search party left.

Sergeant Anders gave the fellow hell, telling him that if it happened again he might better fill his pants than let seven men risk their lives trying to find him. Nobody talked to him for a while; nobody saw much humor in his goof.

Early the next morning, the Second Battalion moved out in attack formation with E Company in front and the other companies following. Naturally it was my platoon's turn to lead again, since we knew the terrain. We approached the roadblock very, very gingerly—only to find the Germans gone.

The two other platoons of E Company turned right at the crossroads and headed for the company objective, over a mile away at the edge of the woods overlooking the Siegfried Line near Miescheid. The little hamlet was about two hundred yards away, across open fields beyond the edge of our woods, and the Siegfried was just behind it. Our company was another three hundred yards back in the forest, and that is where we dug in awaiting the big jump-off into the Siegfried.

Our E Company was spread out in defensive positions on the left of the road and F Company continued the defense to the right. Lieutenant Piszarak's First Platoon was dug in nearest the road, and my platoon was to their left. Lieutenant Mason's Third Platoon was on the left flank, and Lieutenant Lloyd's's Weapons Platoon filled in the rear, with company headquarters in the middle. We placed a pair of men every ten to fifteen yards, covering between three hundred and four hundred yards along the front.

My platoon had just begun to dig in when we were suddenly attacked by about forty Germans, who ran at us shooting, taking cover behind trees as they moved in.

We instantly dropped our shovels, lay down in the shallow beginnings of our foxholes, and fired back with all we had. All they seemed to have were single-shot, bolt-action rifles, and these quickly proved no match for the volleys of our Browning Automatic rifles (BARS) and semiautomatic M-1s. The Krauts were stopped about seventy five yards in front of us. They probably came upon us by accident, and they didn't seem organized. It now looked as though they might be regrouping to continue the attack, so I called for artillery.

Our artillery forward observer, a very young chap who was new to us, started off by giving us a real thrill. His first rounds were not the standard High Explosive. They were lethal white phosphorus, designed to burn through anything. They also fell short, hitting high up in the huge maples directly overhead. Smoking hot metal rained down all around us.

I screamed at him to cease fire and raise his guns, and his next rounds were right on target, bursting in the trees just over the Germans, seventy five yards out from us. About a dozen of the 105s blasted in over the Germans with a thunderous racket, and that ended any attack plans they might have had. They collected their wounded and took off to the rear.

The forward observer apologized for the short rounds. He actually had called for smoke shells to point out the target but got thermite instead, and thermite sometimes does fall short.

It was there in that green forest that we ran into the most frightening weapon of the war, the one that made us almost sick with fear: *antipersonnel mines*. By now I had gone through aerial bombing, artillery and mortar shelling, open combat, direct rifle and machine gun firing, night patrolling, and ambush. Against all of this we had some kind of chance; against mines we had none. They were vicious, deadly, inhuman. They churned our guts.

They were planted a few inches below the soil and covered by leaves or natural growth that left no sign. Not a bit of ground was safe. They went off if you stepped on them with as little as five pounds of pressure, or if you moved their invisibly thin trip wire. The only defense was to not move at all.

A mine usually blew off one leg up to the knee and shattered the other, which looked like it had been blasted by a shotgun at close range. If the man was not killed instantly, he needed immediate attention due to shock and loss of blood.

Soon each of the line companies had lost men to mines, and the rest of us were afraid to walk anywhere. A call went out to the engineers and the pioneer platoons, which had specially trained men, who cleared paths through mine fields. Each path was about three feet wide and was marked by white tape. The specialists used mine detectors very slowly and deliberately; yet despite their care, an engineer lost his leg in one of the cleared paths.

After that tragedy they began to probe every inch of ground with trench knives, gently working the knives in at an angle, hoping to hit only the sides of mines. This way they came upon many devilish little mines handmade from cottage cheese–type crocks and sealed with wax. Their only metal was the detonator, which was too small to be picked up by mine detectors.

The engineers and pioneers worked day and night for several days on what had to be one of the nastiest jobs of the war; each probe could be a man's last.

One night the captain of H Company, the Second Battal-

ion's heavy weapons company, came up to our area. He
was a big, heavyset, dark-complexioned man, and he was
very concerned about his company's mission. He was
looking for advance positions for his heavy machine guns
so they would have clear lanes of fire on long-range targets
behind the enemy's lines. This overhead fire was intended
to harass the enemy during the rifle companies attack on
the Siegfried.

The captain went about his task conscientiously, even
though it was somewhat disheartening: he never could see
where his bullets were landing. Heavy machine guns were
much more effective on defense.

The captain talked about his plans perhaps a bit more
than necessary and paced about in what seemed a nervous
manner. Less than ten minutes after leaving me, he strayed
off a marked path and had a leg blown off up to the knee.
At least he was alive, we figured gratefully, and he would
be going home.

A few nights later, just as I was getting ready to lead a
reconnaissance patrol into the Siegfried, Captain Newcomb
and I were told to report at once to battalion headquarters;
Colonel Walker had some new ideas to give me for the
patrol, and a short delay wouldn't make any difference.

It was a night of almost total blackness, by far the dark-
est I had ever experienced. The thick, tall pines were by
themselves enough to cut off reflected light, and above
them was absolutely nothing. The sky was completely
overcast, and we couldn't even see our hands when we
waved them before our eyes. The only way we could stay
on the dirt road was to walk in the deep tire ruts. Captain
Newcomb wondered aloud how I was ever going to lead a
patrol under such conditions.

We knew we had arrived at battalion headquarters when
we heard the metallic click of a safety going off a rifle,

followed by a frightened voice's demand for the password. The guard then led us to Colonel Walker's tent, a few yards off the road among some thick pines.

As soon as we got beyond the blackout curtains we had to shield our eyes against the bright glow of the Coleman gas lamp. Gathered around Colonel Walker were his staff officers: Major Samuelson, Captain Tom Harrison, Captain Kerr, and Lieutenant Simon. The colonel came quickly to the point. He told us that division wanted to know more about the enemy, and so they needed a fresh prisoner. He therefore had changed my reconnaissance patrol to a combat patrol.

I was to take about twenty men and move into the town of Miescheid astride the Siegfried to our front. My mission was to engage the Germans in a fight—using trench knives, bayonets, and grenades. We were to inflict as much damage as possible, then quickly take a prisoner and get out.

Our purpose was to determine enemy strength and, through a prisoner, find out what kind of an outfit we were facing. Colonel Walker made it clear that taking a prisoner was of utmost urgency.

I was shocked at the idea of leading twenty men into a black abyss and was well aware that hand-to-hand combat was about the last thing they wanted to do. On the other hand, I knew Colonel Walker would accept no excuses. I did venture to ask him, however, if he was aware that it would be difficult to find more than two bayonets in the whole company and very few more trench knives.

Angrily, the colonel turned to Simon, the supply officer (S-4), and demanded the reason for the shortage. Simon replied that when the veterans got wounded they either took their weapons with them or left them in the field. New replacement troops were not coming up with bayonets or trench knives, and his own requisitions were being scratched.

Colonel Walker at once ordered a full report from his company commanders on the number of bayonets and trench knives on hand. Then he told me I was to round up all the weapons I could from E Company and proceed as ordered.

Captain Newcomb and I were very quiet as we stumbled blindly along the ruts heading back to the company. We decided it would be useless to take only volunteers; there wouldn't be any. The captain suggested I immediately call out my first two squads, of twelve men each, ready to move out on patrol.

None of the men were more than fifty yards from my foxhole, but it still took over a half hour for them to assemble their gear and find their way to me in the total darkness.

I carefully explained our mission to the men sitting on the ground around me. Immediately a voice came out of the blackness: "Lieutenant, what are the consequences if I refuse to go on this patrol?"

Before I could answer, another spoke up: "I don't give a damn what the consequences are. I'm not going!"

I quickly ordered a stop to all such talk, saying that I knew who the complainers were (I did), and that I had better not hear any more from them. I stated very firmly, in a tone no one could mistake, that I didn't like the orders either, but that I had been ordered to lead them on this damned patrol, and that we were all going, like it or not.

That was the one time any man ever dared question my orders. I was glad I had acted quickly to stop the discussion before it got out of control. It had been close to becoming a serious problem! The fear of those damned mines was sure to be half the trouble.

No one uttered a peep after that, and I went ahead with the patrol orders. We agreed on a system of sound signals, making use of a pocket comb, and a few minutes later we started out.

Never, I think, was there a combat patrol like that. The only way I could control twenty men I could not see was by deploying them in a long, snaking single file. Each man groped around until he had hold of the belt of another man, and then I felt my way to the front of the column. Somehow I was able to make out the needle of my compass, and I slowly drew the line ahead as I stumbled over the uneven ground.

We bumped into trees, bushes slapped us in the face, and we tripped over roots. Once someone fell flat, losing his hold on the belt in front; for a few minutes we had two lines. I stopped my section and quietly groped back to look for the other line. We found one another through the sounds of our comb signals, and soon we were all one line again. I was so busy, I never gave a thought to the mines.

Several times I had to stop and go back along the whole line to warn each man to be quiet. Then a new problem developed. Someone started to cough and it quickly spread along the line. I bawled the men out because of the danger their noise put us in, but I couldn't see them in the blackness, and it all seemed so futile.

By the time we reached the edge of the woods and came to the open fields, I realized my orders were impossible and decided to salvage what I could of the asinine patrol. First I went back to my original mission, a reconnaissance patrol rather than a combat one, and I selected five men who had not been rebellious coughers. I was sure I could control that many, and from then on we would be out in the open and extremely vulnerable.

Once we were out of the thick pine forest we could make out one another's shapes as far as four or five feet away. Leaving the other men with orders to stay put, our small patrol set out across the field in diamond formation, with one man slightly ahead of me in the lead.

It wasn't far across the fields, and in a few minutes we saw the dark outlines of buildings in Miescheid. Normally a tiny crossroads settlement of innocent farmhouses, it now sat atop the Siegfried Line, with formidable rows of dragons'-teeth tank traps in front.

We did not know what sort of ambush we might be walking into, and we were scared as hell. We had to force ourselves to move from one shadowy building to the next in the deep blackness. We couldn't even make out where the windows were, and we listened carefully for any sound of the enemy. We even tossed pebbles to attract some response but we got nothing at all.

After a while I was satisfied we had done all we could, so we withdrew quietly back to the woods, picked up the others, and returned to the company. I told Captain New-comb exactly what I had done and why, and he told me not to worry about it.

"Get some sleep," he said. "You've earned it. I'll give the whole story to Colonel Walker."

I crawled into my foxhole and tried for sleep but was too keyed up. The patrol had been total frustration from the very beginning, the only success being that I had brought the men back alive. I hoped Colonel Walker would not insist on my trying it all over again.

Next morning I rehashed it all with Captain Newcomb, and I told him I expected to catch the devil from Colonel Walker, but the colonel never mentioned it at all. Probably he had been out later and realized what a hopeless night it was to go anywhere.

Later that morning a six-man patrol led by a lieutenant from battalion headed through the woods toward the old farmhouse at its edge. They were in diamond formation, and their route was about one hundred yards to the left of ours the night before.

A few minutes after they had passed us we heard a rifle shot, followed shortly by several thumping explosions. Then someone yelling for a medic. My platoon medic and I at once headed toward the sounds, and some of my men followed.

When we got close, the lieutenant yelled at us to stay back. Mines! He said they would all try to crawl back to us. It seems the point man had been shot, and the other five had gone forward to help. All five stepped on mines and lost limbs. The lead man was dead, shot by a sniper.

The young lieutenant kept his cool. He lay where he fell and carefully directed each man to crawl out of mine field back along the paths they had taken. Each man somehow managed to get out on hands and knees, dragging his shattered stump.

It was horribly gruesome. Five young men lying there with mutilated legs. Thank God for the initial numbness that gave us a chance to help them before the pain hit. It took quite a while to get them bandaged and sent on their way, even though we had help right away.

We taped off the entire area and marked it "MINES" as the last man, the lieutenant, was evacuated. We did not attempt to get the dead scout. Certainly there was no use in risking men for one already gone. I have often wondered who that brave young lieutenant was and how he and his men made out.

How lucky we were to have missed all the mines! But I was weak and shaky for many hours afterward just thinking about how close we had come to them. It would have been even worse in our case, for we would have been helpless in the total blackness the night before.

* * *

One day we heard the pillboxes to our front were going to be bombed by our P-47 fighter-bombers. To get a better view of the dive bombing, less than a half mile from our area, some of us walked through the woods and the mines to the old farmhouse we had found on our night patrol.

We climbed up the back side and lay with just our heads above the roofline. Grandstand seats on the fifty-yard line. It was a tremendous show. We watched spellbound as the P-47s came over at ten thousand feet and then, one by one, tipped their wings and dived straight down at the pillboxes.

The drone of the planes' engines became a thunderous roar as they sped earthward. My heart seemed to stop, and I held my breath waiting for them to pull up out of the dives.

When it seemed suicidally late they released their bombs and somehow managed to level off just a few hundred feet from the ground. The bombs hit smack on top of the seven-foot-thick concrete-and-steel pillboxes.

From our angle, we could see no damage at all. No roofs were caved in, no huge cracks appeared. Probably the Jerries had hellish headaches from concussion, but nothing was visible. All the great show did was raise dust.

Later in the war we heard the Army had developed a special 155mm shell for our Long Tom artillery. This shell was to be fired like a rifle bullet, point-blank into the pillbox, and was designed to penetrate before exploding. Unfortunately, they weren't around for us to use.

The next day we were moved back about a mile into reserve. While in this area, three of us went deer hunting in the woods to our rear. One of the men got a deer, and the cooks gave us a nice venison dinner.

While out hunting, I saw my first buzz bomb. I had heard a lot of them go over, and at night we could see the balls of fire shooting from their tails, but none of the men with me had ever seen one. The unmanned missiles traveled so fast that by the time the roar of their motors directly overhead reached us, the buzz bombs were a half mile beyond. I just happened to be looking out across a valley and spotted one leaving the area. It looked like a long, sleek plane with stubby wings.

A few minutes later our deer hunting ended abruptly when we ran into a German patrol larger than our hunting party. We fired a few rounds to scare them off and made a hasty retreat.

All my patrols of the past weeks had apparently impressed someone. Lieutenant Colonel Walker transferred me back to battalion headquarters and promoted me to the job of Battalion Intelligence Officer (S-2). I was now responsible for getting all possible information about the enemy.

Finding out enemy strengths and weaknesses, his gun emplacements, mine fields, recent changes in his defenses, was not a desk job. We had to dig up this intelligence ourselves, and the only firsthand source was patrolling.

I was not surprised, therefore, when Colonel Walker told me my first job was to capture a German soldier. I was to send out patrols day and night—and get a prisoner, no matter what. We had to find out what kind of unit was facing us. The colonel told me that division demanded the capture of a prisoner as our top priority.

He also said I could commandeer anyone in the battalion. In addition, I was in charge of an all-volunteer platoon that was used only for special patrolling. The men of the special platoon were expertly trained, and their patrols were led by an excellent staff sergeant.

Colonel Walker mentioned Gallagher of G Company as a top man. I had heard of "Gal" but had never met him.

The Colonel repeated that he must have a prisoner.

Nothing short of success would be accepted. Conspicuously absent from his orders were suggestions on just *how* to get the job done. He made it clear that that was up to me.

At first I was stumped. At least I knew I couldn't sit and wait for a German to walk in and surrender, so I had to go out and find one. To get myself started, I studied the map diligently. This led absolutely nowhere, for I had used the map many times before and found nothing new in it now. Then I was hit by an inspiration.

It suddenly struck me that the German commander should be concerned with the routes we might take when we launched our inevitable attack. So how would *he* look at the map? I put myself on the other side of the map to try to get his viewpoint, asking myself which routes would be most likely for the Americans.

I examined wooded cover, natural draws, fence rows, buildings, open fields, roads, and any other terrain features. Several natural approach routes offered good cover, and the shortest one looked to be the best bet, since it would give the Americans the least exposure. This approach would require us to go over two hundred yards of more or less open ground to reach the head of a draw that led close into the German lines.

If the German commander read the map the way I did, then it seemed logical he would have an outpost at the edge of this draw nearest us. To prevent myself from jumping to conclusions, I carefully studied the other routes. In the end, I came back to the shortest one and also decided the Germans probably would have plenty of mines in front of the outpost. Also, I assumed, the commander would have at least one machine gun in the outpost.

By now I was planning as though this German position really existed, and I figured it would have to be taken by surprise at night with a large enough force to do it quickly. Most importantly, I needed an experienced man to lead this expedition.

The best man available was First Lieutenant Gallagher, who was summoned to battalion headquarters. He was given an outline of his mission and an explanation as to why I had chosen that spot. He saw the logic, and we began to make final plans. We quickly agreed on limiting the force to one squad armed only with rifles and grenades. We wanted the men to be able to move freely, and Gallagher felt he could use his twelve best men and get the job done quickly.

We discussed enemy defenses and known mine fields. Both of us felt the ground immediately in front of the outpost probably would be mined, and therefore we decided the approach should be made from the flank, even though the route was longer. Gallagher hoped it might be easier to surprise the Germans that way.

We then estimated the time for getting out and back and allowed a half hour safety margin. Timing was crucial; since quite a bit of the route was open farmland we couldn't afford to get caught out there in daylight.

The one-way distance from Gallagher's G Company to the outpost was almost a mile. Most of the trip would be on the road in the woods, which led to open fields, and much of the last two hundred yards would have to be crawled, even at night.

We agreed Gallagher should start at 2:00 A.M. and begin his return trip no later than 5:00 A.M. That should get him back in the woods before daylight. We estimated the German outpost would have six to ten men, and Gallagher was confident he could take them if he and his twelve men could achieve surprise.

Gallagher now returned to G Company to work out the

details of selecting his men, briefing them on the mission, and working out signals and the exact plan of attack. Then they all tried to get some rest before the guard woke them at 1:30 A.M.

The night was clear with some stars and occasional clouds. Fortunately there was no moon. Gallagher had memorized the map, and he led his men right to the spot we had marked as the outpost, without being detected. They could make out the dim outline of a machine gun emplacement and were just able to make out a German sentry sitting against a tree facing his front.

Crawling forward very gingerly, Gallagher carefully positioned his men alongside the outpost. They came across a field-telephone wire and cut it, and then they waited patiently for cloud cover to move in even closer.

Gallagher then gave the signal to throw grenades and break into the outpost. The surprise was complete, but even then the Germans fought back until they realized the hopelessness of their situation and quickly surrendered.

The entire outpost of six men and a machine gun was captured, and Gallagher lost no time in disarming them and heading for home. As they moved out he made the Germans lead the way. Two of the wounded Germans were supported by their comrades.

In the darkness the prisonors didn't recognize their own mine fields, and suddenly there was a tremendous blast a few yards in front. One of the Germans had stepped on a mine and had his foot blown off. Gallagher allowed the Germans to give him quick first aid and then had them pick up the wounded man and carry him along.

Time was getting dangerously short, and carrying the casualty slowed the patrol down, but there was nothing else to do. Gallagher found out that the German corporal spoke English, and so he told him that if the Germans led them into any more mine fields he would shoot them all. There were no more mines after that, and the whole patrol made it back without the loss of a man.

I was delighted with our success on this first mission and told Gallagher what a terrific job he and his men had done. Colonel Walker thanked both of us for a job well done and said he would recommend Gallagher for a medal. I don't know if he ever received it. Sweating out someone else's patrol was a strange experience for me.

Most of the next day was spent with an interpreter from battalion, trying to dig information out of the prisoners. The division intelligence officer (G-2) was elated with our catch, and he sent up a team of interrogators.

One of the prisoners was a Pole who had been forced into the German Army and been told to help fight the Americans or else be shot. He had been waiting nervously, eager to be captured. Meanwhile he made a real effort to learn as much as possible about his unit so he could pass it on to us if the time ever came.

He told us everything he knew, marking defensive positions on the map, locating the mine fields, and naming many of the officers, their ranks, and their commands. He also marked in gun positions, supply dumps, and pillbox locations, and he told us the food was poor and that a lot of the men had dysentery.

The German corporal in charge of this outpost was quite interesting. He was a Regular Army man and a staunch Hitler fanatic, a genuine Nazi. He spoke English rather well, though he had to stop and think first, and this made it a little difficult for him to be as arrogant as he tried to appear.

At first he would give us only his name, rank, and serial number in curt, clipped words. Gradually he became more relaxed and gave us more indirect information than he realized. When I asked him about the Germans' food situation, he replied; "What in hell do you expect after five years of war?" The Polish soldier had already told us how poor the food was, and this remark confirmed it for us.

The corporal asked me one question I have never been able to forget. He wanted to know whom we had elected as our new president. I told him the election wasn't until November (the conversation was in October, 1944), and I asked why it was important to him whom we elected. He said he hoped we would elect a new president because many Germans felt the war might not last so long if we had a new leader.

I wasn't quick enough to ask him to explain just what he meant. My only conclusion was that the Big Three—Churchill, Stalin and Roosevelt—had agreed to accept nothing short of total unconditional surrender, but that many Germans might be ready for some sort of conditional surrender very soon.

With all the new information provided by the captives, division G-2 set out on a wide-ranging propaganda attack. They printed leaflets bearing the names of German officers and described how well the officers were eating and what a good time they were having with the fräuleins.

The leaflets said that many Germans would be killed or wounded in a few days when we attacked. The propaganda people suggested the best way for a German soldier to survive the war and get back home to his family would be to bring in the pamphlet and surrender.

Pleasant music was played to the Germans over loudspeakers, along with persuasive talks in German. The pamphlets went over in artillery shells, and the wind scattered them all over the enemy area. As I recall, over one hundred Reich soldiers came in with the pamphlets and surrendered.

* * *

A week or so later the sergeant who led battalion's special patrol platoon was sent out through G Company to check out the exact location of several pillboxes and a long row of dragon's-teeth concrete tank obstacles.

The tooth-shaped, reinforced cement blocks were about three feet at the base and tapered to a point about four feet high. They were built in rows about three feet apart to a depth of twelve feet and stretched across many open fields adjacent to roads. Tanks thus were forced to use the road; this made them easy targets for the antitank guns in the pillboxes near the road.

The intelligence the sergeant brought back from his night patrol did not agree with what Colonel Walker already had, so the colonel ordered me to personally check it out. Apparently, aerial photos of the area did not agree with our maps. For some damned reason, I was ordered to go out and get the answer in broad daylight.

The sergeant who had led the patrol the night before went with me, and we made our way through G Company to a fence row at the edge of the woods. The next five hundred yards were open fields clearly visible to the enemy, the only cover being the grass itself, which was a foot high.

It was midday as we crawled out into the tall grass, cradling our rifles in our arms. For what seemed hours we squirmed forward through the grass on our stomachs and elbows, covering well over five hundred yards, scared as hell all the way. Finally we could see the pillboxes slightly to our left and only two hundred yards away, across a small ravine.

We could see the Germans very clearly as they moved about in the open areas around the pillboxes, and several other pillboxes were nearby. Fortunately, our hiding place was about ten feet above the enemy's ground level, and we stayed as motionless as possible in the tall grass.

I slowly edged my map out from inside my shirt and carefully drew in the pillbox locations, raising my head ever so gradually, just enough to see. To mark points on the map I used back-azimuth, or reverse compass readings. I simply picked two spots on the terrain in front of me and found them on my map. Then I sighted these two objects through my compass and used compass readings to draw a line from each object back toward my position. The intersection of these two lines had to be my position on the map. Once I had my spot located, I could draw in all the fortifications.

I stuffed the map back into my shirt, and then we very carefully crawled back to the woods, expecting machine gun bullets any second. When we reached the woods, we breathed a sigh of relief and made our way very quickly back to battalion headquarters.

A World War II battalion headquarters in combat is difficult to describe because they varied so much. Typically, the actual headquarters was where the commanding colonel set up his command post (CP). He might use a tent about twelve feet square or a log-covered bunker. Headquarters personnel might consist of the battalion commander (usually a lieutenant colonel), his executive officer (a major), and captains for administration (S-1), adjutant in charge of operations (S-3), and supply (S-4), with a first lieutenant for intelligence (S-2).

The battalion command post would usually be surrounded by a headquarters company that provided clerks and personnel for mail, supply, communications, medical support, cooks, pioneers, drivers, radiomen, and others. Also found at headquarters were officers from the various units that might be attached to the battalion; e.g., tank units, tank destroyer units, artillery, engineers, chemical warfare units, etc. The battalion commander's staff saw that the line companies and units attached to the battalion were supplied as needed.

Many times a battalion commander would have a moving or forward command post, which might be only a foxhole from which he and his staff worked with his two radiomen. The forward command post might be almost on the front line and was usually within a thousand yards of it. The forward CP would move with the front line.

My report confirmed the sergeant's earlier one, and Colonel Walker was pleased with the extra details on my map. It also confirmed that certain aerial photos were up to date. This was valuable information because, even though we never did get to attack there, it later became useful to our successors.

Then it happened. My short term as S-2, as part of the elite, abruptly ended. Colonel Walker called me in and told me he was sorry, but it was necessary to transfer me back to a line rifle company. He was well pleased with what he called my outstanding job as S-2, but my combat experience was needed desperately in the F Company because Captain Clang and some of his officers had met with a freak accident. He also mentioned that Captain Newcomb had wanted me back in E Company and had offered to trade two of his officers to F for me. I don't know whether this was blarney or not, but it did make me feel a little better. I had been S-2 on the battalion staff for only ten or twelve days.

The freak accident that eliminated those officers was not only tragic, it was downright stupid: one of the lieutenants was demonstrating how to fire a rifle grenade, which is very much like an ordinary hand grenade except that it is fitted at the muzzle end of the rifle so that it can use the gases from a blank cartridge for propulsion of about two hundred yards. A blank is used because the bullet from a live round would explode the grenade right at the end of the rifle. And that is exactly what happened. Luckily, no one was killed.

Now I was a platoon leader again in a new company with a new captain and not a single man I knew. I hated to start all over again, but I tried hard not to let it show. The captain was a big man who appeared to be experienced, but I never really got to know him. I believe his name was Captain Flanigan. This time around I, at least, was experienced myself, and the men were aware of it.

At about this time I heard of another serious accident, this time with men from my platoon in E Company. The last to leave the front lines, a whole squad of them hitched a ride in a single jeep, piling on top of one another inside and hanging on to the fenders and bumpers outside. The driver had to use the cat's-eye slits on the headlights, and he did not see a bomb crater at the edge of the road. When one wheel went over the edge, the unbalanced overload tumbled the jeep to the bottom of the crater, on top of the men. The driver was killed, and many of the men were badly injured. Jackson, the old reliable BAR man who had gone through so much combat, broke his back.

I was gradually getting better acquainted with the new platoon, though it was awfully hard to stop comparing them to the men of my old platoon, because we had been through hell together so many times and knew what to expect from one another. But these new men also proved out.

One day some of the men found a cultivated field nearby and dug up some nice large white potatoes. Then they scrounged a large can and some cooking oil from the kitchen, rigged it over an open fire, and soon filled the air with the delicious aroma of french fries. After weeks of K rations, they were the freshest, most tasty food ever created—and some of us couldn't stop eating. The grease was a little too much for us, and we paid for it later one way or another.

Somehow I managed to come up with a severe sinus infection, and my face and ears ached until I could hardly bear the pain. The doctor gave me pills and nose drops, and after a few terrible days, it all suddenly cleared up. This was fortunate for me because the weather was turning cold, and soon we would be in the Hürtgen forest. We didn't know what that name would come to mean.

We had been in the inactive area for almost a month, and the change had been wonderful. Actually, we were getting in top-notch condition for our next battle. We would need that conditioning, and then some. For that particular engagement, nothing was sufficient.

XI

SLAUGHTER IN THE HÜRTGEN FOREST

Long after darkness on about November 10, 1944, the Fourth Division leapfrogged some thirty miles farther north along the German–Belgian border. This was to be a highly secret maneuver, so elaborate pains were taken to erase all signs of our identity. Divisional and regimental numbers were blocked out on all vehicles, and the green four-leafed ivy shoulder patches of which we were so proud were removed from our uniforms. All personal letters bearing the division number were burned.

Our blacked-out trucks took long, confusing detours to the rear to mislead local enemy agents, and we arrived at our new post before dawn, sleepless and miserable. It was something of a shock early that morning to pick up the English-language propaganda broadcast of Berlin Sally, welcoming the Fourth Division to its new position in the Hürtgen Forest. Actually, the deduction was simple: They knew where the Fourth had been, they knew when it left with erased identity, and they knew when an unidentified unit arrived thirty miles north. Berlin Sally broadcast daily to us in English, trying to pack all the propaganda she could into a few sentences. We could occasionally pick up her program on our walkie-talkies.

We bivouacked in very rugged, roller-coaster terrain deep in the forest east of Zweifall, Germany, near the middle of the Hürtgen, a one hundred-square-mile forest of extremely steep hills, rough ridges, and deep ravines covered with oak, maple, birch, scrub oak, white pine, and jack pine. Some growths of hardwood were over one hundred feet tall; pines of mixed heights of about ten to fifty feet were planted in closely packed rows. Now and then we would see a giant stand reaching up almost one hundred feet.

The country was obstacle enough in itself, yet the Germans had two additional advantages. They always knew exactly where we were, having just left there themselves, and thus easily called down shelling on us. They also had prepared in advance a series of defensive positions. After they had made our attack as costly as possible, they simply pulled back a few hundred yards to their next emplacements—and bombarded the ones left to us

Their new line usually gave them command of everything in front, being perhaps on an upward slope or near the lip of a ravine. Their bunkers were made of thick logs with a few feet of dirt on top. The bunkers were almost immune to artillery, which had to arc in overhead. They might as well have been concrete. Tree bursts bothered them very little, and there was no chance of our tanks getting anywhere near them for direct fire. The infantry had to take them the hard way, going in after them one at a time, sometimes through barbed wire.

Why the Hürtgen forest was not bypassed is still a major question. Possibly the Allies feared the Germans would open the floodgates on the Ruhr dams just to the forest's south. Opening the gates would have flooded much of the land to the northeast. Some experts feel that the dams could have been captured and the forest still bypassed, but it is possible that the Allied leadership felt that the forest could also have been used as a base from which the Germans could launch a major counteroffensive.

At that time, none of the officers I spoke to raised any question about the Hürtgen's strategic value. We were ordered to fight there and assigned sectors to take. We knew the going there had been very difficult. Several American divisions had fought there for almost two months, and none had been able to make a complete breakthrough. We were told that a breakthrough to the Cologne Plains was essential in order to allow our tanks to move across open ground and on to the Rhine, about thirty-five miles away.

It was decided that another major effort would be made. This time the battle-hardened Fourth, Twenty-Eighth, and Ninetieth Divisions, with extra tank and artillery support, would attack abreast. The main effort was concentrated to the front of the First Division, just north of the left flank of the Fourth Division. The attack would begin with a very heavy bombing mission designed to wipe out the Germans facing the First Division.

The German High Command was, of course, aware of our objectives and ordered us held up at all costs. Several experienced German divisions were sent in along with masses of artillery. We heard there were as many as seventeen battalions of artillery. Later we had reason to believe it.

The days had been growing shorter right along at that time of year and in the tall, dense forest daylight faded away around five in the afternoon. The blackness lasted until almost eight in the morning. Winter also came early that mid-November and proved it with dreary rain, a dousing of early snow, and a miserable chill.

Normally, each man carried a blanket and shelter-half

(half of a canvas tent), so that he and a buddy had a complete tent and two blankets between them. But the weather was so bad we had the men set up in three's so each could share a tent, an extra shelter-half to lay on the ground, three blankets, and the warmth of three bodies. We also always slept in our woolen clothes, and even through them the ground felt rough and was piercingly cold.

While waiting for the weather to clear for our bombers we rechecked weapons, stored up some rest, and also received enough men and officers to bring the unit back to full strength.

We awoke one morning to a deep hush and crawled out to find two inches of new snow. The ground we had been scuffing up was hidden under a pure white blanket, and the gaunt, leafless hardwoods now sported limbs topped with soft ermine. Our world was suddenly clean, fresh, and uncorrupted, and it seemed senseless that we were not deer hunting back home in Michigan but at war with people on the next ridge.

November 16 came clear and cold, and masses of our heavy bombers did their jobs on the Germans some five miles northeast. This was beyond our division's zone so it did not help us directly, but we must have received some side benefits from the reduction of the enemy's overall strength.

While the bombing was still underway, my platoon moved out by itself ahead of the battalion. We followed a two-lane track to the north and ran into no opposition. The only sign of danger was a few booby traps strung in the trees to the right of the trail. The trip wires were in plain sight, but if we had been a little careless or come through at night we would have triggered them. I radioed back to the captain to warn him.

After about a quarter mile, we turned to our right and formed a long defensive line along the ridge, facing north.

Once we were in position, the rest of the battalion advanced straight ahead behind us, so that we were strung out defending the left flank of the whole battalion, led by Lieutenant Colonel Glenn Walker.

Second Battalion immediately ran into a tough German defense, veterans who fought savagely from thick log bunkers and gun emplacements protected by barbed wire. From dug-in positions facing us, they put down brutally accurate mortars and artillery on our men out in the open and chewed us up with direct machine gun and rifle fire. Our casualties were dreadful. Most of our losses were inflicted by artillery and mortar shells exploding in the trees above us.

Normally, artillery shells come into the ground at a sharp angle, and their shrapnel fans out and slightly upward to the front, much of it going harmlessly into the ground or straight up into the air. When a shell explodes overhead in a tree, almost half of its shrapnel spreads out and downward like rain, and it is infinitely more lethal.

The best defense is to stand upright against a big tree, thus exposing mostly your helmet and shoulders. Instincts are strong, however, and many men could not stop themselves from hitting the ground as usual. Actually, it didn't always make much difference, because mortars drop straight downward, and their steel splinters fan out in all directions. Thus you get hit from all directions, even from below with mines.

My platoon was very lucky to have a defensive job on a quiet flank that opening day. A few stray tree bursts came in, and they did give us our first two casualties, but we saw no other sign of the enemy. All day long we heard the heavy fighting behind our right flank. We knew the rest of the battalion was catching hell, and we were pretty jumpy.

At dusk, which was only a little after 5:00 in the thick woods, the fighting stopped, and my CO ordered me to rejoin the company. By the time we assembled it was dark, and the only way we could get back was to trail one hand on the field phone wire. We stumbled along over roots and small depressions and slashed through the underbrush, and then we piled up against some barbed wire. It took some time to cut through the wire and bend it back in the darkness. We then followed the phone line and soon were with F Company again.

The company was digging in to the rear of the battalion as the reserve, and Captain Flanigan, F Company commander, said E and G companies were dug in a few hundred yards in front. "Have your men dig in along the right rear, and let's hope for a good night," he said as he went back to his command post, which was little more than a foxhole with his phone and radio nearby. Most commanders tried to locate their CP's near the center of their company.

The dense pines ended a few feet south and bordered on a large, open stand of hardwoods. I decided to stay just inside the pines for protection. The pines were so thick that the lower boughs nearly touched ground, and at night they almost completely blotted out any faint light.

Very carefully I began to place my men in pairs about ten feet apart along a rough perimeter. This was difficult because I couldn't see the ground. Then, suddenly there wasn't any. I dropped several feet into a void and lay stunned at the bottom of an old German foxhole. My wind had been knocked out, my chest ached, and my teeth had been jammed. I couldn't see a thing and must have been in shock as I dragged myself out of the hole. Then I had to go right back down again to grope around until I found my helmet.

After all the men were in place, my runner and I began to look for the German foxhole I'd found, so we wouldn't have to dig our own. We fanned out slightly and cautiously, felt our way but finally had to give up and dig our own shelter. At daylight we were pretty disgusted to find we had missed it by only ten feet, and then we learned how lucky we had been.

Some of the men were interested in my mishap and went down in the hole themselves to poke around. They quickly found something they hadn't expected. The foxhole actually was the entrance to a dugout, and still inside were four terribly frightened German soldiers, who couldn't surrender fast enough. They had spend a dreadful night fully aware that we were all around them and had hoped they would get a chance to surrender before someone as nervous as they were tossed a grenade in on them. For my part, I couldn't help thinking how lucky I had been that they weren't fanatics who would have finished me off as I lay stunned at their feet. I tried not to recall how hard my runner and I had looked for that hole with an eye toward using it as shelter.

Second Battalion continued its attack eastward early next morning, with companies E and G leading and F trailing along in reserve. The lead companies fought feverishly to break through a second line of log bunkers, and we clearly heard the clatter of machine guns and rifles, the endless explosions of mortars and artillery, as both sides pounded away.

Our casualties were prohibitive, and the wounded had to be carried out on stretchers in a continuous stream, since not even a jeep could find a path through the dense forest.

The front-line companies frequently were held up for long periods, and during those times F Company was caught without foxholes. We also picked up more shelling than we would have if we had been able to keep moving forward. Once, when we were in a thick grove of thirty-foot-tall reforestation pines, a shell hit a tree only twenty yards ahead and we all dove for cover. Almost instantly another shell took the top off the tree right overy my head, and I was knocked silly.

I got up and ran like a madman. I must have covered seventy-five to one hundred yards before a glint of consciousness got through. My head was reeling and my hearing was gone, but I turned around and made it back to the platoon. Five or six of the men had been hit, three very seriously. One had a grapefruit-sized hole in his back, and air sucked through his punctured lung.

Our medic worked quickly on the wounded while I moved the rest of the platoon ahead and out of the area before any more shells came in. We were lucky only those two had landed on us; a barrage might have finished us off.

A few minutes later a messenger came to my platoon and announced that I was now in command of F Company. That morning we had started with six officers, but we were down to just myself and a second lieutenant. I was told Captain Flanigan had been killed and all the others wounded.

Battalion headquarters also had been hit severely, with Lieutenant Colonel Walker and his entire staff being casualties. Captain Newcomb from E Company took over the battalion until Major Blazzard arrived.

During this unsettled period we again had a long wait on the forward side of a hill. The front-line companies were about three hundred yards ahead on the next hill. Our hill somehow had only a few trees, but clumps of bushes did give some concealment.

While we were in that semiexposed position, P-47 fighters swooped over our heads to strafe the woods beyond our front lines. To our surprise, we suddenly were bombarded by the empty brass casings from the 50-caliber machine guns. They whistled down all around us and would have done plenty of damage to anyone without a helmet. We had always known those things went *somewhere*, but we had never been attacked by them before. A couple of the men picked up empty cartridges and pocketed them as souvenirs.

A little before dark I received orders to move F Company up to the front and dig in to the right of G Company. As I was doing this an officer appeared and pronounced himself our new company commander. He took over and began by ordering me to have the men dig in along the edge of a gully to our right rear.

My experience told me this was a dangerous position, so I suggested he have us move farther up the hill because gullies usually were natural targets for German artillery. He refused the advice and insisted we dig in where he'd said at once.

We had barely started our foxholes when, to my disgust, the enemy artillery plastered our gully, one terrible shell after another. I immediately stood and flattened myself against the thick trunk of a big beech tree and yelled at the men to get up and find trees. A few of them had time, but many were hit before they could move.

Our new commander broke down in tears, blubbering about how it was all his fault. He kept at it, and when I realized he was completely out of control I called battalion to report the situation and was told to send him back to the aid station.

Very soon another officer was sent to take command of the company. He was a good man, a combat veteran who had been wounded earlier. Though not yet fully recovered, he was being rushed back into a special hell called Hürtgen.

He was just not ready. On a cold November day, beads of sweat plastered his forehead; his fingers trembled so much he couldn't manage to light his cigarette. Next day he went back to battalion headquarters and was sent on to the rear. It must have been hellish to come back to the front lines after a serious wound, and I'm glad I never had to go through it myself.

Since headquarters apparently had no one else to send up, I was left in command of F Company once more. I felt totally inadequate. I was sure I could handle a platoon of forty-some men in combat, but I was overwhelmed by the responsibility for a whole company, with its four platoons and a headquarter section. It would have been easier to work up gradually as executive officer before becoming company commander.

Around noon I was ordered to report to battalion command post, which was only three hundred yards back. There, in an old German log bunker, I met our battalion commander, Lieutenant Colonel Thomas Kenan. Also present were Captain Faulkner, the new commander of E Company, Captain Toles of G, and Captain Newcomb, now battalion exec. I was rather proud that three of us— Newcomb, Toles, and myself—had all served together at one time in E Company.

Colonel Kenan told us our attack would continue in the morning and that First Battalion would be on our left and would jump off at the same time. Our objective was the edge of the woods southwest of Grosshau, about 1,500 yards ahead. The plan was for E and F companies to attack abreast and spread out along each side of an east–west fire trail. Company E was to attack from its present position, and F was to move up through G, now abreast of E.

The First Battalion was about one quarter mile away on the left flank of E Company, but my F Company's right flank was completely open, so far as we knew. The woods ahead were mostly thick reforestation pines about twenty-five feet tall and so dense we couldn't see more than twenty feet ahead.

I knew it would be difficult to control men we couldn't even see most of the time, and this while we were under fire, so it seemed an awful risk to thin our lines by spreading out so widely. As a brand new company commander at my very first meeting with experienced company commanders before a new battalion commander, did I wait to find out what the others might think or did I brashly stick out my young neck?

"With all respect, sir," I heard myself saying, "I don't like this plan because I think it would be a major mistake to spread out so thinly with our flanks unprotected. We're very short on officers and noncoms, and, in my opinion, control would be extremely difficult. With unprotected flanks, we have to be able to move very fast."

The colonel looked startled and, after he'd swallowed, asked if I had any suggestions.

"Sir, why don't we hit in a column of platoons? Hit hard and quickly and punch a hole through fast. That way we have our men closer together, we can control them, and we can defend better if we get hit from a flank. If we move fast enough, we might get in ahead of a lot of the shelling."

I was sweating a little as Colonel Kenan looked around at the other officers and asked what they thought. They quickly supported me. My hat was off to the new Colonel, he would listen to suggestions and be willing to follow them. Many a battalion commander would have cut me down on the spot. The colonel thanked me and said we would use my suggestions. We worked out some details and returned to our company areas as the colonel wished us luck.

Back at F Company, I briefed my four platoon leaders. I now had two second lieutenants and two staff sergeants in charge of platoons. One of the lieutenants was just back from the hospital but seemed in good shape.

It was important, especially considering the lack of vision in the woods, to know our exact jump-off point in the morning, so I sent a platoon leader up ahead some three hundred yards to make sure of G Company's location. His platoon would be leading the attack in the morning. He was back in a short while; he assured me everything was under control and that he could find his way easily in the morning.

He also brought back the tragic news of the loss of my old friend from G Company, First Lieutenant Gallagher. It was Gal who had led that excellent patrol to capture German prisoners for me when I was battalion S-2 (Intelligence Officer). He had been at the head of his platoon when it was caught in a crossfire by German tanks, and he was killed. Gal was one of the finest platoon leaders ever to serve in combat with our army, a man deeply respected by his men.

Next morning broke clear and cold as I led the company out into attack the first time as its commander. As planned, the lead platoon went up through G Company to the line of departure and, by radio control, E and F companies jumped off together.

I followed my second platoon across the north–south road and into the thick woods. After I'd moved in about one hundred yards, something suddenly bothered me, and so I pulled out my map to check our position. It was lucky I did, because the map showed we were to the left of the fire trail instead of to the right and that we were actually in E Company's territory. This meant we were forcing E to their left, into a ragged gully.

Now the entire company would have to swing back south and get on the right-hand side of the road where we belonged. I radioed the platoon leader to push his men to the right beyond the fire trail immediately and then to continue ahead parallel to the trail to our final objective. He acknowledged the order, and we stayed in place waiting for his move.

A few moments later I looked up to find the lead platoon tearing headlong back to us like frightened deer. When they were near enough, I jumped in front of them, waved my arms, and ordered them to stop right there. I was mad enough to use my rifle on them, and it must have shown, because the men all hit the ground and hid behind tree trunks and stared back the way they had come.

I walked right up close to the most senior man visible and was practically spitting in his face as I demanded to know what he thought he was doing—trying to start a stampede? I raised my voice and told him he'd better not ever again move to the rear without permission. I had not heard any enemy action up front, so I asked just what all the running was about. He said they had run into a big German tank and were pulling back so we could hit the tank with artillery.

That being the case, I asked Lieutenant Caldwell, our artillery observer to go back with one of the men to spot the tank and lay some artillery fire on it.

While they were gone I started to make the rounds and quickly discovered that the rear elements of the company were missing. Normally, the company executive officer would lead them up behind the rest of the company, but we had no exec. They should have been following on their own, but apparently they weren't that eager. So I went back to the road we had crossed earlier and whipped the men out of the shell holes they were hiding in and sent them up to the main body of the company, which was still where I had left it.

I had been gone less than fifteen minutes, but it had been costly. The fine young redheaded second lieutenant who led the Second Platoon had been shot between the eyes. He, of course, never knew what happened. There he was, fresh from the hospital, his first day back on the lines, and he was dead before he even saw a German.

We were still out of position, and now that all my officers were gone I called on Staff Sergeant Servat and Staff Sergeant Seltzer to lead the two attacking platoons. Lieutenant Caldwell, the FO, meanwhile reported that the rampaging German tank was only a log sticking out over a stump. He was chuckling, but I had lost my sense of humor.

I ordered the two lead platoons to attack to the right until they crossed the fire trail and then turn left, or eastward, and keep up the attack. The Germans on the high ground near the trail were well dug in, and they opened up viciously with rifles and machine guns as soon as we were within range. The air was moist and heavy, and the savage explosions of the individual rifles and continuous drumming of the machine guns pressed down on our senses. Bullets whipped by us, sometimes tossing up dirt or clipping off twigs and sometimes clinking off helmets or tugging at clothes. We sweated in feverish excitement.

We had all hit the ground at once, and now no one could move. Our position looked hopeless. I crawled forward until I got to the nearest platoon leader, and I told him to get his men going by fire and movement. This was slow and painful, but it seemed the only way, since we were too close for artillery support.

"Fire and movement" is an old military technique that requires a few men to crawl or surge forward a few yards to the next cover while everyone else lays down heavy fire on the enemy to keep him occupied. The next group then scrambles forward while the others cover it with fire. And so it goes, with the platoon leader directing traffic. This uses up an awful lot of ammunition, and it also is about the roughest thing an infantryman has to do. Casualties are sometimes high.

Actually, it's suicidal to stay in place where enemy fire can seek you out; the only real safety is in getting ahead and driving off the enemy. The lucky ones pick up wounds just bad enough to send them to the hospital and its comfortable beds and three hot meals a day. Usually it takes a man a few seconds to realize he has been hit, and then his first emotions are great satisfaction that he has done his job honorably and intense relief that it is all over for a while. Especially if it's a light wound.

At that moment I found my men were being pinned down by one very stubborn machine gun in a bunker out of reach, so I worked my way back to my 60mm mortar section. The noncoms who led this section had been wiped out and not yet replaced, so I asked a likely private if he could fire the mortar. He said he wasn't sure but he would give it a try. I showed him the target in a clump of trees 150 yards ahead, and he and the men fired a round. The explosion knocked the mortar barrel over backwards, sent the 60mm shell straight up overhead, and forced us to run for cover. He had set the mortar up to fire almost straight up, and that meant the shell would fall quite close to the mortar.

That was enough for me, so I went looking for Lieutenant Caldwell. He was able to call in a few 105mm artillery rounds but refused to try a barrage because we were so close to the target. These shells, plus a few near misses with rifle grenades, finally gave the German machine gun crew the right idea, and they withdrew.

At this point I was beginning to realize the full gravity of our situation, and I decided to inform Colonel Kenan. I spoke very carefully on the radio as I explained to him that

all my officers were gone, that we were getting loaded
down with wounded needing evacuation, that our ammunition was almost gone. I said I didn't see how we could
continue in this condition against such a formidable enemy
defense. It seemed to me I was completely objective, simply listing the plain facts, and that my assessment was correct.

Colonel Kenan then taught me a powerful lesson in positive thinking, one I've never forgotten. In a calm, matter-
of-fact voice, he said; "Wilson, ammo is on the way over
now. I know what you're up against, and I know *you can
and will* continue to advance and take that line of defense."

Without another word, he broke the connection.

I was furious. The guy back in his CP was asking the
impossible. It was crazy.

Then the bearers arrived with bandoliers of ammunition,
and somehow we took on new life. Lieutenant Caldwell
laid down some more artillery ahead of us, and we moved
out again. Just before dark we knocked out the last German
breastwork and cleaned out that defensive line.

The surviving enemy pulled back a few hundred yards
into the woods where the pines were very close together,
leaving us in a relatively open area of scattered hardwoods.

Darkness came quickly in the forest, and we had to stop
and dig in for the night while we could still see what we
were doing. Because of the German artillery and mortar
fire we had to get below ground and also get a log roof
over our heads. The Germans, of course, did the same
thing, and whenever their abandoned shelters fit into our
line we used them gratefully. Most of us weren't so lucky,
and so, after an exhausting day, we had to start digging.
Such is life in the infantry.

Our advance for the day had been about five hundred
yards, and E Company on our left had gained about the

same. It was extremely costly yardage, possibly the most expensive real estate in the world, and we never could have gone the other 1,500 yards to our original objective.

During the night we received a few riflemen and three officers as replacements. One officer had some experience, another was a former sergeant who had earned a battlefield commission, and the third was a very big, rough recruit; Second Lieutenant Smith.

Young Smith kept me awake quite a while that night. He had probably heard plenty of the truth about our losses, and he was so nervous he couldn't stop talking. Rather than try to turn him off, I let him wind down. There was plenty of shelling to keep me awake anyway.

At daybreak I got up and made my way along our lines, checking every man. Mortar shells continued to drop in our area, most of them bursting overhead in the treetops as I made my rounds. It occurred to me that this business of being up and around checking on the men and showing them that you were still there was one of the reasons casualties were so high among officers.

I came upon one man lying face down, dead, in the bottom of his foxhole. I didn't know who he was, so I reached down inside his shirt for his dog tags, and my hand came upon a gruesome mess of cold blood. He was one of the replacements who had arrived after dark. He had died even before he had a chance to fight. Many never made it up to the front lines due to the heavy shelling that hit in the rear areas. This was the Hürtgen.

By now our supply lines were in a terrible mess. The jeep trails were mined or so muddy as to be impassable. All our food and ammunition had to be carried, and this meant that the recruits joining us after dark were loaded down with boxes of supplies.

Our medical staff also had taken a severe beating, with

most of them killed or wounded. The few remaining stretcher bearers were ready to drop from exhaustion.

The German mortars continued to drop in relentlessly. Some became deadly tree bursts, and some made it to the ground; since they were coming straight down and faster than sound, there was no warning. By the time you heard the explosion you were already hit or else had escaped.

During one of my rounds I was caught in the middle of a barrage, with one shell exploding in a large oak directly overhead. My right arm stung, and I looked down. A sliver of shrapnel was sticking out of my right forearm. It was about a quarter inch thick, and a half inch protruded. When I pulled it out I found that about an inch had been buried below the surface. The medic sprinkled sulfa powder on the wound, then bandaged it up. At the time it didn't particularly bother me; that came later. I must have been pretty stupid, because it simply never occurred to me to go back to the aid station, about five hundred yards to the rear.

One of the new men asked if he could try out his rifle. He hadn't had a chance to zero it in, and he asked if there were some Germans he could get a shot at. I assured him there were indeed Germans in the woods ahead and told him if he went to our outpost fifty yards in front he might well get a shot.

A short time later he returned excitedly and bragged that he thought he'd gotten a couple of Germans. That would have been over two hundred yards through thick woods, so I rather doubted it.

Later that morning we were ordered to continue the attack eastward toward the far edge of the woods, our original objective. Companies E and F were still to lead the way.

I called my new officers together and explained that we

would attack in column of platoons. I emphasized the importance of speed, because we had to move in close to the Germans to get out of the shelling. I thought we could knock a quick penetration through the German defenses and continue to drive hard for the edge of the woods. This would undoubtedly make the Germans slip off to our sides, particularly our open right, and also to our rear, and I strongly warned against a possible German counterattack from any quarter.

To guard against probable enemy reactions, I assigned defensive positions for each platoon in our new area at the edge of the woods. I didn't think we would have time to mill around, so I told each platoon leader in advance exactly where he should have his men dig in and clear out fields of fire to his front; they were to cut off tree limbs that might obscure or obstruct their view of the enemy to their front and flanks. Then I repeated everything, particularly about the Germans' custom of counterattacking. By then I seemed to be respected as a veteran.

Both companies jumped off on schedule, and the shelling picked us up at once. As the artillery screamed into the treetops above us I pushed my company right out to the front. Evidently the Krauts were caught off balance by our rush, and they took for the rear with only a few shots at us. I knew the dangers of staying in place too long, so I whipped my men ahead even though I could tell by the sounds of firing that E Company was falling behind. They were probably being pinned down by heavy artillery barrages.

They were being shelled from the front, just as I had expected. If they had moved out fast, the way we had, they probably would have escaped most of the shelling.

We didn't dare wait for E, so we pushed on rapidly and reached our objective, the edge of the woods, in about a half hour. We were about a half mile ahead of everyone and exposed on all sides.

The three rifle platoons immediately began to dig in as arranged, and I assigned the weapons platoon and the headquarters section the rear of our lines. I also designated what would be the inner side when E Company joined us. We were in a rough square, about 150 yards to a side.

The fir trees there had been planted very close together by the local foresters and had grown to a height of about twenty feet. We couldn't see more than about twenty yards in any direction, except over the open farm land that was our front. I went around to make sure the platoon leaders were having their men cut off the lower limbs of the pines to give them longer fields of fire and prevent the enemy from sneaking in too close.

I had just finished my rounds and was starting to help Lieutenant Caldwell dig our foxhole when the audacious young fellow who had so eagerly tried out his rifle the day before came charging wildly up to me and stammered, "Germans! Germans!" and pointed to the rear. If only he had fired that rifle at them, some of his buddies might have had enough warning to save themselves.

Before I could move a step, the clatter of machine guns and the *b-r-r-r-ip* of burp guns sounded almost on top of us. The men on the rear line were only partly dug in, and they dove for the ground. These were mostly replacements, and they were shocked and nearly paralyzed by the suddenness and fierceness of their first action. Very few of them even attempted to fire back.

Lieutenant Caldwell and I began firing our rifles and yelling at the men to start shooting. Then I told Caldwell to keep trying to get them to shoot while I went up to the front—actually back to the front—to get more men.

Bullets cut through the branches and zipped all around

me as I ran back. Every damned man I came upon was trying to hide in his foxhole or under a tree, making no attempt at all to fight back. I rousted a bunch of them out and got them to follow me, running as low as possible under the whizzing bullets.

It was easy to tell where the Krauts were from all their firing, and I led the dozen or so of my men out to the side and killed a couple of them, wounded three, and took a prisoner. A few managed to get away.

Actually, it turned out to be only a combat patrol, but they were so heavily armed with automatic weapons that they sounded like a whole company. They sure raised hell with us for a time.

With the excitement over, I got the men back to cutting branches to clear fields of fire. I told them that was far more important than digging foxholes. They had found out the hard way.

Normally I would have continued to work on our defenses, leaving the wounded to our very capable medic, but I couldn't find him anywhere. Then I heard muffled moans from a nearby foxhole and went over to find my new young Lieutenant Smith lying shot to death, with his body blocking the entrance. I tugged at his limp, two-hundred pound body but couldn't budge it due to my bad arm, so I yelled for help. His body was riddled with German bullets; he must have died instantly. All our talking the night before would never serve any purpose, although I couldn't help wondering if he might have had a premonition.

Underneath Smith's body was Sergeant Servat, who had been terribly wounded in the face. Somehow the gutsy sergeant was still conscious. A third man was at the bottom of the log-covered hole, and it was our missing medic. He was quite unhurt but completely pinned down by the other two. He quickly went to work.

First we sent the walking wounded, including the Germans, toward the rear. Then the medic worked on a man hit in the gut, and I did what I could for Servat. I tied bandages around both sides of his face and asked if he thought he could make it back to the forward aid station some 1,200 yards away. He nodded, and so I pointed him on his way, telling him he was bleeding internally and that he mustn't stop to rest but had to keep moving to save his own life. There were no stretcher bearers. Somehow he made it. It must have been the longest journey of his life.*

The man with the stomach wound needed to be evacuated, but the stretcher bearers were all casualties themselves. I offered to rig up some kind of stretcher and send two men back with him, but he didn't want to be moved. He said he was sure he would be okay until a jeep could get that far. I wish I had insisted, because he died that night from shock and loss of blood. The medic and I second-guessed ourselves and felt pretty sick about it.

My arm was so sore that it was almost useless. I couldn't grip a shovel handle, so I ordered the German prisoner to dig my foxhole. He was about forty, and a couple of times he wanted to stop and rest, but I was so damned mad at the deaths and wounds he and his buddies had caused that I took it out on him a little and wouldn't let him stop. Then I had him cut some thick pine logs to make a frame for the top, and on this frame he spread big pine boughs, then his rain cape, and then a thickness of dirt as extra protection against tree bursts. About a foot of small pine boughs made a wonderful mattress at the bottom. This was the best foxhole I ever had, being high enough to sit up in and wide enough for two men to stretch out in. We weren't used to such elegance.

---

*My wife and I met Servat and his wife in New Orleans in 1960, fifteen years after the war. I still don't see how he could have dragged himself back to the aid station that awful day in the Hürtgen.

Lieutenant Bowman, heavy machine gun platoon leader from H Company, was sent up to us with his two sections and four water-cooled machine guns. They added tremendously to our defense. I let Lieutenant Bowman share my deluxe foxhole because Lieutenant Caldwell had decided to dig in closer to the open field in case his artillery was needed.

Just before dark E Company made it up to our left. They had had a rough day. This left only our right flank exposed, and I had already moved our own light, air-cooled machine guns over there and cut some wide and deep openings through the pines for better observation of enemy movement. We were well dug in and could hand out a tremendous amount of damage if attacked.

The fronts of both E and F faced eastward across big open fields, which were about halfway between Kleinhau on our southeast and Grosshau on the northeast. Both of these villages lay in the open farmland about three quarters of a mile apart, and we were about one quarter mile west of the main north–south road connecting them.

First Battalion's A, B, and C companies were all on line to the left of E; those companies had taken heavy maulings and were in very bad shape. We were all so short of officers and men that we made no attempt to move ahead for the next few days. We made ourselves as comfortable as possible, staying close to our foxholes because of the frequent systematic shelling day and night.

Meanwhile, F Company received one hundred replacements and one officer, bringing us up to a total of 150 men, which was only about ten short of full combat strength. I was still shy a weapons platoon leader and an executive officer, and so I had to take on the executive's job of assigning the new men. Each man was interviewed briefly to find out his MOS or Military Order Specialty; most turned out to be simply basic riflemen.

* * *

Both my radiomen had been casualties, so I quizzed each man on his knowledge of radios. Battalion had loaned me one radioman but wanted him back as soon as possible, and he sure was eager to return. Finally two men, who appeared to be buddies, told me they could do the job. It seemed they had been ham radio operators but knew nothing about military radios, and I decided to keep them in mind in case no one turned up.

After the screening was over, I had to go back to those two. Then I told them to finish their foxholes and report to the regular radioman for instructions.

I told the battalion radioman to teach them only the fundamentals and how to change batteries. He kept them busy the rest of the day and toward evening convinced me they could handle it, so I let him scamper back to his real assignment at battalion, where they'd been working shorthanded; he had seen enough front-line duty.

Day and night the shelling never ceased. The Germans, of course, knew exactly where we were regrouping, and they wouldn't let us rest. Our log roofs could take care of any shrapnel, but two of our men were killed instantly, torn to pieces by a rare direct hit, as they slept.

One day we were startled by the thunderous roar of what seemed like a freight train overhead, and a huge shell landed with a tremendous blast about seventy-five feet to my left side. It plowed a crater eight feet deep, ten feet wide, and fifteen feet long. This was within our lines; we were shaken.

This was the biggest one that ever landed near me, and I reported it to battalion. Some artillery officers came up and measured the hole and calculated from its depth and angle that it came from a giant railway gun about sixteen miles back. They must have put some counterfire out there for we never got any more incoming rounds from that gun.

We were lucky enough to have a rather quiet night, and I managed to catch up on sleep. Next morning Lieutenant Bowman and I were indulging in a K-ration breakfast when the smaller of the two new radiomen plummeted into our foxhole. He was shaking violently, and tears streamed down his face. His whole frame quivered with the spasms, and he was barely able to tell me between sobs that he couldn't take it "up here." He just had to get the hell out; I had to let him go to the rear. He sobbed like a baby during the entire outburst and beat his head on the ground.

I tried to calm him down and reason with him, but all he could do was sputter through his broken sobs, "Please, please let me go." He was beginning to get under my skin, so I dropped the soft stuff and told him angrily that I had been in front-line combat for over five months and no one would let me go back. Since he had just arrived, he sure as hell wasn't going back.

This only brought on more hysteria, and he said he would desert. I told him that was one way of ending it all quickly, because he would be shot as a deserter. He said he didn't care. Then I told him how ashamed his parents would be, and he still didn't care. Nothing seemed to work, though somehow he became a little calmer, and then he shocked me with his remark: "I'm just a dirty, no-good, yellow, Jewish SOB."

I didn't give a hoot about his background but was horrified to hear a man demean himself so abjectly. All this was enough for me, and I sat back completely stumped and let Lieutenant Bowman try his hand.

I hadn't had time to analyze, yet somehow this fellow didn't ring true to me, and I was determined to get to the bottom. It was pure luck, however, that led me to a way to draw him out. With nothing particular in mind, I began to probe about his past. When I got into college sports, and he began to wipe his eyes, I knew this was the right track.

He said he had played football in high school and had led his team to conference championships. I congratulated him on what must have been a fine job of leadership and followed up by remarking that he must have had a really great team for them to play together so well.

Then I tried to tie it in to the present by suggesting that he think of combat as similar to football. Now, however, it was my turn to be quarterback, and our team really had taken an awful mauling in the first half. We had used up our entire bench and desperately needed every single man to help us win. I went on to say he might have to go out for a pass, or make an end run, or maybe just block on the next play. Right now I wasn't sure where he would be needed most, but a radioman could be very important.

By now he had quit crying, and in a perfectly normal voice he said that it had never occurred to him that this was a team effort, but he could see it and would try hard to carry out his assignments. Our talk ran on a little longer, and then I sent him back to his foxhole.

It seemed he hadn't quite given up the idea of leaving the hellish trap we were in, for he tried to get back to see me several times that day, but I wouldn't let him in my foxhole. Once some shells landed nearby, and that sent him scurrying for his foxhole. Finally he stayed there.

The dramatics weren't quite over, however. Later that day the other radioman, a big guy over two hundred pounds, crawled into my foxhole, and he, too, was crying. On his hands and knees he blubbered and begged me to let him go to the rear. By now I had become something of a drama critic, and his performance was far inferior to that of his smaller buddy. I blew my top and shouted at him that the two of them were trying to play me for an idiot, and I'd had it with them.

Surprisingly, he readily admitted it and even went on to describe how they had spent a few hours the night before planning the charade. It seems they had both been in plays at college and had had some training. In spite of myself, I had to admit the first guy was quite an actor. I had to marvel at his talent in producing such big tears and in shaking convulsively so realistically. He was every bit the equal of M*A*S*H*'s Corporal Klinger.

I got rid of the big guy quickly, telling him I would have him shot on the spot if he gave me any more trouble. He dried his tears at once and promised he and his buddy would do their jobs.

This was my first encounter with an overt attempt to fake battle fatigue, and instead of seeing the humor or allowing for circumstances all I felt was a sickening shock. Oh, I knew that everyone had a breaking point, but I had just assumed that everyone naturally was doing his best up to that point. This may seem a bit naive, but I do think it was the way most of us felt. Most of the men I knew in World War II seemed to accept their role to fight for home and country without complaint. I don't recall a single person who questioned our involvement. We were not gung ho but quietly went about our duties. Perhaps that is why the occasional shirker stood out.

I have witnessed real emotional breakdown under the enormous physical and mental pressure of combat, and for those cases I have the most heartfelt sympathy. It is awful to see men go into convulsions, froth at the mouth, gibber incoherently. Many later responded to rest and treatment, and some were returned to the front—time after time. Some of the poor guys never did make it back to normalcy, even long after the war. But I knew of only two men who ever made a completely successful return to the battlefield.

Our Thanksgiving dinner was hand-carried up to us by men from the service company. Our cooks had put together giant turkey sandwiches, and they were a treat compared to

K-ration Spam, even though we, of course, received none of the usual fancy trimmings. It wasn't all celebration, however, for we learned that some of the food carrying party had been hit on the way up. Though this happened all the time, we never quite learned to accept it. We had been fighting in the Hürtgen Forest for twelve days, the worst combat I had yet encountered.

Late in the afternoon of November 29, 1944, I was ordered to get my men ready to move out and to report at once to the battalion CP. This sounded like good news, for we had heard rumors that we were to be relieved.

My runner and I picked our way a quarter of a mile back along the fire to trail to the big log-covered dugout Colonel Kenan used as his command post, and as soon as I entered I was struck by the thick gloom. Colonel Kenan, Captain Newcomb and Captain Toles all nodded at me gravely; no one was smiling. The colonel handed me a cup of coffee, as though to the condemned.

Colonel Kenan wasted no time. "Wilson, I've got a tough job for your company tonight. B Company has been attacking Grosshau all day and they're now pinned down in the open ground a couple hundred yards west of town. They have a lot of casualties and need help at once. Regiment insists we take Grosshau tonight in order to relieve B Company and also because possession of Grosshau is vital to tomorrow's attack plans."

He went on to say that the balance of First Battalion was holding the high ground north of Grosshau and that they had their hands full just hanging on.

The colonel continued in a quiet, calm voice: "Take your company northeastward along the edge of the woods to your left. Try to make contact with B Company as soon as possible. You may have to send in a patrol, because their radio is out."

So far this was not in the least attractive. A night patrol

trying to get through to B Company could easily come unexpectedly upon other Americans, who frequently shot at sounds in the darkness. It was, nonetheless, our only choice.

It seems to be the practice of commanders to use their most experienced men for the tough jobs. While this might appear unfair to the men asked to undertake repeated risks, the commander knows that using his best men gives him a better chance of getting a difficult job done with the least losses. Lieutenant Colonel Teague, our regiment's most experienced battalion commander, was often called on for tough assignments by Colonel Lanham.

Now I was being given a very difficult and dangerous assignment. I wondered how many such jobs I could survive. On reflection, I could think of five or six times I had been given tough assignments because of other jobs I'd performed successfully.* I do not blame anyone for this method of assignment; on several occasions I used it myself. But it does tend to put a high price on successful performance.

"Now, Wilson," Colonel Kenan went on in a fatherly manner, "I'm aware of your shortage of experienced officers and know it will be tough to go in at night with so many recruits, but we do need Grosshau tonight."

He paused a few seconds to let this sink in. "My first concern is B Company. If you could even get a radio to them, then perhaps we could make plans for getting in medical help. After that, remember—we absolutely must have Grosshau tonight. Then, with Grosshau and Kleinhau in our hands, we can use our tanks to take Gey, only a

---

*For example, at Saint-Lô I led the second day's attack because I was the last one to lead the previous night; as we approached Germany my platoon led the combat patrol to the Siegfried Line and led again in our first attack through the line; I was called on to lead nearly every patrol from our company during September and October, 1944; my platoon led the jump-off attack the first day in the Hürtgen forest. Other examples can be found in the text.

couple of miles northeast of Grosshau. We will be counting very heavily on you."

The colonel went on to tell me he would be moving his CP up as soon as possible. We checked watches, the current password, and the location of the forward aid station. I couldn't help but notice that no mention at all was made of what our battalion's three other companies would be doing while F Company was out there in attack. The Colonel wished me luck, and I took off quickly.

Also absent from my orders were any suggestions on just how to get this job done. That was strictly up to me. I think I was flattered. As I walked back to the company with my runner I tried to get things straight in my own mind.

I knew the location of all friendly forces from the positions clearly marked on the map. Many unknown items confronted me coldly. We were all aware that the Germans held Grosshau, but I had no idea of where their defensive line was and whether it extended outside the village.

Night attacks are very difficult and usually require a lot of planning. To control and direct men so they shoot the enemy and not their own is a major concern. Exact directions and signals that are easily seen or heard must be worked out. Radios and other equipment must be secured and checked, passwords have to be assigned, the order of movement determined. With experienced men and officers who know them well, night attacks are still one of the worst assignments possible.

We did not have any of the proper qualities, and time was also against us. Our only advantage was the ability to move in the darkness. I hoped my new officers would be able to follow instructions and that I would be able to stay in contact with them.

When we got back to the company area, the officers had the men almost ready to move out, since they were also aware of the rumor about our being relieved and sent to the rear; I wasn't eager to give them my news. I sympathized with them as I repeated our attack plan. Even in the twilight, their shock and dismay were apparent as the dangers and risks sank in. Slowly their faces returned to normal as they realized the necessity for the attack. Yet I could almost hear them saying to themselves, "Please, tell me this isn't so, tell me it's a nightmare."

I went over the big picture once again and then got down to details, keeping them brief. Control of the men is paramount. I had to appoint a leader for every six men. If there weren't enough sergeants, I would have to appoint acting sergeants at once. I told the men to keep me informed by radio of everything they did. I admonished them that they wouldn't be able to see much, so they had to be extra careful. They might run into friendlies, so they couldn't shoot too quickly. If any man moved from where he was supposed to be, he was to check with me at once. We then double-checked passwords, watches, and radios.

When I felt we were ready, I moved the company out in column of platoons, with the First Platoon leading. I went with the First Platoon, following the lead scouts along with the platoon leader. We passed through the front of E Company and headed northeast along the edge of the woods in the general direction of B Company.

We had gone about three quarters of the way when our scouts abruptly fell flat and shouted out a challenge. The password that came back was delightfully welcome. By great good fortune, we had run into a small group of walking wounded from B Company itself, along with a couple of stretcher cases carried by German prisoners.

The sergeant leading this small group had only a slight arm wound, and he asked us the way to the aid station. I gave him directions and then asked if he knew how we could contact B Company, since their radio was out. He said he could tell us, but that the route was pretty risky because of the open ground. So we tried the radio again at short range, but with no luck.

Then I asked the sergeant if he'd go with one of my men and take a walkie-talkie to his captain, and he agreed to give it a try.

It seemed only a few minutes later that we got through to B Company on the radio, and I was able to get the complete tactical situation from their captain. The Germans had several strong points to the captain's front, making a frontal attack very hazardous. The captain said the Germans were well dug in and were also using the cellars in town for protection against our artillery. He had seen plenty of action on the west side of town where he was, and also on the northwest, but he didn't know about the south. He hadn't seen any action there and thought it might be our best approach, if we could get across the open ground.

I thanked him for the very important information. Based on this, I told him we would enter the village from the south, near its southwest corner. He wished us luck and said they would try to hang on until help arrived.

Using a flashlight under a couple of coats, I showed my officers the general layout on the map. From our position, about five hundred yards southwest of town, we would head due east until we were even with Grosshau, when we would turn northward. One platoon would lead off the attack and take the southwest corner of town and then continue northward in hopes of getting behind the German front-line defenders. The second platoon was to follow right behind and then turn to the right when it reached the north side, thus getting behind any defenders up there. The third platoon was to follow along until it got to the edge of town and then was to turn to the right and take care of the south side. There were only two blocks in the town, so we planned to mop up quickly. We hoped no civilians were in town. In the darkness, they could easily be killed by mistake.

After another strong reminder to the officers to keep a close hand on their men and to keep me informed, we shoved off. The moon was not yet out, and far across the wide fields the ghostly shape of Grosshau seemed to beckon. We crouched low to reduce our silhouettes as we quickly filtered across the field. In a few minutes we came upon a small cemetery on the southwest corner, and, to my immense surprise and relief, not a shot had been fired. I couldn't believe it.

A few minutes later the lead platoon jumped off in attack. They came upon the Germans from the rear, as hoped, and took them completely by surprise. Apparently they were exhausted themselves and had given all their attention to their front. I couldn't understand why they had had no defense at all on their south flank, but I was deeply grateful.

The moon was still behind the clouds, and in the full darkness it was difficult to keep close track of the men as they went from house to house to root out the Krauts. We had only a few flashlights but still managed to find sometimes two and sometimes up to eight Germans sleeping in each cellar. Some of them didn't show up until daylight.

In a half hour we had the town secure, a job made easier because no civilians were found. I radioed Colonel Kenan, who was profuse in his congratulations as he told me the rest of the battalion would be moving up shortly. Meanwhile, I had set up my main defensive line on the eastern side of town, close to the important north–south road. We were prepared for a German counterattack.

Around midnight I felt everything was completely secure, so I tried to get some rest in a nearby cellar. I was just getting comfortable and starting to reminisce about how incredibly lucky we had been to take Grosshau so easily when a messenger roused me to get me up to the front line.

There I found Caldwell quite bothered and upset. The forward observer agitatedly pointed to the ridge out front and slightly southeast of town and asked if that didn't look like Germans to me. With the help of field glasses and in the light of what was by then a very bright moon, I clearly made out a column of what could only be enemy soldiers. They were wearing German long coats and were marching in single file toward the northeast, about five hundred yards to our front.

Caldwell complained that he had fired a couple of rounds at them but that when he had ordered a barrage his battery had turned him down. His commanding officer explained that his map showed that the hill was being held by Americans.

So I trained the field glasses on the marchers once more, and in addition to their long coats I saw that they were carrying long-handled shovels, which our men rarely had. I then called Colonel Kenan and asked his permission to fire, since both the artillery FO and I were positive they were Germans.

The colonel called me back in a few minutes and told me he had checked it out and had to deny permission. He said a unit from the Fifth Armored Infantry claimed they had men on that hill. I protested so heatedly that the colonel told me to send out a patrol to check firsthand.

One of my new lieutenants led a small patrol across the road and along a small ditch toward the marching column, and I watched intently through my binoculars. They got within fifty yards of the marchers and radioed back that they were definitely Germans. He could see the cut of their helmets, their long coats and long shovels, and, most convincing, that they were carrying their wounded toward the

German front. And they were speaking German.

Colonel Kenan still was reluctant to let us fire, and he ordered me to send out another patrol—this time to the Fifth Armored, about a half mile south on the road to Kleinhau. The patrol leader returned in about an hour and reported that the CO there stated flatly that his men were dug in on that hill and that he was sending more people up there.

I was frustrated and disgusted; Caldwell was furious. The Fifth Armored didn't know how to read its map, but absolutely nothing could be done about it. I went back to sleep.

My play-acting radiomen had performed surprisingly well that night—as radiomen. They made a few mistakes, but they got right into things and were pretty excited. They did their own jobs and even volunteered for extra work when we were in town. I was quite pleased.

That night also was a pleasant surprise. The Germans let us sleep. There were no mortars, no artillery. And there were no counterattacks. I almost thought that this respite might be due to their not even knowing we had taken the town, for it had been quick and almost noiseless.

Early next morning I was summoned to a meeting of company commanders at battalion headquarters, now in Grosshau, and our attack orders were very simple. Captain Toles would lead G Company on the right, and I would lead F Company on the left. We were to cross the open field and advance up the hill to our front, the same hill the Germans had marched along, immune to our artillery, the night before. After covering this ground, about eight hundred yards, we were to enter the woods and continue the attack eastward along a small fire trail, with F to the left of the trail and G to the right.

Meanwhile, First Battalion would attack parallel to us

and about a half mile to our left. Our objective was the far edge of the woods about two miles ahead, just west of Gey, gateway to the Cologne plains.

Since friendly troops, namely the Fifth Armored Infantry, were supposed to be holding the hill ahead, we were to use the top of that hill as the line of departure for our attack. It all sounded simple enough, but to me it was too good to be true, because I couldn't get out of my mind the suspicion that the Germans we had seen the night before might not have gone very far. I expressed my concern but was assured, albeit by people who had not been there with me and Lieutenant Caldwell, that everything was okay.

Captain Toles moved his company up next to mine, and we jumped off as planned. As we headed across the open slope I kept my men spread way out and watched the ridge line very sharply. It seemed odd to me that the American troops on the ridge were not at all visible from the rear as we approached. Our progress the first three hundred yards was almost a stroll, almost like a training exercise back in the States. "States?" What a strange word, and what an impossible distance in the past.

Then it happened. The sky fell in, and we were in hell. German artillery and mortars, machine guns and rifles, and the murderously direct fire of the tank-mounted 88s all hit us at once. Everyone dove to the ground and then crawled to the nearest shell hole or depression. There was no time to think; we simply reacted. Our infantrymen began to fire back with their M-1s, and Lieutenant Caldwell was able to get some artillery on the Krauts, who were well dug in. Now we were paying for the inexcusable stupidity of that armored captain who couldn't read a simple map.

It may seem strange that our headquarters did not appear to believe our report of the enemy troops. One must keep in mind that a captain had stated his troops were on the hill. No one was willing to take the chance of shelling our own soldiers based on the night observations of another officer. If we had taken a prisoner, our story probably would have been accepted. However, when in doubt, the colonel had no choice but to refuse the request for artillery. Sad, but true; we had to overcome one more mistake.

This battle raged on insanely, impossibly, for hours as we slowly moved forward. In my five months of considerable combat of all kinds I had never had to endure such a heavy, mercilessly accurate barrage of shells and bullets.

The Kraut artillery forward observer was on the heights above us, and he had perfect vision of our every move. They had let us get so far in the open that we couldn't pull back in daylight, and our only protection was the irregularities in the field itself. I know the FO had me spotted, because I had to keep moving around while trying to push the men forward, and I was marked by my radioman (and his antenna), who followed a few feet behind.

It was almost a game, and the German FO was very good at it. No sooner had I changed position and allowed twenty or thirty seconds for the range on his cannon to be adjusted than the shells would start dropping in all around me. He was extremely accurate. He already had the exact range and only had to make very slight adjustments.

The mortar observer was just as good as the artillery. I would look up quickly for a new shell hole, get up and spring ten or twenty yards, and dive into the new hole. After about a half minute, the mortar shells, which had to go way up and then drop almost straight down, would pepper the area all around me.

Once my radioman and I plunged into a shell hole about three feet deep and six feet across, and we had hardly settled when the mortars began to explode very close to us. Even if it had been possible to hear their vertical descent, the other battle noises would have drowned them out. This became my single worst experience of the war. Because the shells came in so fast, I judged they must have had eight or ten mortars zeroing in on us. About one hundred shells came down in an area that couldn't have been much more than fifty feet on a side. Why they never got a direct hit I'll never know.

A third man piled in on top of us, and we tried to bury ourselves in the bottom of the hole, praying out loud as we held on for dear life. Handfuls of dirt, chips of stones, and spent shell fragments kept hitting me in the back. The only thing that saved us was the softness of the plowed fields. There could be no tree bursts out there, of course, and the soft dirt let the shells penetrate a bit before exploding and then absorbed much of the force. We were lucky the ground there had not yet frozen. Of course, the fact that there was no direct hit was also a factor in our survival, for which we thanked Providence.

And it was on that terrible open slope beyond the hamlet of Grosshau that young Lieutenant George Wilson, commanding officer of F Company, Twenty-second Infantry, came to the very edge of his breaking point. I had to fight with all I had to keep from going to pieces. I had seen others go, and I knew I was on the black edges. I could barely maintain the minimal control I had after fourteen or fifteen days of brutally inhuman fighting in those damned woods; I had reached the limit of my physical and emotional endurance.

The barrage abruptly ended, and a problem with my radioman, the larger of the two buddies, snapped me right out of my morbid thoughts. He was crying again, though this time with reason, and he begged me to send him to the rear. It wasn't the best time to bother me, and I couldn't take it from him. I turned on him angrily and pointed my rifle at his chest, saying that if I heard one more word out of him I'd shoot. He stopped bawling instantly.

A few minutes later in the next barrage, as a kind fate

would have it, this radioman was wounded slightly in the arm, and I had to send him to the rear. And then I became my own radioman.

His buddy, the smaller man with the SCR 300 longer-range radio, which was used to relay messages, was still back in Grosshau with my headquarters group. But a little later, when I tried to relay a message through, I couldn't reach him. The medics later on listed him as a battle fatigue case.

When I look back, I don't see how anything could be worse than the punishment we took that day. The Germans had waited until we were out in the open with only shell holes and the undulations of the plowed field for protection, and then they let us have it with artillery, mortars, rifles, cannon, snipers, and—worst of all—the direct fire of machine guns and 88mm High Explosive (HE) shells from tanks right in the line.

The tanks at the edge of the woods would shoot HE shells into the ground just ahead of the attacking infantry. After that the Germans would machine gun the fallen men. I could move only a few men forward at a time. Only those who were fast and could find a hole to dive into after fifteen or twenty yards made it.

The toughest thing for me that terrible, insane day was to hear stricken men all over that slope crying out for a medic who no longer was there. Our marvelous, courageous medics had been working right out in the open wherever they found a wounded man, and they had all been wiped out. Normally the medics were spared being shot at by German infantrymen. However, artillery, cannon, mortar, and tanks could not be so selective. Anyone in the area could be hit; often it was the misfortune of the medics and stretcher bearers to be caught in an area being shelled. At these moments I was furiously bitter at that armored infantry captain who had insisted his men were on the hill, and I don't think I could have been trusted near him.

Whenever I could get to any of the seriously wounded, I would tell them their only hope was to somehow crawl back to the aid station. Some of the bad ones actually made it. I don't see how.

One man made his way over to me, and he was unable to talk because his chin had been shot away. I pointed to Grosshau and urged him to get there as soon as possible. It was all I could stop to do for him then.

G Company, on my right, seemed to be falling behind, so I called Captain Toles on the radio and asked if he could come up on line with my company, so we wouldn't be a salient the Krauts could concentrate on. He told me they would be dropping back even farther. Then I received no further response.

Later I found out that Captain Toles had been seriously wounded and that another of my old friends formerly of E Company, Lieutenant Piszarak, had been killed. Piszarak and I had joined E Company the same day back in July near Carenten, France.*

Without leaders, G Company just didn't move, and many of the men drifted back into Grosshau. Colonel Kenan had me send Lieutenant Greenlee to take command of G, but he got there too late. So from about noon onward, my company fought on by itself.

We were nearing the crest of the hill, and what was left of my forward platoons was being blasted by the tanks in the woods, cutting them down like a giant, bloody scythe.

---

*After the war, at camp Butner, near Durham, North Carolina, Captain Toles explained to me with tears in his eyes how sorry he was he just couldn't get G Company that far up. He had heard me on the radio that last time but lay there gravely wounded and couldn't answer me. All his officers were gone, and there was nothing he could do.

Lieutenant Caldwell got some artillery on them before he was wounded, and I called for fighter planes. Soon some P-47s came over and strafed the hilltop and dropped a few bombs. This helped quite a lot because it forced the German tanks to take cover deeper in the woods.

During what may have been the peak of the shelling, the man leading my left platoon went berserk and had to be sent to the rear. This forced me to call forward a young officer who had just joined me that morning before we jumped off. Since he had had no chance to get acquainted with his men, I had left his platoon in reserve. Now I needed him and told him to bring his platoon up through the left platoon and continue the attack.

He immediately began to cry, and he sobbed out that he couldn't do it. Coming in fresh and going out onto that hill looked to him like an execution. He might have been right. But I had no choice in the matter and had to send him to the rear.

Thus, for the second time in ten days, I was the only officer left in the company, and most of my noncoms (sergeants and corporals) were gone. I appointed one man a sergeant on the spot. I had long since lost count of how many times I had had to make such instant appointments and promotions. I told him to try to get some of the men on the left moving again while I did the same on the right.

About a half hour later this new sergeant came over to me and pointed to the only building left standing on the hill to our left. He asked if we had anyone in there. He said it looked like someone was up in what was left of the chimney. I raised my field glasses and sure enough spotted a sniper as he was pointing his rifle our way. I yelled at the sergeant to duck and instinctively pulled him down into a shallow trench dug by the Germans, just as the sniper's bullet kicked up the dirt beside us. Then I told the Sergeant to get some of his men shooting at the SOB.

He got up and walked nonchalantly about twenty yards to his nearest men, knelt down, and pointed up to the chimney. This he repeated to the next group of men, and then he casually walked over to a shellhole for himself.

Just as he reached the lip of his hole the sniper dropped him with a bullet to the head. Damn it, why hadn't he hustled? The sniper might well have missed. His men quickly got the sniper, who also must have been the mortar FO, because after that the mortars didn't bother us anymore.

All my leaders were gone again. I didn't even have a corporal left. Sergeant Bert Smith, the forward observer for the 81mm mortars from H Company, was still with us, but he was busy directing his mortars to fire on any target he could find.

Our day-long infantry attack, along with great help from our artillery, had driven the Germans out of their foxholes and one big log-reinforced dugout at the edge of the woods. As we entered the woods, a quick look around at our strength made me shudder when I saw how few men had gotten through. And with G Company apparently out of action back down the hill, I realized we were sitting out on the proverbial limb; it wouldn't take much for the Germans to snip us off once they appreciated our weakness.

So I kept on doing what I'd been doing all day almost automatically, making quick decisions. There had been no help at all during the battle, and it never even occurred to me to ask for any now. I was still on my own, and my judgment told me to get out of what could have been a trap, so I moved the remnants of F Company back some two hundred yards over ground we had taken and up a slight slope to a former German trench. This would force the enemy to attack uphill and across open ground to get to us.

I sure hated to give up ground that had been so expensive, but I didn't see its value if we didn't survive to hold it. Perhaps I should have called Colonel Kenan and requested that he send up E Company to help out after dark, but decided I had to deal with the problem immediately.

We moved back to the long trench without any problems, and, although we all were close to physical and emotional exhaustion, each man began spontaneously to deepen the trench, which was originally about two feet deep. Some got it down to about five feet before they felt safe. At least the ground was soft and scooped out easily.

I had reported by radio to Lieutenant Colonel Kenan and was told to hold where we were. No mention was made of sending up help. I still wonder why E Company wasn't sent up immediately.

We had started out that morning with about 140 riflemen, a couple medics, three noncoms, four company officers, one attached artillery officer, and one attached sergeant from H Company. We had lost all the medics, all the noncoms, three of the four company officers, and the artillery observer. And we had lost *ninety* riflemen. This was, and still is, the most terrible day of my life. The ordeal was beyond human endurance, and I cannot understand how fifty of us survived.

On the top of the sickening pain of our losses was the nagging bitterness that it probably all could have been prevented if Lieutenant Caldwell, the best FO I ever saw, had been permitted to wipe out the Germans before they could dig in. What a difference it would have made to F and G companies. The losses at G must have been similar to ours. If that Armored Infantry captain had only been able to read his map, that particular battle would never have taken place. Yet, again and again, headquarters denied us the action we, who were on the spot, could have taken to such advantage.

We had fought all day without food, and now some of us tried to force down a cold K ration, but few of us were hungry. The night of November 30 was cold in that German trench without blankets or overcoats. Wearing only a field jacket, I was so cold that I could not stop my teeth chattering. Although I was completely exhausted, physically and emotionally spent, my nerves wouldn't quit. I could not sleep. The horrible events of the day kept churning around and playing back vividly as life.

I was sickened with grief at our losses, and yet it had happened so quickly that the total effect was numbing. The loss of one man is deeply depressing; the loss of ninety is just overwhelming. In fact, I was overwhelmed by the courage of those men, most of whom were very raw recruits, and it gave me a sensitive, even touchy, feeling of pride in the fighting qualities of our twenty-second Infantry. Emotion was all most of us had left.

As I lay there in the chill, unable to relax enough to sleep, I couldn't help dwelling on some of the things that naturally bothered me. Why hadn't G Company come up on line, and how badly had they been hit? And where was E all this time? Was it too risky to send any more men out there to help us? Were we being written off and abandoned? More to the point, and this is what may really have been keeping me awake, did the Germans realize our helplessness, and would they counterattack during darkness and wipe us out?

Since I am only human, I have to mention how pleased I was to hear from friends at battalion that there was talk that I would be recommended for the Distinguished Service Cross (ranking just below the Medal of Honor) and also

would be put in for captaincy. I didn't know about the
DSC, but I sure felt entitled to promotion to captain, the
normal rank of a company commander. As it turned out,
due to circumstances I never understood, nothing ever
came to pass. I never thought much about the medal, but
being passed over for an earned promotion did rankle.

As dawn approached I got out and made the rounds to
make darn sure everyone was alert for an enemy attack. At
about this time of day—it now was December 1, 1944—
Private Mays, our former radioman who had been
wounded, rejoined us, and with him came a young retread
officer. Retreads had been trained for rear echelon work,
and now, in the emergency, they were given some quick
infantry training and sent up to the front.

At this time our First, Second, and Third battalions
were given the code names Red, White, and Blue. My new
lieutenant told me Colonel Kenan's orders were for me to
hold in place while Blue Battalion went around our left
flank and continued the attack. We were to be alert for any
enemy action on the rear or right flank of Blue and to stop
any such attack. I heard myself wonder aloud, *"What the
hell with?"*

It was a tremendous relief to learn another battalion
would be leading the attack, and I kept in close contact
with Colonel Kenan over the radio. Blue jumped off as
planned and made it into the woods on our left with ease.
Apparently the Germans hadn't worried much about that
flank. An hour later Colonel Kenan radioed me that Blue
had run into a battalion of German defenders and was now
having a very rough time. Blue was concerned that the
enemy might work around between my position and theirs
and attack Blue's rear, so Colonel Kenan ordered me to
move F Company, all fifty of us, up into the woods ahead,

go in five hundred yards, and then set up defensive positions facing southeast in order to cover Blue's right flank and rear.

This normally would have been a simple exercise in control, but it was not easy with only one spanking-new officer and no sergeants or corporals at all. The squads were down to three to five men each instead of the normal twelve, and no squad had a leader. In our exposed position it was impossible to regroup, so I decided to lump all the riflemen into one platoon for the new lieutenant and leave the rest of the company for me. It was too bad Officer Candidate School never taught us how to operate at considerably less than full strength, for that's the way we always seemed to be in actual combat.

I called my one and only lieutenant over to my position in the center of the trench and gave him the story of his new platoon of all riflemen, with no sergeants, and I told him to lead them about one hundred yards into the woods and wait there for me and the rest of the company. I would lead the company myself from there on. Then by word of mouth we passed the orders down both sides of the trench. I couldn't help wondering what sort of message the men at the end received.

It was a bright, clear midmorning when I signaled the lieutenant. He at once jumped out of the trench and at the top of his voice yelled: "All you riflemen, come on, let's go!" He started at a trot toward the German lines and after a moment looked back over his shoulder at a sight that should have given him heart failure. Not one single rifleman was following him.

This young retread lieutenant then made a big sweeping motion with his arm, yelled "Let's go!" at the men again, and continued trotting forward with hardly a break in his stride.

I think I was holding my breath, then suddenly some of

the men on both sides of me began to climb out of the trench, and soon the whole platoon of riflemen was running after him. They disappeared into the woods without a shot being fired.

This was one of the most courageous acts I had ever seen, and I recommended the young lieutenant for a Silver Star, but I never found out if he received it. I felt like giving him mine.

When the lieutenant and his riflemen reached the edge of the woods, I ordered the rest of the men to stay spread out and follow me. The Krauts evidently had been surprised by the quick rush of the first wave, but they certainly were ready for us. We could even see the flashes of their cannon a half mile off to the left front, and within seconds the shells were blowing up all around us. I was on a direct line to the cannon, and the shells were so big and were coming in so low that I could actually see some of them flying through the air. This gave most of us a split-second warning, and we could dive out of the way.

It didn't help one of the men, unfortunately, and he took a direct hit in the chest. His whole upper body disintegrated, but by some weird motor reaction his legs kept going a few steps. I almost threw up. I had seen that particular shell and where it was headed. I had yelled at the man, but he never heard me in all the other noise.

It was quite a surprise when we reached the woods ourselves and looked around, expecting to be greeted by our new lieutenant, but found no sign of him or his platoon. I left my few men with Sergeant Bert Smith, the mortar FO, and went forward with my radioman to look for the rest of the company.

We moved forward carefully through about four hundred yards of scrub oak and saw no sign of them. Suddenly we heard noises to the front and edged forward slowly. There we found some German soldiers in a small gully working to free a Tiger tank that was mired in the mud about fifty yards below us. Very slowly we backed off. We didn't have a bazooka, and we couldn't be distracted from our main purpose of finding the only riflemen we had.

All at once a chorus of small arms fire broke out that sounded like it was about two hundred yards ahead in a patch of thick pines. "I'll bet that's our boys," I remarked to Mays. "You're probably right, Lieutenant, but if we get caught up there and we lose you, what will the men do?" In my heart I knew this was the plain reality. If the new lieutenant was in trouble, he would have sense enough to pull back. And two of us alone couldn't help him much, so Mays and I headed back.

As soon as I rejoined my small group I had them all pick out old German foxholes, because the shelling might pick us up any moment. Up ahead the small-arms fire became even more intense, with most of it seeming to be German weapons. It's hard to describe what distinguishes different firearm sounds, but after one has heard them a while it's easy to tell the types of weapons apart.

While we were enlarging a shell hole one of the lieutenant's men, a Latin-American, came tearing up to us, all out of breath. He was so excited he chattered out his first sentences in Spanish. I stopped him and calmly told him to speak slowly in English and tell me what had happened.

"We just ran into a lot of Germans, and the lieutenant sent me to get some help. Quick!" he blurted.

"I don't have anyone to send," I told the messenger. "Go back and tell the lieutenant to get back here as soon as possible." He took off again running.

Ten minutes later he returned with the lieutenant and no one else. They were the only two who had managed to escape. The lieutenant was slightly wounded.

He told me they had moved into the pines as I had

ordered and immediately had run into a whole German
company. This misunderstanding startled me. I had clearly
told him to get into the woods and wait for me there. I
couldn't believe that anyone would not consider scrub oaks
to be woods. Now it was too late for discussion.

Anyway, his men had taken cover under the pines when
the shooting started and had tried to hide. He hadn't seen
anyone shoot back at the Germans. Some were wounded,
and others began to surrender. They were hopelessly out-
numbered and out of control, and there was no way a single lieutenant could save them. The best he could do was
ignore his wound and get away. Thus, in just a half hour,
he had lost about thirty-five men, killed, wounded, or captured.

What had happened there was about the norm for inexperienced men with an inexperienced leader, particularly
men who had been unsettled by the most terrible baptism a
man could get. Perhaps we had been asking too much of
human beings, and that mistake was catching up with us.
Men work best in small squads under a leader of their own,
and there had been no way to bring this about in that open
field in a trench under German fire.

The lieutenant went on to the rear to have his wound
treated, and I never heard of him again. He had had a
chaotic, traumatic three hours in combat, and it must have
given him plenty of fuel for memories.

Now we were down to only twelve men, including Sergeant Bert Smith of H Company and myself. Again I was
the only leader. What in hell could we do if the Germans
somehow found out how weak we were and came in on us?
Probably make them pay as dearly as possible, and that
was it.

We began to dig in and try to roof our foxholes. Some
of us leveled off the bottom of a bomb crater that was
about six feet deep and twelve feet across. We needed

poles to stretch across as a roof, and we cut scrub oaks. This was not easy, since we had neither saws nor axes. All we had were trench knives, so we selected the smaller trees only three or four inches in thickness and chipped away at them like beavers. Somehow we finally got enough poles to crisscross the crater; then we laid raincoats on that latticework and piled dirt on top to help absorb shrapnel. It looked like a pretty strong roof, and it later proved itself.

In two days' fighting, we had gained about eight hundred yards. In twenty-four hours my company had lost 138 men of 150. With only twelve men, we stayed in place that night.

The night was nice and quiet, and I slept for a few hours in spite of the gnawing cold. Next day I moved about one hundred yards to a very well engineered German shelter and made this my headquarters. And soon E Company moved up beside us, and things seemed to be taking a turn for the better.

We took up positions to cover the left of the firebreak road, and E Company took the right. The men were busy most of the day digging and covering their foxholes. Some men had to stay alert for possible enemy action; thank God, none developed.

Later that day a mortar landed smack on top of the roof we'd made over the bomb crater. The men inside were shaken up and got something to think about, but no one was hurt. A little more dirt on top and the roof was as good as new.

During the day we received sixty-six new replacements and a couple of new officers. My orders were to remain in place and set up a defense, so I had the men dig in along the ridge that was our front. Now we had seventy-eight men, and we felt much stronger, although I knew we were far from being a fighting unit.

We were getting an awful lot of incoming mortar shells,

and mortars don't have much range, so I knew they had to be fairly close by. Our new artillery forward observer sent up the Piper Cub, and it circled around but could not spot any mortar batteries. I borrowed his map and found a few ravines and partial clearings within two thousand yards, natural places for the Germans to have mortars, which fire in a high arc and so must have a position with no trees overhead. Because of their high arc, mortars usually had to be within a mile of their targets. The Piper Cub was sent to check them out. Soon we were pleased to get his "Bravo, bull's-eye" over the radio. His artillery batteries made quick work of the Kraut mortars, and we were able to breathe a little easier.

On December 3 I got word that another company from a different division was coming up to relieve us, and I spread the word; I knew it was the truth, since it came from Colonel Kenan. And sure enough, at 9:30 that morning the captain of this relief company came up to check out the area with his officers. I toured them around my defensive position and cautioned them not to bunch up because we probably were under observation and would draw fire.

They paid no attention to the warning and continued to move around in a tight group, and in less than a minute the shells began to whistle in. One landed not far from the captain, and although he had not been hit, he claimed he couldn't get up. Some of my men had to carry him into my dugout.

This relief company was something of an eye-opener for me because they were by far the worst bunch of infantry I had ever seen. They had served so poorly on the front in the swamps near Saint-Lô that they had been transfered to siege duty around Brest from July until November. They still were not fit for combat.

They had a full complement of officers, and even one

extra, and were up to full strength in noncoms and enlisted men. After a while the captain announced that he just couldn't carry on. His exec must have been of the same stripe, for he didn't stir himself to take over.

I finally told the executive officer he'd better get moving to bring his company up from Grosshau, and when he hesitated I told him flatly that I was going to move out and that he might have to fight the Germans to get the position back.* This got his butt in gear, and in about an hour he was back with the rest of this truly pathetic company.

Privates in this company called their officers by their first names. With this sort of familiarity, it seemed to me, there was no sense in taking orders. And they didn't. There simply was no discipline. I even heard a sergeant tell a lieutenant to go to hell, and I think I might have sided with the sergeant. What should have been an easy exchange became a real problem with men milling around, refusing to go where they were told.

We wasted no time getting together what was now F Company and heading back over that bloodstained hill and through the shattered ruins of Grosshau, only a quarter mile to our rear. We continued on through three or four miles of shell-splintered, mutilated forest to Second Battalion's bivouac area.

We were going in the right direction, but I was so totally played out, so emotionally spent and physically exhausted, that putting one foot in front of the other was a chore. I didn't think we'd ever get there.

I was in something of a daze, probably from delayed shock. I was thinking that of all the men who had started out with me in the F Company attack a few weeks back, I was the only one still able to walk out of those awful

---

*Actually, I couldn't move out until relieved by them, so I prodded the company's executive officer to get moving and bring the men up.

woods. I might also have been crying. At any rate, my vision was misty, and I didn't see my old friend from E Company, Supply Sergeant O'Malley, when he came up to me as I shuffled along the trail.

O'Malley threw his arms around me in welcome and then insisted on taking all my gear—rifle, bandoleer, canteen, trench knife—and carrying them the rest of the way. I tried to say something to him, but I became all choked up and couldn't.

Our division had been in many battles, but none more costly for the ground gained. We had taken about four and a half miles of forest in our sector, reaching the Cologne Plains, our objective. Our replacement division was engaged there for several more weeks. Perhaps because of the unexpected development of the Battle of the Bulge some two weeks after we broke through the Hürtgen, our gains were never exploited. One might rightly say that the battle of the Hürtgen forest was a major military error. The First Army's losses there must be recorded as the most severe of any American army fighting in Europe during World War II. Yet it is not considered a victory, nor is it even known to most Americans as a battle.

I didn't know what F Company's losses were in the Hürtgen until Francis Thiefels, the company clerk, told me they were about 167 percent for the enlisted men alone. This means that we had started with a full company of about 162 men and had lost about 287, including replacements.

Casualties among the company's officers probably were about double that of the men. I personally recall the loss of twelve officers, and I think we lost a few others, for a total of perhaps fourteen or fifteen.

It was very difficult for me to believe that of all the men and officers who started out on the front lines in F Company with me, I was the only one who finished. And I had been wounded twice but never evacuated. All I could do was shake my head and wonder.

Of over thirty officers in the Second Battalion, it appears that Captain Newcomb at battalion headquarters, Lieutenant Lee Lloyd at E Company, and I were the only ones who survived the entire eighteen days of battle. Our only purpose in fighting there had been to help finish the efforts which had been made by several other divisions. Fighting with us in this last phase of the battle of Hürtgen forest were the First, Twenty-eighth, and Ninetieth divisions, and part of the Fifth Armored Division. The fighting had been going on for over a month when we arrived. Our goal was to reach the Cologne Plains at a small town named Gey. The objective lay only four and a half miles away, but it took eighteen terrible days to reach. All the divisions taking part in the battle were badly mauled.

The total losses for the Twenty-second Infantry Regiment with a complement of the Fourth Infantry, which was part of division in the Battle of the Hürtgen forest, were approximately three thousand men.

Killed In Action (KIA) - Enlisted men: 126 - Officers: 12 - F Co.: 3*
Wounded In action (WIA) - Enlisted men: 1,782 - Officers: 77 - F Co.: 8
Missing In Action (MIA) - Enlisted men: 489 - Officers: 8 - F Co.: 0
Non-Battle Casualties (NBC) - Enlisted men: 178 - Officers: 6-F Co.: 1
Totals: Enlisted men: 2,575 - Officers: 103 - F Co.: 12.

This came to about 100 percent loss for the three battalions in the regiment. It was an awful beating—a terrible

*F Company losses are based on officers only. They are from my personal recollection. We started with six officers, so we had 200 percent losses.

price for that damned patch of woods, a total of about five miles.

In bivouac our men soon settled down for the night. Someone thought to set up a pup tent for me, and I crawled in. Still in the same dirty clothes of the last eighteen days, without either a shave or a bath, I didn't feel much like a conqueror or victor of any kind. Outright exhausted, I soon was sound asleep.

That was the Hürtgen.

XII

REST FOR THE WEARY

On a crisp, bitterly cold December 4, three weeks after we had entered the forest, the battered remains of the Twenty-second Infantry plus its frightened replacements boarded the usual two-and-a-half-ton, 6 × 6 trucks for our seventy-five-mile trip to a quiet sector of the front lines in Luxembourg. We were told no fighting had occurred there since September and that we could R and R there and obtain more replacements.

For the few of us who had survived the Hürtgen, it was as delicious and unbelievable as a release from a long prison sentence. No longer did we have to flinch from the scream of artillery and its shattering explosions; no longer were we forced to wonder if the next minute would be our last. The relief was so overpowering, yet once again I found myself fighting back tears of grief for our terrible losses.

As the convoy headed out mine was the dubious honor, of riding in the open jeep of the commanding officer of F Company. Still below half strength with its seventy-six souls, of whom sixty-six were new recruits the final day of the Hürtgen, F Company limped away from the scene of one of the nastiest battlefields of World War II. According to Army records, our heaviest losses in Europe occurred there.

The convoy covered over one hundred miles, passing through many villages and small towns and then Luxembourg City itself. I can understand why so many of us have returned to those battlefields, for there is where we came of age, there is where we went through our rite of passage. I recall names such as Zweifall, Eupen, Houffalize, Bastogne, and Arlon. Under other circumstances, and perhaps in the early fall when the hardwoods were in full color, it could have been a most enjoyable, scenic excursion. Now it was dreary, gray, bleak, cold, miserable winter.

Convoy travel was usually irritatingly slow and fitful. No one along the line ever knew why there had to be so many stops, why the convoy couldn't get going again quickly. The halts were always exasperating, particularly since we knew there probably was no other traffic, certainly not civilian. It took us all day to travel about one hundred miles.

At least when we were stalled the wind wasn't so bad. Once we started up again the wind whipped through the open cabs of the trucks and the jeeps and bit right down to the marrow. It had never seemed that cold when we went hunting in the freezing wilds of Michigan, though we were better dressed then and weren't riding in open cars. My feet were so icy that they began to hurt. They weren't in particularly good shape; I hadn't been able to change socks or even take my shoes off for three weeks.

Finally I had to do something about it; perhaps my actions made a little history—I am probably the only one ever to have built a fire on the floor of a moving jeep. I simply emptied a K ration box and set fire to the wax box.

This helped my hands, but I couldn't get my feet over the fire long enough to help. The driver looked at me a little strangely but didn't say anything.

Forwarding units had gone ahead the previous day to arrange our exchange of position with the 331st Regiment of the Eighty-third Infantry Division, and my company wound up near the Moselle River in Luxembourg about twelve miles southeast of Luxembourg City. My command post was in Oberdonwen, Luxembourg.

We were now part of a sector of the German western front known as the Ardennes, which two weeks later became part of the Battle of the Bulge. For almost four months, as though by tacit agreement, there had been little activity, except for occasional minor patrols just to keep an eye on the area. For us it would be a rest and training area. We were just a shell of the old Twenty-second Infantry, and we would now rebuild, train the new men, and absorb them into a fighting unit. We hoped.

In the same area, the rest of the Fourth Division had very loose defensive positions along a twenty-five-mile stretch of the Luxembourg–German border, west of German troops facing the Sauer and Moselle rivers. Each rifle company covered at least a mile of the front. My F Company had an exceptionally large area. By road it was over five miles from one of our outposts to the company command post. In addition, we had several outposts between which we had to keep patrols roving.

The terrain was rugged, with many winding roads, steep slopes, and deep valleys. There were many gaps in our defense, and it would not have been difficult for the Germans to penetrate quite a distance into our territory without being stopped. Our line was very weak; at best it would only be an early warning system.

We were not the only ones so vulnerable, for the entire seventy-five miles of the sector was held by divisions chewed up in the Hürtgen that were then only at token strength. What we were doing was apparently the only thing that could be done with such damaged divisions, and no one seemed overly concerned. The Allied High Command was well aware of the circumstances and took the calculated risk.

To me it was a most unaccustomed luxury to live in bare, unheated houses. It might be cold sleeping on the floor, but it was dry and out of the wind and weather. We also had kitchens with us, and regular hot meals were a sumptuous treat the new men did not yet appreciate.

Once all the men had been housed and fed, I decided it was time to look after myself. After three weeks of the dirtiest sort of existence in the Hürtgen and a long, nasty convoy, I was somewhat ripe. I asked the cooks if they could scare up some hot water for me. They scrounged around and came up with an old ten-gallon copper tub in which they heated water on the gas kitchen range.

They carried this marvelous bathing contraption upstairs into one of the vacant rooms. I dropped my old clothes in a heap and crammed as much of myself as possible into the warm water. Very soon the heat began to defrost my poor feet, and the pain became so severe that I had to get out of my wonderful tub and change quickly into clean clothes. Then I shaved off three weeks' growth and went down the stairs, where I was met with the nervous stares of men who wondered who this resplendent new officer might be.

My feet were so swollen the next day that I couldn't get my shoes on. They continued to hurt for an entire week. Colonel Kenan sent the battalion surgeon over to examine me. He rubbed my feet a little, gave me some Epsom salts, and told me to soak in hot water as much as possible.

I was still without a second-in-command. I asked Colonel Kenan if I could have Lieutenant Lee Lloyd, my old friend from E Company. The Colonel arranged the transfer.

Lieutenant Lloyd took over at once as my executive officer, running the patrols and outposts and also all the company details while I was still struggling with my poor feet. Toward the end of the week, when I was able to move again, Lieutenant Lloyd took me on a jeep tour of our lines. All I could do was shake my head at the futility of ever having to defend our position against serious attack, should it come to that.

Oberdonwen was a very old, typical middle European village. The farmers' houses and barns were more or less backed up against one another for mutual protection, and the surrounding land was farmed in all directions. Unlike the usual American practice, isolated farm homes were rare in much of Europe. I would have guessed that at least one hundred people normally lived in that communal village; all had decamped, except for the Catholic priest and a few of his helpers. They stayed in the convent, apparently living off supplies stored in the cellars. They were not at all friendly—possibly out of wariness for the Germans so close to the border, possibly because of the normal fear and resentment toward any invaders—so we left them alone. We were living in their homes, after all, yet they were not our hosts.

We had not had any enemy action at all in that part of the line; it was therefore something of a surprise to learn from Colonel Kenan that we were to be pulled back even farther behind the lines. Second Battalion was now regimental reserve, and we came back a few miles into the Schrossig-Moutfort area, where we occupied some barrackslike buildings. The buildings were heated and had hot showers, and though they were not fancy, we loved them.

On December 14 Colonel Kenan phoned to tell me that he thought I ought to take a few days off. It seems that Regiment had acquired a nice house in Luxembourg City, supplied a cook, and set it up as a temporary escape for those most needing a change. At first I wasn't particularly interested, because I already had passable living quarters; and, being somewhat conservative, I wasn't wild about floating in liquor or chasing women. Not that I disapproved for others. The colonel insisted, however, and sent over a jeep and driver to pick me up. I knew I couldn't have left the company in better hands than Lieutenant Lloyd's, so off I went for a few days Rest and Recreation.

The winding blacktop road went through some picturesque villages and pretty countryside. After a short while we came upon the pleasant view of the city on its rather high plateau some miles ahead.

We went almost up to the main business section. The driver stopped before an imposing, modern two-story brick home and said, "This is it, sir." There I was greeted by four other officers from the Twenty-second, none of whom I'd met before. Our sole bond was that we'd had our fill of the Hürtgen and probably had no business having survived it. We respected one another because of the horrible experiences we had shared.

Luxembourg was a rather large, beautiful old city, after Paris by far the biggest I'd seen on the Continent. Even though it was shelled every day for months by a German railroad gun about twelve miles away, it seemed a most peaceful, tranquil retreat from a very distant war.

After settling my few belongings in the lovely wallpapered room assigned to me, I stretched out blissfully for a short nap on the big double bed. I couldn't believe it—a real bed with a genuine mattress, white pillows, and white linen!

It was only a short walk downtown. We all went out together to see the sights. The local citizens were all openly friendly, and many of them spoke English. Schoolchildren also spoke to us freely; English was a required subject in the schools.

As part of my adjustment to civilian ways, I treated myself to a dish of ice cream and a movie. It was an old Western with the soundtrack in French and subtitles in English.

I couldn't wait to try out my warm, comfortable bed, and it did give me a night's delicious sleep. Hot pancakes and syrup for breakfast was another treat. Good coffee, table and chairs, and silverware made the whole meal a delight.

The next day we met four very nice fighter pilots over coffee in one of the little cafés. We compared notes and had a great time talking with them. There was not the slightest bit of envy or rivalry. They even offered us a chance to shower in their quarters, not realizing we had our own. We parted with friendly waves and mutual encouragement to keep up the good work.

It was a bit of a shock to find my battalion jeep driver waiting for me when I returned to quarters. He had orders from Colonel Kenan to get me back to my company at once because of activity on the front. My R & R thus ended abruptly, and I headed back to what had by then become, for me, the real world.

XIII

BATTLE OF THE BULGE

Second Battalion was in its usual turmoil, everyone scurrying around getting packed for a quick move. Colonel Kenan told me to get right down to my company. He said the only information he had so far was that the Germans had made a sizable attack against the Twelfth Infantry. The Fourth Infantry Division had three basic infantry regiments, the Eighth, Twelfth, and Twenty-second. As the Twenty-second Infantry reserve battalion, we were temporarily assigned to the Twelfth Infantry. We would be fully briefed once we got on the scene.

It was December 17, barely two weeks since we had pulled ourselves out of the Hürtgen forest holocaust and we were about to be thrown into something again. I worried about how unseasoned F Company was. With only four officers and eighty-four men, the company was eighty men short of full strength as well.

Thanks to Lieutenant Lloyd, the company was already mounted in trucks and ready to move when I arrived. In forty-five minutes we arrived at the assembly area about a quarter mile south of Beck along the road to Berberg, and I hurriedly joined the other company commanders for a briefing.

Colonel Kenan told us the Twelfth Infantry had been hit pretty hard along most of its front and that a fierce battle had developed at Echternach on the left front. German units were known to have bypassed Osweiler in the center and Dickweiler on the right.

The Allied High Command had gambled by using a very thin defensive line along the Belgian, Luxembourg, and German borders—only five divisions defended the entire seventy-five-mile front, which would take at least twelve divisions to defend properly, and none of them was ready for combat: the 106th Division was fresh from the States and had no combat experience. Many of its weapons were still in crates. The First, Fourth, Twenty-eighth, and Ninetieth divisions had taken part in the battle of the Hürtgen forest and were at about half strength; it is easy to understand why many units were overrun in the initial fighting. One company of the Twelfth Infantry was trapped in Osweiler. Our main objective would be to attack at once and get to Osweiler to rescue that company.

The colonel asked if any of us had ever fought with tanks. I waited while no one spoke up and then admitted to having been in the Saint-Lô Breakthrough. So he gave my company the job of working with a company of tanks from the Nineteenth Tank Battalion of the Ninth Armored Division.

The colonel's plan was for a two-pronged advance on Osweiler, with the main body of the Battalion—Companies E, G, H, and Headquarters—approaching directly southeast along the road to Osweiler, and with F Company going south one mile to Berberg to pick up the tank company and then heading eastward through Herbon to Os-

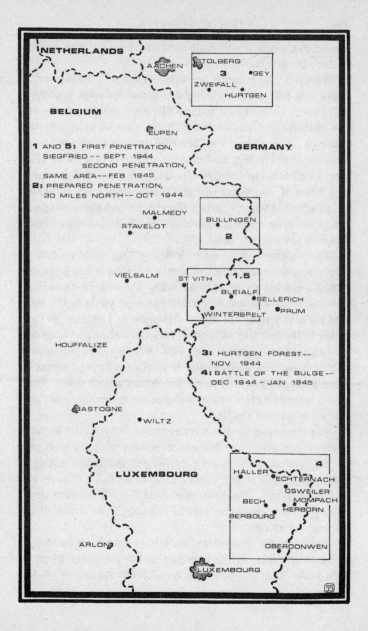

NETHERLANDS

BELGIUM

AACHEN

STOLBERG

GEY

ZWEIFALL

HURTGEN

3

EUPEN

GERMANY

1 AND 5: FIRST PENETRATION,
SIEGFRIED -- SEPT 1944
SECOND PENETRATION,
SAME AREA -- FEB 1945
2: PREPARED PENETRATION,
30 MILES NORTH -- OCT 1944

MALMEDY

STAVELOT

BULLINGEN

2

VIELSALM

ST VITH

1.5

BLEIALF

SELLERICH

PRUM

WINTERSPELT

HOUFFALIZE

3: HURTGEN FOREST --
NOV 1944
4: BATTLE OF THE BULGE --
DEC 1944 - JAN 1945

BASTOGNE

WILTZ

4

LUXEMBOURG

HALLER

ECHTERNACH

OSWEILER

MOMPACH

BECH

HERBORN

BERBOURG

ARLON

OBERDONWEN

LUXEMBOURG

weiler (see map). I was cautioned that the Germans might already be near Berberg.

Within a few minutes we were on the way to Berberg, about one half mile south, where the tanks were waiting. As soon as I'd assigned men to ride each tank we took off for Herbon, our first objective, three fourths of a mile to the east. Everything was peaceful and normal until we went through Herbon, and then we passed several dead GIs on a small ridge to our right. Judging by the positions they had fallen in, my guess was that they'd been gunned down by an armored vehicle, rather than by footsoldiers, and this made us even more cautious as we followed the blind bends in the winding road.

The weather thickened to a heavy fog, with visibility down to about two hundred yards even on open ground. When we came to the sloping fields just west of Osweiler we sent tanks and infantry a few hundred yards to the left and right to probe. We found a platoon of Germans in the fields to the left and took them prisoner. They had spotted us beforehand, however, and had already called down artillery. Now they were trapped in their own fire and seemed quite happy to join us behind the shelter of our tanks. The artillery couldn't follow our movements in the fog, and this spared us a lot of shelling.

The fog began to thin a little, particularly on the higher ground, and my naturally cautious nature made me suggest to the tank captain that he break out the bright orange panels to be put on the backs of our tanks to identify us to friendly aircraft. The tank man didn't think it necessary, saying, "Those guys can't fly in this soup." He was probably right, I thought.

I was on the ground to the left of the road directing some of my men in the handling of the prisoners when I heard the roar of plane motors. Four American P-47 fighter-bombers began to swoop down on our tanks and men on the hill three hundred yards to the right of the road. The first three planes came diving in at very low altitude, but when almost on top of the tanks they pulled up abruptly, wagged their wings, and flew away. The fourth plane, unaccountably cut loose his bombs about one hundred yards from two of our tanks, and his napalm bombs scored direct hits, engulging the tanks. Orange flames shot up from every part of the tanks and surrounding ground, and black smoke rose in an ugly cloud that drifted away.

The two tanks were lost; all the men in them and those close by were killed almost instantly. Napalm burns all the oxygen out of the air and causes quick suffocation. It was over in a few seconds, and we couldn't do anything except watch helplessly.

The tank captain ordered the orange panels displayed at once.

Thanks to the partial concealment of the fog and the lack of much enemy resistance, we made it into Osweiler about 2:00 that afternoon, December 17. A few survivors from L Company of the Twelfth Infantry were holed up in town, and their lieutenant seemed quite relieved to collect them and march them back down the road to Berberg.

When I radioed Colonel Kenan that we had secured Osweiler, he told me to set up the strongest possible defense and be very alert for counterattacks. We would be on our own, he said, because the rest of the battalion had been attacked and was fighting against a very stubborn enemy. The main battle was about a half mile northwest of us, to our left rear, and we could hear all the shooting. I knew we'd be in jeopardy if the Second Battalion was annihilated.

Osweiler was another typical small farm community. Its

sturdy brick and stone houses occupied a small valley with
open hills on all sides. Most of the houses seemed to have
good cellars, which were where we would live because of
the artillery.

Our main concerns were the three roads coming into
town from the east and south. Lieutenant Lloyd and I
climbed up to the top of a five-story narrow wooden school
building to get a better view, and we could see the open
hills clearly for about three hundred yards but had no idea
what lay beyond. According to our map, Dickweiler was
about three quarters of a mile south of us near the Sauer
River.

The nearest patch of woods, about a quarter mile north,
bordered a ravine or valley near Rodenhof and spread westward beyond where the Second Battalion was in battle. We
were so exposed and vulnerable on all sides that I realized
we'd have to send out patrols so we'd at least get some
warning of attacks.

First we placed in position the tanks we needed to defend the roads and kept the rest of the tanks in mobile
reserve for emergencies. Then we placed the riflemen and
our light machine guns and mortars in houses close to the
tanks to give them support. Every man had his job.

After dark the tank captain became a little restless and
decided to pull his tanks out of town and back two miles to
Berberg because, he said, they needed gas. I tried to per-
suade him to stay, but it was a delicate situation. I was in
command of the small combat team, yet he was my superior in rank. He therefore decided to ignore my persua-
sions, so I was forced to radio Colonel Kenan.

The colonel got the captain on the radio and told him to
move no more than two tanks at a time to the rear for gas.
The captain protested that it would be too dangerous to
send two tanks by themselves and also that it would take
too long. The colonel then told him to have his gas trucks

meet him halfway, but that under no circumstances was he to move more than two tanks at a time to be filled up.

The captain had to comply, but he was mad as hell. His mood didn't bother me because all I cared about was defending the town; I *needed* those tanks.

The Second Battalion was unable to disengage itself from the Germans all night. Early the next morning, December 18, Colonel Kenan ordered me to send a platoon of tanks and some infantry to release the entrapped battalion. Visibility was still poor due to the heavy fog, so poor that our tanks accidentally opened fire on the leading elements of G Company. Later I learned that G Company's Greenlee saved what could have been a tragedy by running toward the tanks and waving his maps.

Because of the extra firepower of the tanks, the Germans were driven far enough back to allow the Second Battalion to break through the Germans and join the rest of us in Osweiler. Colonel Kenan quickly reinforced our defenses and sent out patrols north, east, and south. No contacts were made, so we had an enjoyable, peaceful night.

Next day Colonel Kenan called a meeting of company commanders and for the first time was able to give us an idea of what was happening. At the time, and even to this day, it was pretty damned scary. These were not strong combat patrols or company- or battalion-strength attacks we were getting; rather, a whole big section of the German front had erupted in a massive, desperate surprise offensive. We happened to be at the southern edge of a huge German spearhead, and it was utterly vital that we hold our ground and thus force the German penetration northwestward, away from the critical airfields and supply depots of Luxembourg.

At about this time Division G-2 (Intelligence) had information that the Germans had a pontoon bridge across the Sauer River, about three quarters of a mile to our northeast.

Two brave volunteers took a long-range radio and went through our lines and on into the hills beyond. Their mission was to direct artillery fire onto the bridge, and cold as it was, they stayed out a couple of nights giving the Germans fits. Finally they were forced to return home when the Germans began to send out search patrols that were getting awfully close. That was some tough mission, and my hat was off to those two men.

Second Battalion was still attached to the Twelfth Infantry Regiment. Their commander, Colonel Chance, needed more information, so he ordered us to send patrols to greater distances. Therefore, on December 19, Lieutenant Lloyd led a patrol northward toward Rodenhof. The fog had thickened, and visibility was down to less than one hundred yards at midday.

Lieutenant Lloyd returned with his patrol in about an hour. Less than a half mile out of town, and just west of Rodenhof, he had found a large concentration of Germans. Colonel Kenan immediately relayed this intelligence to Colonel Chance, who apparently was not much of a conservative, for he just as quickly ordered Colonel Kenan to leave his strong defensive position in Osweiler and get out and attack those Germans that very day.

As I should have expected, the colonel ordered my company to move out first on foot, with Lieutenant Lloyd leading us to the head of a small valley just a couple of hundred yards southwest of Rodenhof. We were to take up positions facing north and to begin firing on the ridge directly in front of us at 4:00 P.M. From our positions on the forward slope of the ridge we would be firing at the Germans across a valley about two hundred yards wide.

This firing was intended as a diversion to keep the Germans occupied while the main attack swung in from my left rear and then continued straight ahead through the valley and ridge into Rodenhof. My company's firing was, of course, to stop on signal as the attack advanced.

Lieutenant Lloyd led us to our firing positions without confusion and without detection; we were there in plenty of time. At exactly 1600 hours we commenced firing across the small valley. Due to the heavy fog it was impossible to tell just where our barrage of bullets was going and what effect, if any, it might be having on the unseen enemy. Certainly the shooting made a tremendous noise and must have given the Germans the impression of a powerful attack coming their way.

At 4:00 P.M. companies E and G jumped off abreast. As they advanced we clearly heard the staccato barking and ripping of German machine guns; E and G must have been meeting very stiff resistance. In part due to the vicious enemy fire, in part due to inability to maneuver in the fog, our battalion attack soon petered out. Both attack companies were still back two hundred yards on my left flank when they began to dig in.

With the attack aborted, we were isolated way off on the right flank of the battalion. Thank goodness for the experience and the cautious nature of Lieutenant Lloyd and myself, for we didn't just stand around waiting for battalion to make another move or give us orders. Instead we had our men dig in at once as deeply as they could. We were down to about sixty men, or about one third full strength, and we shaped our defense in a rough horseshoe reaching to the edge of the woods at the top of the ridge we were on. The hardwoods gave us some protection and a feeling of comfort and security we sorely needed. The area to our right and to our rear beyond the edge of the ridge was wide open farmland. We also decided to place a small outpost on our left flank, between us and E Company.

The late afternoon light was quickly fading, and we'd managed to get our foxholes down only about a foot when the men on the outpost rushed in yelling, "Germans!" The

Krauts came right in on their heels firing rapidly, and one of the outpost men was the first casualty.

For the next half hour we had some of the toughest small arms fighting I'd ever been in, and I was proud our new men held on so well.

These were very stubborn, determined Germans, and they kept right on coming. By then it was completely dark; we couldn't see the enemy, and they couldn't see us. We kept firing at the flashes of their rifles and burp guns; every now and then we could see a shadow moving.

We had the advantage, for a change, in that we were partly below ground and were firing slightly downhill. Also, we were able to toss out grenades as the Germans got closer, and they must have been very damaging to the exposed enemy. For some reason, the Krauts didn't use grenades on us. We were lucky. This was a life-and-death situation, and we didn't have time to think, only to react. The constant explosions of rifle fire and the mad drumming of the burp guns wore on our nerves, but we couldn't stop fighting.

When the Krauts were in real close, within fifteen or twenty yards, they began to yell something that sounded like, "Kamerad Hände hoch."

Lieutenant Lloyd knew German and told me they were yelling at us to surrender and come out with our hands up. I said to tell them to go to hell, so he yelled back what sounded like: "Nix, you *schweiner hundt!*" This made them furious, and for the next few minutes they gave us all they had while we ducked low and fired back.

Suddenly the Germans shot up two small white flares, and we were caught in the glare. I was sure it was to mark us for artillery, and I began to think in terms of moving somewhere, but it must have been a signal to withdraw, because the firing ended abruptly and the Germans disappeared.

We checked everyone and found we had one dead, four wounded, and one missing. All the wounded were able to walk back by themselves to the aid station in Osweiler. One man didn't look or act like a seriously wounded man as he walked up and asked if he could go to the aid station. When I asked where he was hit, he opened his shirt and showed me a bullet hole and then turned around to show me where it came out his back. It had missed his heart by very little. He said he was positive he could make it to Osweiler with the other wounded, so I sent them on their way. They all made it.

The body of the missing man was found later by Graves Registration. Apparently he had taken off during the heat of the battle and, in trying to find safety, had run into some Germans instead. Many weeks later when his folks wrote me for details of his death I simply told them that he had died quickly from bullet wounds.

Now that the Germans had left, we went back to completing our foxholes. No one needed urging. We were out of grenades and low on ammunition, but fortunately the enemy didn't know how vulnerable we were, and they left us alone all night. Within an hour new supplies of grenades and ammunition arrived, so we felt a little more secure.

Of course, I didn't know we'd be undisturbed, so the balance of the night passed very slowly for me. I studied every shadow, every movement of the wind, every noise of the field and forest for warning of the enemy. My nerves would not relax.

With the first faint light of dawn we made out some odd mounds or lumps to our front and left flanks, and these were German bodies. Two of them were almost on top of us, only five to ten yards out, and several others were scattered behind them. Someone said he'd counted ten altogether, which seemed about right. Normally seven or eight are wounded for every man killed, so the grenades and all our firing might have accounted for seventy or eighty casualties, not including the KIAs left behind.

We had probably been hit by a rifle company, though I doubt that in the darkness they were able to concentrate their strength on us. One of the bodies was that of a young, fair-haired lieutenant; possibly the loss of this leader led to their withdrawal, for they had almost had us overrun.

Fortunately for me, I did not know our true situation at the time. Sometime later I was looking at the tactical map, which showed F Company to be the absolute extreme tip of the entire Allied holding position at the lower southern edge of the Bulge. To our east and north were nothing but Germans: on the east was Germany itself, on the north was the seventy-five-mile gap in our line made by the German penetration. The edge of this bulge ran roughly northwestward from my position and about fifty miles deep. To the south was Osweiler, held by battalion Headquarters and H Company plus a platoon from Third Battalion. Between us and Osweiler was a large gap through which the enemy could have encircled us at any time. Only to our west, with E and G companies, was there any reasonably close help. In our new line of defense we were holding the bottom hinge to the gate the Germans had opened in our line—the one known as the Bulge.

The defense of this small salient was still my responsibility, and my experience and Lieutenant Lloyd's came in very handy. Together we studied the terrain and the map, and we both felt the area east of Rodenhof was the most likely approach route for a major enemy attack. The only way we could stop the Germans in this hostile country was through artillery, so we carefully marked off and numbered on our map twenty of the most promising target areas they might attack, then radioed the coordinates back to our artillery. If we ever wanted to direct fire on those targets, we had only to pass to artillery the prearranged target number.

We very thoroughly covered Rodenhof and its eastern approach valley. That done, we put it all aside and hoped we'd never have to use it.

The weather suddenly became a vicious enemy. The soft, clean, beautifully white and pure snowflakes that the poets love so well settled down on us in abundance. Over a foot of this loveliness accumulated in twenty-four hours, and we were miserable. We had no shelter but had to keep pushing the stuff away to keep it from melting on us and, above all, on our weapons. Then the weather turned bitterly cold at night, dropping to as low as ten below zero.

Our hardworking and usually reliable supply people had not yet caught up to us with winter equipment. The trunks of our bodies were not too bad off, because we did have long johns, wool uniforms or fatigues, field jackets, and wool overcoats—to keep warm, we wore everything we had. Our heads suffered, however, because all one had under the steel helmet besides the plastic liner was a small wool beanie. No earmuffs, no hood, no face covering, no scarf. Our hands also suffered with only wool finger gloves. No mittens, no outer shells. Of course, none of our things were fur-lined.

The other extremities that were in trouble were our feet. We did have four-buckle overshoes on top of our regular GI leather shoes, but we were very uncomfortable with only one pair of cotton socks.

Worst of all were the long, cold nights when all we had were chilly foxholes from which we'd scooped out the fresh snow. No blankets reached us, no shelter halves, no sleeping bags. We were undergoing the type of weather reserved for mountain troops or ski troops but without their superb winter equipment. Winter wear did not reach us until early January, 1945.

Lastly there was the general malaise of gradually losing one's resistance to everything, of never being able to get warm, day after day after day. Perhaps there's a medical term for this ailment, but I think the word "misery" will do. It must be experienced to be understood.

The merciless cold and our inability to move about and stimulate circulation soon led to a nasty new problem. Trench foot became near epidemic. This commonplace, rather colorless name hid the truly hideous nature of the disease: Cold, damp feet in tight boots caused poor circulation, and blood stopped flowing to toes and feet, causing tissue decay—and for many, unless circulation could be restored, the only remedy was amputation. Some victims lost toes, some lost a foot. For these people the war was, in effect, over, and they were safe. But there was always the lingering, unprovable suspicion that some men deliberately gambled on this variation of Russian roulette.

The battalion medics quickly sent us instructions on how to cope. We conducted daily foot inspections during which we looked for swelling or discoloration. We warned the men about tingling sensations or numbness and urged them to massage their feet as much as possible. Of course, we explained that trench foot was only a problem of circulation, that the worst things were coldness, dampness, and the tourniquet effect of tight lacing. And everyone was issued an extra pair of socks and was ordered to change socks every day. Despite our precautions, we had our share of trench foot casualties.

Probably the most vulnerable man in the entire company was me; I'd only recovered from frostbite a few days before. After all the combat I'd been through, I was damned if I was going to set this example as a way to get out of the fighting. I rigidly followed the medics' suggestions. I didn't have soap, but I rinsed my feet in cold water in my helmet once a day, drying them with my old socks. Then I put on my fresh socks and washed out the old ones, wringing them as dry as possible and then putting them inside my shirt against my body to dry. They had to be turned inside out several times, but they eventually did dry. This laundry method could have given me pneumonia, but fortunately it didn't.

Water itself was a problem. We had only treated water brought up in five-gallon cans from about three miles back. The cans were so cold that even during that short haul ice formed on the surface. We usually got by on two canteens a day. The first canteen was for a warmish cup of coffee or chocolate in the morning and for washing in our helmets. The second canteen had to last the rest of the day.

Canteens that were carried in the normal position on the hip were useless because the water froze, so some of us got wise and carried our canteens under our coats and thus had some water for later in the day. Some of the men ate snow directly, and some melted the ice by holding their canteens between their legs for a while.

Since we were in such exposed positions on the front line, we were not able to build wood fires, and our only source of heat was the burning of our K-ration cartons, which were slightly larger than Cracker Jack boxes. Such cooking was a tricky business, and we learned it by trial and error.

First one got a cup of water. Then he got out of the wind in the foxhole and opened the ration box at one end only. Next he used the key and slightly opened the can, which held eggs for breakfast, cheese for lunch, or meat for supper. Meanwhile, he emptied the other stuff out of the waxed carton and then lit it carefully at one end, nursing the flame to burn gradually around the lip of the box just like a wick.

With the oven going, one hung the partially open can of food by its key, which was hooked over the lip of the canteen cup, and carefully held both over the small flame. In the few minutes it took the fire to exhaust itself a cup of coffee or chocolate became piping hot, the food got warm enough to eat—and one's hands thawed.

As in most culinary art, little things made the difference. If, for instance, the K-ration box was stood on end and was turned to burn slowly, it would give off a good deal of heat; but when torn into pieces and gradually fed into the fire, it gave off very little heat.

We also developed other refinements in the art of survival. Our foxholes were just wide enough for two men to sit up facing each other with each one's feet shoved under the other guy's butt. They were deep enough to give our heads about a foot's clearance below ground level. In this way we escaped the surface wind and also trapped enough warm breath and body heat for continued survival.

At night we took our arms out of our coats and hugged our bodies, and that seemed to help. Perhaps, to complete the scene, it should be mentioned how we handled the normally routine calls of nature. This would become a particularly urgent personal problem during times of enemy action, such as shelling, or when the prevailing west wind was too penetrating and freezing to expose a bare derriere. (Try it yourself sometime in a gale.) The choice at times would be a form of constipation or, in cases of extreme emergency, measures too indelicate to mention.

Somehow and by some grace, most of us got through the beastly weather for five long days and five very long nights from December 19 to Christmas Eve, 1944.

F Company's earlier role as decoy in Second Battalion's attack changed abruptly as we found ourselves in the forefront of an incoming attack. Our lookouts were shocked to discover a swarm of German tanks and infantry coming out of the Rodenhof valley headed directly toward us. It looked to be at least a full battalion attack with double tank support. Those monsters crunched over the snow with ease, with some of their infantry riding on the tanks, some following. They clanked along relentlessly right out in the open, as though they didn't care whether we saw them or not. They looked like a bunch of steamrollers to us. A chill went down my spine, and my scalp tightened as though my hair was standing on end.

After a second's initial paralysis, I grabbed the radio and reported the attack to Colonel Kenan. I asked that he clear all radio channels to the artillery. He wished me luck and immediately ordered everyone else off the air.

Next I sent the invaluable Lloyd, then my only officer, up front about fifty yards with a walkie-talkie to be our forward observer. Then I got out the map and radioed to artillery the numbers of the prearranged targets that covered the Rodenhof valley.

From then on Lloyd and I became spectators to the greatest show ever. It seemed like only a minute before we heard over our heads the sibilant gurgle of shells plowing through the air. Ah, but it was such sweet music! Moments later we saw the electric flash and quick spumes of smoke and debris as the 105 and 155 shells landed among the enemy.

When I had earlier called our 105 artillery battery and given them the map coordinates for targets to our front, it apparently passed the coordinates on to the division 155mm Long Toms, 4.2mm mortars, and the cannon company. Later, when I requested fire on a particular target number, all units laid on salvo after salvo. A salvo called for each gun in a battery to rapid-fire four rounds—i.e., sixteen rounds from each battery on each target. In addition, H Company's forward observer, Sergeant Smith, directed his 81mm mortars at any target he saw. As the Germans moved about trying to avoid our artillery I just called in another number—within moments fire was screaming down on them.

It was a dose of Hürtgen hell for the Germans, but we were almost savagely ecstatic as we enjoyed every moment while our artillery shelled them. Artillery at its best was flying in the right direction, and even though some of those rounds seemed to rock our treetops in their passing, we were too happy to care.

To us the artillery strike was more deliverance than conquest. Those people could have killed us all. They had overwhelming strength. Without even bazookas and with only our rifles, our position was both helpless and hopeless.

Hundreds and hundreds of explosives had hit those Krauts, and I didn't see how they could take much more. After fifteen or twenty minutes they gave up and pulled back out of view and out of range. Ours was the deepest gratitude for our artillery, and when Colonel Kenan and the artillery commander later called us, we told them our feelings. It was great to have a team.

During that night and the next one we heard the clanging noise of horses and wagons going out into the battle area to collect the dead and wounded, and probably to salvage whatever equipment they could. Actually, the tending of wounded had begun as soon as the shelling had stopped, with the German medics and stretcher bearers getting right out there. Anyone left on the field overnight would have frozen to death. Meanwhile our 4.2mm and 80mm mortars continued to shell Rodenhof and set several buildings on fire.

The Germans never seemed to give up, and soon they began to shell us again. This time the target was Osweiler, where they must have known our headquarters to be. They were not using ordinary artillery, but rather the six-barreled rockets that quickly earned the name "Screaming Meemies."

These spine-chilling things were launched with a piercingly shrill, eerie screech that by itself scared the devil out of us. The awful sound carried for miles, it seemed, and was so widespread we couldn't pinpoint its source of trajectory, though we knew it must have arced up pretty high.

The new German rockets were larger than our 155mm shells. They had an awful wallop and were causing havoc for Colonel Kenan and his people. He had to keep moving his headquarters from cellar to cellar and once took a direct hit but was saved by a reinforced concrete basement.

The colonel was fed up with the murderous things, and one night he radioed us to ask if we had any inkling where those damned rockets were coming from. Lloyd and I already had a pretty good idea, because we had been watching the sparks from their tail assemblies as they streaked overhead. We had also seen their muzzle flash, and I had taken compass readings and timed it from the first flash to the explosion in Osweiler.

Colonel Kenan was delighted and asked if we'd like to take a shot at them. He said he'd talked to Division Artillery and that they'd put some Long Toms—155mm artillery—at his disposal when he had a target.

The next time the Krauts fired their rockets Lieutenant Lloyd timed them while I took a reading on the flash, using a couple of trees to line up the direction for my compass. The artillery commanding officer used the time we gave him, drew an arc on his map, and estimated the target in the vicinity of Echternach, about two miles distant.

I then suggested he fire a few rounds of white phosphorus. I lined up my trees again to get the target, and while I could see the explosive flash from the Long Tom's smoke the firing angle was such that I couldn't tell if they were on target. After a few rounds at different distances I felt they were pretty close, so I told the commanding officer to fire for effect—i.e., each gun in a battery of four guns was to fire four rounds on the same target.

All those big shells began exploding just about where we figured we had seen the muzzle flashes, and I yelled "bull's-eye!" The Long Toms continued to pour it on for several minutes. Those big guns must have fired four or five times the usual salvos. I wouldn't have wanted to be on the receiving end of all that.

Of course, we never did really see those rocket launchers, and I don't know how close the Long Toms came; but if they didn't hit anything, they sure must have scared those Krauts, because there was no more firing on Osweiler, to Colonel Kenan's great satisfaction.

During the morning of December 24 we received the delightful news that a combat team from the Fifth Infantry Division would be coming up to relieve us. We were ordered to change our radio frequency to their channel so we could speak directly to them. This led to something of a comedy of errors, because our battalion call letters were the same as theirs, and every time I tried to reach my battalion, the Fifth Division people were convinced we were clever English-speaking Germans. As a result, frantic calls kept interrupting us to tell battalion to ignore our sabotaging calls.

Finally, on Christmas Eve, we were replaced, and my frozen, exhausted men happily marched the quarter mile back to Osweiler. To us it was the best possible Christmas present. There we packed the entire company—all twenty-three of us—on one two-and-a-half-ton truck and my jeep, and we moved back some two and a half miles to the little village of Berberg that we'd come through earlier.

It didn't seem much like Christmas Eve. There were no Christmas lights at all in the settlement, no lighted Christmas trees, not a cheerful note or carol in the air. We moved quietly into unheated, deserted buildings and were grateful to be out of the wind and snow. And then, marvel of marvels, our cooks had arrived ahead of us and provided a nice warm meal with plenty of hot coffee.

After dinner the men were trying to get settled in various houses and I was reading some mail from home by candlelight when Christmas came early and Providence gave us an enormous present—one hundred new men and three new officers.

Several trucks delivered the new replacements—raw recruits direct from skimpy basic training and three partially trained officers. The officers were all emergency transfers into the infantry from other branches. They had been given two weeks' basic training then declared infantry officers. They were nice guys, and I hoped they would live long enough to discover what the infantry was really about and not take too many men down with them while they were learning. It was bad enough to be a green front-line officer, I knew, but to be green to the infantry as well must have been hell. They had been trained in antiaircraft or other Army branches and so were not familiar with infantry procedures. It was as if they didn't speak the same language of the rest of us.

The enlisted men were even worse off, for only a little over six weeks before they had been civilians. After five weeks of condensed basic infantry training at Camp Blanding, Florida, and a week on trains, ships, and trucks, they had been thrown out into the cold at Christmas time.

Lieutenant Lloyd and I divided up the new men among the new officers and assigned everyone places for the night. This took several hours, and we didn't bother trying to do any more than get them all bedded down.

Our great cooks meanwhile worked through the night to surprise us with a full-scale Christmas dinner with all the trimmings. It was almost too rich for those of us accustomed to K rations; some of us ate too much. I don't know how the cooks managed to include all the new men, but they did, and we complimented them.

The replacements had been thrown into the breach so unprepared because of the Army's crippling, debilitating losses in the Bulge. We discovered that these men had been on the rifle range only once; they had never thrown a grenade or fired a bazooka, mortar, or machine gun.

Company F was in deep trouble. It was tough enough sending thoroughly trained men into combat. When I thought of all the training and experience I'd been blessed with, if that's the word, I was sick about those poor men.

Lieutenant Lloyd and I talked it over and decided that, even though we were in reserve and were supposed to be recuperating, we had no time for rest. It would be suicidal to take those men into battle. We had to give them some intensive training while we had the chance.

So we had the supply sergeant scrounge up several extra boxes of .30-caliber ammo, hand grenades, bazookas, and mortar shells. We set up our own firing ranges, and everybody, including the new officers, got a chance to fire a rifle, throw a live grenade, shoot a bazooka shell, and try out a machine gun and a 60mm mortar.

Then we had classes and work sessions on the absolutely essential basics. We told the men how important their foxholes were for survival, that they had to start digging in almost every time they stopped. We talked about how to protect against tree bursts, about the care of feet. In short, we reviewed all the tricks we had learned about survival in battle. We also got into how to use fire and movement in attack and the great importance of grenades in close action.

The men responded well, being keen to learn and eager to try out all the weapons. We used up a lot of ammo, but that wasn't as important as saving lives. Lloyd and I did not see how we could have done without this interlude of intensive training, and each new officer told me privately how much he appreciated it.

While none of the new men was in top condition, one had a physical handicap that I thought was just too much, so I sent him to the rear despite his protests. I admired his spirit and assured him they needed good men back there. The guy had a birth defect in his right shoulder that prevented his raising his rifle more than belt high.

One side effect of having so many green men was that our Non-Battle Casualties (NBCs) rate began to rise. Our first loss was that of a man whose rifle fell over while he was going to the latrine. The bullet ripped a hole in his thigh. It is difficult to imagine how this could have happened, but there were no witnesses, and we had to take his word.

Rumors are an inevitable part of Army life. One that came along seemed to have official backing, and it put us a little on edge. We were warned to be on the lookout for English-speaking Germans dressed in American uniforms. We were to challenge any strange Americans at all, asking for the password, which was changed more frequently than usual. We were to ask questions about baseball and politics, things the average GI would know. The ersatz Americans were said to be spies parachuted behind the lines. None of them showed up in our zone. However, they did show up and cause a lot of problems near Bastogne, where they directed traffic onto the wrong roads, blew up bridges, etc.

On December 29, after our battalion had been in reserve a scant five days, we were sent up to the front again. Our new position was between Osweiler and Dickweiler, slightly to their rear. Since we now were the reserve company, we were able to make our command post in an isolated farmhouse and keep our kitchen in the same building.

Most of the men had to stay in foxholes; at least they didn't have to chip them out of the frozen ground, since they could use holes already in place. They quickly learned the rigors of outdoor living. Our strongest outpost was near the river southwest of Dickweiler; because of all the open ground to be covered, the only way for the twenty-man complement to reach it was after dark.

That meant the men had to stay in place for twenty-four hours before their relief. As soon as they got back they headed straight for the kitchen, which was the only warm place in the house. At times, the 15 × 18 room was impossibly crowded, but the cooks were good sports about it. Usually they had some hot food available and lots of hot coffee, so the men lingered as long as they could.

One evening after I'd checked the crowded kitchen I joined Lieutenant Lloyd, First Sergeant Nagel, company clerk Francis Thiefels, our medic, and a couple of other men in the next room, where everyone was sprawled about writing letters in the light of a gas lamp. I had just started to write my own letter when the room shook and the air was split by a tremendous crackling explosion from the kitchen area. My first thought was that somehow one of the gas stoves had blown up.

Lieutenant Lloyd jumped up and ran into the kitchen, and at the same moment one of the men burst into our room from the kitchen. He was hysterical, and blood squirted from a small hole in his neck. Fortunately, he was a little guy, and I was able to force him to the floor, where I sat on him and held my thumbs tightly over his wound.

The medic moved over to help, but I yelled at him to get out into the kitchen to see if anyone else needed help. I continued to compress the neck wound, and soon the man quieted down. Finally the blood began to clot, and his bleeding stopped. Then I got a tight bandage over the wound and told him to lie still.

Lieutenant Lloyd came running back and told me we had a whole roomful of wounded. "It's a terrible mess, and we're going to need help. Better send for some ambulances and medical supplies."

As First Sergeant Nagel called the battalion aid station I went with Lieutenant Lloyd to assist the medic in the kitchen. It was indeed a terrible mess. The floor was covered with bleeding, groaning wounded men.

We grabbed first aid packs and began cutting away clothing to get at the wounds. Three of the men, apparently those closest to the blast, had deep, very dangerous wounds. Some of the men had so many wounds they looked like they'd been hit by buckshot. Our bandages were limited, so the medic had to weed out the most serious cases first, which was quite a problem in such severely cramped quarters.

Soon the battalion medical units began to arrive, and they quickly moved out the most seriously wounded as we continued to work on the remainder. There weren't enough closed ambulances, so we had to tie stretchers across open jeeps, wrapping up the victims in as many blankets as we could find.

The explosion had occurred around 11:00 P.M., and it wasn't until 3:00 A.M. that everyone was evacuated. It was very cold, so I was glad it was only a mile back to the aid station. Those of us who had worked frantically for those four hours were just about ready for stretchers ourselves.

Once the excitement was over and the wounded—all seventeen of them—were gone, I tried to piece together exactly what had happened. I'd heard a few things from some of the wounded before they had left, and I began to question the few lucky ones who had been in the room but somehow had not been hit.

All the havoc had been caused by one fragmentation rifle grenade that had been dropped accidentally. One of the recruits at the outpost had pulled the pin on his rifle grenade, apparently to be ready for any attack. He had forgotten to replace the safety pin when he returned to the company. The grenade was carried on his cartridge belt, and somehow it slipped out and hit the floor, detonating on impact.

It blew a bowl-shaped hole six inches deep in the paving-brick floor. Grenade shrapnel and fragments of shattered brick ricocheted off the stone walls and the floor and peppered some of the men with dozens of wounds.

Of course, I had to make a lengthy report explaining the seventeen non-battle casualties. I could very easily imagine the nervous strain on a green recruit on the front line for the first time. Yet forgetting to replace a safety pin is inexcusable. At the same time, there was no way I would have wanted to keep the crowds out of their only warm haven.

I was very much surprised about three years after the war to receive a letter from General Lanham, our old regimental commander, then stationed at the Pentagon. The general wrote that a man from my old F Company had written him asking for his help in getting "the Silver Star medal 'Captain' Wilson" had promised him.

According to the man's account, "Captain" Wilson had promised him the Silver Star if he wiped out a certain German machine gunpost. He went on to claim he'd been seriously wounded, had lost the use of one leg and partially lost his sight due to a German grenade, but that in spite of all the wounds he had managed to go ahead and knock out the Jerry position. He'd earned that medal, and even though he'd heard that "Captain" Wilson was dead, he thought he still ought to get it.

I wrote to General Lanham that First Lieutenant, not

"Captain," Wilson was very much alive. I then referred him to my long report of January, 1945, on the seventeen NBCs we'd had in F Company from a rifle grenade accident, pointing out that the man who was asking for the Silver Star was the very one who had dropped the rifle grenade; that tragedy had been his only "enemy" action while at F Company.

I imagine this sorry individual had built up quite a story to explain his wounds to friends and relatives. The effects must have been serious, since he was closest to the grenade. Perhaps he had made up the story to bury his feelings of guilt.

Since our company was still in battalion reserve southwest of Osweiler, Colonel Kenan decided we could spare some men for patrolling. One of my new retread lieutenants who had begun to impress me drew the assignment of leading the patrol up through one of the line companies and then onward toward the enemy lines. His mission was strictly intelligence gathering, to see if he could detect any shifts or buildups in the German positions. He was very careful to inform our front line company exactly when and where he was going through their line, and also about when he expected to come back through the same spot. The current password was also verified.

The patrol went out on schedule and later returned to the same point at the expected time—and was greeted by a blast from a Browning Automatic rifle. The marksman was so scared he emptied the whole twenty-round clip at them as they yelled out in panic, "We're Americans, you damn fool!" Fortunately, because of the darkness, only one man was hit—the lieutenant, who was probably leading. He got a bullet through his hips. Thus all our recent casualties had come at the hands of our own people, and I was almost beginning to wonder who was fighting whom.

As we sent out more patrols so did the Germans—but they added a new wrinkle we were forced to copy. There was still about a foot of snow on the ground, and this white cover captured whatever light there was and made a fine background for spotting the dark, moving blotches that were a patrol. So the Germans draped their men in white sheets and their rifles in white clothes. Dressed in white, they were camouflaged beautifully by the snow at night, which gave them a dangerous advantage.

We asked headquarters for sheets and white cloths from the people of Luxembourg. Once our men could blend into the white background they felt reasonably secure, and the patrols continued.

One night I sent out our white-clad patrols led by another new young lieutenant. They came upon an enemy patrol near the river in the valley before Dickweiler. Our men had all the advantage this time, however, because the Germans were making so much noise that our patrol simply lay in ambush awaiting the enemy's approach. As it turned out, our very inexperienced recruits soon lost the upper hand with all the commotion they made getting into place, and it was the Germans who opened fire first. Our boys didn't fight back very well, but they all managed to escape back to the company, except for the lieutenant, who was wounded and captured. The men all felt pretty rotten about it.

Some of the young officers we had in the Battle of the Bulge were with us such a short time, I never got to know them. I recall only the names of Lieutenant Hunt, Lieutenant Scheiman, and Lieutenant Gesner; I think they were all retreads.

Lieutenant Gesner was particularly interesting. He was about forty and had been transferred out of the OSS because he was thought too old to jump behind enemy lines and work with the underground. He knew a lot of worthwhile survival tricks and took the time to teach us a few.

For one thing, he showed us an interesting way to make a quick foxhole in frozen ground. First he held a rifle about six inches over the ground and fired eight rounds into the same spot. Then he quickly dug out the loose dirt with his trench knife, placed a half stick of TNT in the hole, gently tapped the loose dirt around the TNT, lit the fuse, ran back about thirty yards, and fell flat. When trying to save a life with a quick foxhole, a little extra noise is not too important.

Even before the dirt from the blast settled he was back in the hole, enlarging it with his trench shovel. And there it was, a habitable foxhole made in frozen ground within a very few minutes. This fascinated me, and I put it in the back of my mind, hoping I'd never have to use it with my present green recruits because they'd probably blow themselves up.

Early in January, 1945, we moved once more, this time only a few miles northward to a place called Junglinster, which was about five miles northwest of Echternach. Again we were in reserve, and it appeared, at least in our sector, that the first phase of the Battle of the Bulge was over.

The Fourth Infantry Division had stopped the Germans cold and set a southern boundary to their seventy-five-mile-wide breakthrough. The First Infantry Division, after giving some ground initially, was able to confine the Germans on the northern flank. The veteran Twenty-eighth and Ninetieth divisions, both also trying to recuperate from the Hürtgen, were pushed back several miles but made the Germans pay dearly for the setbacks. The 101st Airborne made its heroic, historic stand in surrounded Bastogne.

Our experienced divisions were all disastrously under strength due to the Hürtgen, the only full-strength division being the wretchedly ill-starred 106th Infantry Division. That division had arrived from the States only three days earlier and had been put in a very sleepy sector of the line so the men could unpack and get the feel of things. There they were caught in the vortex of a panzer charge; they never had a chance.

Once the southern flank of the Breakthrough was settled, the Third Army was able to release Patton's tanks below us; and they rolled through our rear areas and then turned north on their unforgettable, valiant drive to liberate Bastogne.

By now the Germans were stretched out too far. They were low on ammunition, gas, and reinforcements, and they began to crumble and fold back, trying to escape into the Fatherland. Hitler's bold gamble had become his last gasp.

And so, barring a spasmodic burst from the enemy, we hoped for a few days' rest.

XIV

OUT OF ACTION—AND
IN PARIS

Second Batallion was placed in reserve again, and this time it appeared we would finally get some much-needed rest.

Some of our divisions had been attacking eastward toward the Our (pronounced "*Oor*") River. Patton's tanks had rolled back the entire southern edge of the German bulge and was closing in on beleaguered Bastogne, still held by the now famous 101st Airborne.

In Junglinster, Luxembourg, as our company luxuriated in houses apparently abandoned by their owners, we received the wool socks and snowpak boots we'd so desperately needed before. The boots had tall leather tops sewn to a rubber shoe, and they replaced the cumbersome combination of leather combat boots and buckled overshoes. They were not insulated, but they were light and warm with the wool socks, and we were mighty grateful. Wool Eisenhower jackets were also issued, and these fitted under our field jackets for extra warmth.

Also making its appearance, and this for the first time in

my Army experience, was a liquor ration of six different bottles or fifths for each officer. Since I didn't use the stuff except for occasional medicinal purposes, and since I was feeling fine at the time, I called in First Sergeant Nagel and had him split my ration among the NCOs. Some of the officers offered to buy it from me, but I thought they already had enough, and nobody pressed the point—possibly because I was their commanding officer.

At this time Lieutenant Colonel Kenan, who remembered my interrupted R & R in Luxembourg City, insisted that I again try to take some time off. Thus I found myself riding in the lead cab of a three-truck convoy of the battalion's enlisted men bound not for Luxembourg City but for gay Paris itself, for some reason the dream city of almost all GIs.

When we arrived at our hotel some two hundred tedious miles later, I was surprised to find I was the only officer in the convoy. The duty was real Rest & Recreation, with no command functions at all for me. The men were simply told at what time and where to report back in three days and were then turned loose on a city the chief wartime industry of which seemed to be women.

Well, the GIs took off in wild jubilation like a bunch of kids on the last day of school, and I was left to myself, in dignity, sitting on the steps of an old second-class hotel.

It was not long before I found out that it is quite possible for an American to be lonely in teeming Paris, the warm and beautiful metropolis of hundreds of small neighborhood villages, sidewalk cafés, fruit and vegetable markets. It was a city with an excitable, war-weary populace. It was dead winter, five long months after the hysterical, emotional tidal wave of the Liberation on August 25, when we were showered with cookies, candy, flowers, all sorts

of bottles; when we were smothered in kisses and em-
braces; when men, women, and children screamed and tore
about in riotous celebration.

Now everything was strictly business, cold and imper-
sonal. I couldn't read or speak the language, and I felt
more like an interloper than a triumphant liberator. The
liberated weren't above cheating the foreigner, for the few
small purchases I made in English-speaking stores and arranged to have sent home to Michigan never arrived.

The black market was in full swing, and the price of a
dinner in a restaurant was about $25—equivalent to some
$75 or $100 today.

Nonetheless, I was determined to see the sights and get
some variety, even though walking down a snow-swept
pavement without having to worry about mines or tree
bursts or burp guns was entertainment enough for me. I
gaped at the Eiffel Tower. I dutifully inspected the Louvre,
Notre Dame, and other imposing buildings from the outside—for they were still closed to the public. Then I
strolled down the Champs Elysées from the Place de la
Concorde to the Arc de Triomphe and its torch for the
Unknown Soldier of that War to End Wars. Standing at that
memorial, I felt a bitter irony.

I was raised in small towns and in the country, and just
as many city boys had never milked a cow, I had never
ridden a subway. I was intrigued by the Métro. The trains
were clean and swift, and they rocketed along in underground tunnels until they eased into a perfectly clean station.

Another phenomenon that impressed this country lad
was the men's rest rooms. It wasn't so much the relatively
sanitary conditions prevailing that seemed so unusual to me
as the way this was achieved. They were cleaned by
women, matrons who came when they pleased, without

knocking and without thinking the least about it. It didn't seem to embarrass the men either, for they gave no indication that they even noticed the women.

This lack of prudery was more evident on the city's streets, where men's relief stations were practically in the open, tiny, circular brick kiosks around the interior of which urinals spiraled. They were screened in to about shoulder height, but passing women could see the men standing there, and certainly there was no mystery as to what they were doing. Most of the women seemed to pay no attention to the open-air contrivances, which bore the none-too-elegant name of *pissoir* (pronounced "*piswa*"). In fact, some women casually conversed over the barrier as they waited for their companions inside.

While I can't imagine any such device in even the worst slums of an American city, I suppose there is a certain modesty in ignoring a natural function instead of calling attention to it by hiding it. Anyway, that was Paris.

I got to know the subways better than most Americans as I rode from one station to the next. Every now and then I would get off to window shop. The exploration would have been more pleasant if I had had a French translator along, but I managed to stay out of difficulty, at least until the very end. On one ride I was surprised to find that the train was no longer underground when it stopped. It was dark outside, and I suppose that's why I hadn't noticed our emergence. Everyone got out and walked away, and the train showed no signs of moving on, so I got out to look around and get my bearings.

My confusion must have been pretty obvious, particularly with my uniform marking me as a stranger, and soon a very kind lady of about fifty came up and asked in English if I needed any help. I asked if she knew when the subway was going back to town. She smiled sympathetically and told me there would be no more trains until morning, that I had been on the last one.

Then she offered to help me find a room and walked me about a block to the only hotel in that part of town. She spoke a few words in French to the manager and then hurried off to her family.

Early the next morning I took the first subway back to the city, grateful that the little misadventure had not come on my last night in town, when I would have missed the convoy back to Luxembourg. I never would have lived that down, and no one would have believed what actually happened and that no French lass was involved.

I ate breakfast as soon as I returned to the city, and then I started to wander around town. I did a little shopping. Although I was most certainly minding my own business, I was stopped time and again by the ubiquitous ladies of the moment. While I possessed all the standard male urges, I did not find the propositions particularly tempting. The poor souls were not especially attractive. They looked worn and haggard.

Anyway, that too, was Paris in all its variety. A few months later I was to encounter a unique situation in this regard, a situation which came my way in the form of an assignment.

One pleasant surprise as I strolled around was a huge American Red Cross sign on a nearby building, and I thought this might be the place to get a cup of coffee and perhaps some suggestions about what to see and do. The suite was nice, clean, and comfortable, and best of all, everyone spoke English. It must not have been much of a lure for the GIs, though, because I was the sole visitor.

The French Red Cross hostess was a pretty girl with a sweet smile and dulcet voice. We had a pleasant chat on places to visit in the city. After a while she asked if I'd like to have dinner with an English-speaking French family. When I agreed it might be nice, she told me to come back at six. She would arrange for me to meet a couple who had been educated in the States.

I made sure I was punctual, but after waiting in the lobby until almost 7:00 P.M. I got up to leave. Thereupon my pretty friend came over and explained that the couple had just phoned to say they had a sick child. They asked her to give me their apologies. She felt responsible for ruining my dinner plans and told me it was too late for me to get back in time for dinner at my own hotel, but she said that if I didn't mind waiting another fifteen minutes until she went off duty, she would be glad to guide me to a nearby place that was not dependent on the black market.

A little while later when I saw the big "American Officers Club" sign on the hotel she led me to I understood her maneuvering. I really wasn't too upset. She knew where to get a good meal, and I didn't mind the company.

Inside the huge lobby a group of officers was queued up to buy meal tickets. I joined the line, and soon, to my astonishment, got two tickets for only twenty-five cents each. That was the price officers were usually charged for meals when in garrison, but I didn't expect it to apply in Paris, where everything else was so inflated.

With tickets in hand and a young lady at my side, I followed the other officers up a long, magnificent staircase to the dining room. I was flabbergasted, and perhaps a little intimidated, by the luxury of the immense lobby and mezzanine. I was in for a shock, though, when the second lieutenant posted at the door refused to admit us to the dining room. Improper uniform, he said. Then I noticed that all the officers were in full-dress "pinks", I was wearing an olive-drab uniform with an Eisenhower jacket.

Instantly I grew angry, and I asked if he thought I

should go back to the front lines and draw a proper uniform. He was obviously embarrassed and quickly apologized, saying he was partial to the infantry and didn't realize I was fresh out of combat. Rear-echelon people sometimes irritate; how can they stand on formalities? How little effort and time it takes to be considerate.

As we were ushered to a table several senior officers glanced our way, but none seemed to object. I couldn't believe the food, having almost forgotten that such lavish, delectable victuals existed. Along with T-bone steaks came mashed potatoes and brown gravy, green beans, rolls, butter, coffee, and pie. I ate very, very slowly and handled the silverware ever so carefully. The club was a wonderland.

Although no one nodded or smiled at my pretty young French friend, I realized she must have been in that arena more than once, and I certainly didn't blame her. What did bother me, however, was the kind of life our rear echelon troops, especially the officers, seemed to be leading. My mind took a nasty turn as I saw myself, in sudden fantasy, as commanding general of the area, putting all those fancy people permanently on K rations and sending them up for a tour of front-line duty just so they'd know there was a war somewhere. (Ah, daydreams.)

The young woman and I talked for hours, and I gave her an idea of the realities of the front. She went on at great length about the ordeal of French families during the Occupation. Her only brother had been killed by the Germans, and her parents had kept her a virtual prisoner in the house the whole time so the Germans wouldn't see her.

She excused herself just before midnight and took a cab home, saying her parents probably were beginning to get worried. We did make a date for lunch at my hotel the next day. Our trucks were due about one o'clock, and I didn't dare miss them.

The next day she arrived on time, looking fresh and

pretty. It was fun watching her order our lunches, with
wine—which I'd never had with a meal. I was pleasantly
surprised. The arrival of the trucks cut short our luncheon
and necessitated very quick farewells. I could only hope,
and I did so fervently, that the future would turn out happily for the truly sweet little French woman. She left me
with my only really pleasant memory of an interlude in
Paris.

Our return trip was dismal and dull, if rather noisy.
Some of the men were still high on drink and even higher
on their memories of conquest. Most of them had indeed
broken loose, and they could not stop talking about it. According to their unending chatter, they must have been the
greatest studs ever on earth. On and on and on. At least the
trip had been something of a change for them, and for a
while they might not even mind the war so much.

The Second Battalion was still in reserve at Junglinster.
Other elements of the Twenty-second Infantry Regiment
had retaken some territory to our northeast along the Sauer
and Our Rivers. We heard it had been pretty rough crossing
the swollen rivers. Rumors also had it that General Patton
himself had come up and personally pushed the attack forward, though I never did find anyone who had actually
seen Patton.

The German breakthrough had driven a wedge between
the Fourth Division and the remainder of the First Army, so
we had been transferred to General Patton's Third Army.
The general's influence was felt in many ways. Everyone
was required to salute, and officers had to wear their insig-
nia of rank at all times. Such civilities stopped, whether
Patton knew it or not, the moment we got into action. Even
the food, when we were off K rations, seemed better, and
certainly we now could get necessities such as watches,
compasses, and field glasses that we hadn't been able to

order successfully in the First Army. I recalled my resentment back in September when I had read in *Stars and Stripes* that Patton had just received ten tons of new maps and aerial photos, while we in the First Army had to struggle with the maps of 1914.

I felt that General Hodges, commander of the First Army, was just as good a general as Patton, though he certainly couldn't compete with Patton in charisma. The gains of the First Army in crossing France and Belgium in August and September, not to mention the D day invasion itself, certainly equaled those of the Third Army. They just didn't seem as spectacular. There were times when we resented all this, and yet we certainly all rooted for Patton.

We heard Patton was the American general the Germans feared the most, and this we relished. We also heard that he had a very quick temper and that he instantly replaced officers who did not do what he thought were their jobs, so everyone around him feared him. We also heard that his type of leadership was vital to Allied victory, and for that, I think, most of us loved Patton. I think the Germans feared Patton because he was very aggressive and unpredictable. He made them worry about what he might do next, so they had to be prepared to defend their lines more carefully than would otherwise have been the case.

XV

THE SCHNEE EIFEL—SECOND TIME AROUND

Near the end of January, 1945, the Fourth Division headed back northward, having completed its task of holding what turned out to be the southern flank of the Bulge, thus permitting Patton's tanks to go inward behind the flank and then roll straight north to rescue the 101st Airborne in Bastogne. The first day of the trip north was routine convoy. The next day, which was about February 1, we reached Bastogne itself, though by then all the fighting was over.

We, who had done our share of attacking small towns, were nonetheless awed by the total destruction of Bastogne. Everything was leveled except for a few skeletal sidewalls. What had not been knocked flat by artillery had been gutted and hollowed by fire. The dust had not quite settled, and the smoke carried a stench like that of soggy burning mattresses.

The desperate Germans had attacked Bastogne viciously with what must have been overwhelming force. The defenders were shelled with furious barrages from tanks, artillery, and mortars, and as they continued to resist the Germans were forced to bring up reinforcements needed elsewhere and to reroute panzers away from this vital crossroads near the middle of their breakthrough.

Delays would be fatal to the Germans because there were very few days of bad weather to keep Allied planes out of the skies. And the Germans had every military right to success at Bastogne. It was not their fault they'd come upon intrepidly stubborn troops with an indomitable commander, that the rubble from their shelling became breastworks, that the defenders would endure any privations and losses rather than surrender.

It was appalling to me to imagine the fighting that must have gone on there. Many bodies still lay where they'd fallen, partly covered by blankets of snow. One long, wide, gradual hillside was strewn with the carcasses of burnedout Sherman tanks and a few German Tiger tanks. Evidently our losses had been several times greater than those of the enemy, probably because of the powerful 88s mounted on their Tiger tanks. Further on it seemed that our Air Force had gotten in some good licks, for the fields were littered with the debris of German tanks and trucks.

We stopped for the night several miles northeast of Bastogne and were lucky enough to find a few vacant buildings as shelter against the cold. Standing nearby were several German tanks, apparently abandoned because they were out of gas. They seemed to be undamaged, and even in repose they were fearsome, with those wicked 88mm rifles sticking out ten yards, it seemed.

Although the fleeing Krauts had not had time to destroy them, they still might be booby-trapped, and the colonel had warned everyone to keep away. Left to themselves, our men just could not resist those massive souvenirs, and they began to nose around. Some of the bolder ones actually mounted the tanks as crowds of the more cautious gathered around. As some of the curious explored deeper the inevitable booby traps blew up, killing and wounding several of the more foolhardy men. I was not on top of the scene and was grateful that at least none of my men were victims.

The terrain was becoming more and more familiar to me, and I realized we were retracing the route we had taken when chasing the Germans over four months before, in September. We learned that our overall mission was to penetrate the Siegfried Line at the very same spot we'd broken through before. We had first taken this sector in the middle of September, 1944; then the Twenty-second Infantry had moved north to the Bullingen area. From there, in November, we moved north again to the terrible Hürtgen, and then south, to Luxembourg and what turned out to be the Bulge. Now, in late January, 1945, we were headed north in December, again.

While the campaign maps would show that the Twenty-second Infantry did indeed, by some curious coincidence, revisit the same sector of the Siegfried several campaigns apart, in truth it was nowhere near the same Twenty-second Infantry. Most of the present Twenty-second were replacements; of the thirty-odd officers originally in the Second Battalion, I believe only three remained active— Captain Arthur Newcomb, Lieutenant Lee Lloyd, and myself. All the others had been killed or wounded. In addition, we had lost many replacement officers over the last five months.

We were on the same winding country roads through the lovely town of Houffalize on the way to Saint Vith. Back in September, Saint Vith had been a very charming little farming town left unmolested by the Germans, who had not tried at all to defend it. The only signs of war had been a few scars on buildings from stray rifle bullets.

I had been aware of the heavy fighting there during the

Bulge, but I still was not prepared for my next view of the town. Saint Vith was in an open valley, and from the approaches of its southern heights we got a clear view of its total ruin. All we could see were the jagged outlines of the shattered walls that had once been buildings. It was like a nightmarish surrealistic painting. Nothing was undamaged; there was no sign of life.

This time around the Germans had made innocent little Saint Vith a key supply and communications center, and as soon as the skies cleared our own bombers had made it a prime target. I hoped that if any natives had still been in town they had had some warning. Nothing could have survived that bombing. In one area of perhaps two hundred square feet, for instance, I counted five huge bomb craters with rubble all around. I was sickened by the destruction.

Somewhere among all the debris some GI had found a naked mannequin and placed it alongside the road, where it stood out starkly, ghoulishly. The humor might have been a little sick, but certainly was a diversion wild enough to cling to the memory.

Other units of the Army had already driven the Krauts back into the Siegfried pillboxes, so we didn't have to worry about ambush as we rolled along the winding roads from Saint Vith in Belgium across the German border into the town of Bleialf. This was something of an excursion compared to my small, motorized combat team that had probed the same paths in September, not knowing what the next turn in the road would bring and not even knowing exactly where the Siegfried was.

One could not help reflecting on the battles we had fought in the same area in September, 1944. We also wondered how many lives had been lost for what appeared to be no gain after almost five months of hell. How far could we have gone if allowed to attack back then? It is easy to second-guess other people's decisions, but the men responsible for the big decisions had a lot to worry about before and after any major campaign.

There was also a big difference in the roads themselves, for now they were solid with ice and snow. The retreating Germans had not had time to plow snow. Their tanks and trucks had just pushed ahead as fast as they could, and there was a six-inch base of ice and compacted snow.

Our tanks could negotiate anything but the steepest hills and sharpest curves, and one such obstacle came just east of the hamlet of Buchet, very close to the Siegfried. The rubber treads and steel cleats of the tanks could not get enough traction on the steep inclines and could not make the sharp turns because in changing direction one tread was braked to become a stationary pivot while the other tread kept moving. The trouble was that the pivot kept sliding on the ice.

The engineers had tried setting off primer cord explosives to break up the ice, but all that did was leave small burn marks. They then sent out a call for extra manpower to dig corrugations that would aid traction, and F Company was elected, since we were in reserve. I was told to have my men use their entrenching shovels to chop out small grooves or ditches across the road about every foot of the way. This particular hill was over a half mile long, so we were out there hacking away all night.

Every now and then we had to take cover against *Nebelwerfer* shells screaming overhead; but the worst discomfort, aside from fatigue and the cold, was the ice that kept getting chipped up into our faces and the occasional hitting of one's own foot or shin with a shovel. It was a very tough night for us, but at least we had the satisfaction of seeing the tanks' tracks biting into the ice trenches and pulling them up that hill before dawn. We were given the next day off, away from the fighting, and we stayed in reserve slightly to the rear.

The Twenty-second Infantry, with its First and Third Battalions leading the attack, once again sliced through the Siegfried Line at the same spot it had before—just east of Buchet and slightly north of Brandscheid. The infantry advanced by fire and movement supported by artillery and the fire of tanks, and with the use of hand grenades and flamethrowers when the men got close enough. Some pillboxes had grenades dropped down their smokestacks; others had their apertures blasted by flamethrowers. At least one was plowed under by a bulldozing tank. The Germans never should have started this business. We proved once again that fortifications can be taken.

The Second Battalion moved on through our First and Third battalions and headed southeast, going into defensive position east of the fortified village of Brandscheid. This time, in contrast to its frustrating fight in September, the Third Battalion swept right into Brandscheid and took many of the pillboxes from the rear.

At that, Brandscheid was not a joyride for the Third Battalion, for even after they had taken the town and were being relieved after dark by a battalion from the Ninetieth Division, they were hit by a strong counterattack. The Germans swarmed in on top of the normal confusion of men trading places, and soon hand-to-hand combat was taking place in the darkness, with some Americans being killed by others. For a while our troops were afraid to move, but after a time the enemy was sorted out and driven back.

Next day the First and Second battalions continued the attack eastward toward Sellericher-hohe. Soon we came to the edge of some woods and looked out on a valley and hillside that brought back a frightening recollection to a few of us. This was the place where the German artillery had massacred a battalion back in September. We had been up on the hill on what was now our left front, and we'd been helpless spectators in grandstand seats as the attack battalion had come out of those very woods and swept the Germans before them in what looked like a classic exercise in tank-infantry support. It wasn't until they'd gotten way out into the open that the Germans brought down deadly barrages of artillery that tore the attackers apart and finally sent them in stampede back to the woods.

To cross the same valley where so many had been casualties that September wasn't a pleasant prospect, and I was glad that most of our people didn't know its history. We certainly were forewarned, however, and we made sure our men were well spread out and alert to incoming Kraut shells. This time the wet slush and mud prevented us from taking any tanks along, and we were therefore less of a target in the open. We had also heavily shelled the hills ahead before we attacked.

We did run into some well-entrenched Kraut infantry, but with the help of our artillery we were able to overrun them, and we made quick work of taking Sellericher-hohe and its roads and ridges.

Lieutenant Gesner, the OSS castoff, really distinguished himself as a good, tough infantryman. He was all over the place, moving his platoon. I saw him using three different weapons—a carbine, an M-1 rifle, and a Thompson .45-caliber submachine gun. He seemed to be firing a lot more than most officers, and instead of stopping to reload he'd trade guns with one of his men or pick up a fallen man's weapon. They all thought he was great. One time when he ran out of ammo at the edge of a trench he jumped in and began to club a German with his rifle butt. The poor German quickly threw his hands up.

* * *

While at Sellericher-hohe we ran into and were victimized by one of the major defects in the Army's generally reliable system of rank and command. The man with the higher rank always gets the nod over one with lower rank, with absolutely no regard for qualifications. This assumes that all promotions are fair and deserved, that all majors are better than all captains, that captains better than first lieutenants, and so on. This procedure is partly excusable in the sense that there's really no way of knowing which man is better qualified—until he's tested.

The worst part of this system, ironically, was the end to which the entire army effort was pointed, combat itself. In combat, which is what the army is supposed to be about, the testing was quick and conclusive. Yet those who qualified—yes, even survived to be useful—were not quickly promoted, even when there were existing vacancies in rank. Thus Captain Newcomb, who was serving so beautifully as battalion exec., which position called for a major, was always in danger of being bumped by an inexperienced new major. This sort of injustice was legion among combat officers, but complaints about it are not the petty griping they may seem; experience was a matter of life and death in combat.

Anyway, the problem struck us at this time. The Army had lost so many higher-ranking officers in the Hürtgen and in the Bulge that personnel officers scoured the corps of rear echelon and garrison officers and shipped them to the front as infantry replacements instead of promoting qualified men already doing the jobs. This is not to imply the new men were not good people; they simply were not experienced, and most of them were deeply embarrassed and uncomfortable at these circumstances beyond their control.

So Captain Newcomb was replaced by a major and sent

to take command of F Company, and I was reduced to company executive officer which forced Lieutenant Lee Lloyd down to platoon leader. Everyone was unhappy, particularly Lieutenant Colonel Kenan, who was not responsible for the assignments but had to live with their results. But it was a reunion of sorts, for Newcomb, Lloyd, and myself; we'd all been together in the old E Company.

Captain Newcomb was very quiet when he arrived to take over command of F. He was the only D day officer left in Second Battalion, and he had long since deserved a majority. Lloyd and I were a little depressed. In fairness, it is probable that those people who should have been pushing our promotions had been too busy, yet the memory of Colonel Lanham's words, "If you survive, I'll promote you," was beginning to irritate.

From Sellericher-hohe, Second Battalion's attack continued eastward, with one of the rifle companies drawing the nasty job of taking Hill 553 (hills were named for their elevation). This hill was directly in the battalion's path to both Obermehlen and Niedermehlen, and from its height the Germans could control with artillery all the approaches to both towns. In addition to elevation, the Germans also had the advantage of concealment in the two sizable patches of woods near the crest.

A few hours before dawn, our attack company went up the open slopes of Hill 553 in full darkness and was lucky enough to surprise the defenders and rout them. Before there was enough light for the company to completely set up their defenses, the Krauts struck back in a furious counterattack led by bellowing SS troops. Our men were quickly thrown back off the hill, though most of them made it back to where they'd started.

This misadventure was no fun for the attack company,

and it turned out to be even less fun for us, because Captain Newcomb was called to battalion headquarters and ordered to retake Hill 553 at once, in broad daylight. The advance just had to continue, and it couldn't unless we had that hill. Colonel Kenan gave him the use of tanks and tank destroyers but said they'd have to stay on the road because the ground was thawing and the heavy tanks and tank destroyers (TD) might get mired in the mush.

Captain Newcomb asked me to go with him to reconnoiter possible approaches, and the two of us walked several hundred yards southeastward along the road from Sellericher-hohe to Niedermehlen. The uphill side of the road was thickly lined with trees, and the banks were high; we were able to move about easily behind this cover, from which we had a good view of Hill 553 and its surroundings. From our concealment we used field glasses to study 553 and its patches of woods from a distance of about a thousand yards.

After a while Captain Newcomb, the old pro at about twenty-seven, veteran of every battle since D day, turned to me and said, "This looks like the place to jump off from. We can move the tanks and TDs along this road and use them to give us support fire."

We discussed using heavy barrages of artillery but decided to use the direct fire of tanks and TDs as the primary weapon, with the artillery in support. The other attack company had told us about the formidable log bunkers up there, and we figured low-line direct fire would be more effective.

We brought our men up against the high bank of the road out of sight of the enemy and lined up the tanks and TDs along the flat stretches, giving them specific target areas in the patches of woods. They would be firing directly over the heads of our advancing men, and they'd use high-explosive shells to keep the Germans under cover while peppering the area with their 30-caliber and 50-caliber machine guns. The artillery FO was also with us, and he had the same targets.

Captain Newcomb then had the men spread out widely, and he personally led them out onto the open hill slope as I directed the tanks and TDs to commence firing. The only problem in the beginning was the stunning shock waves from the 75mm and 90mm rifles of the armor as the men were still close in. Many of the men had to sling their rifles so they could get both hands up over their ears. The rolling thunder of the big guns made it impossible to tell whether the enemy was firing back; I could not see any evidence of incoming artillery.

With Captain Newcomb in the center and the platoon leaders and their platoons spread out to his left and right and behind him, the attack moved in orderly fashion with everyone walking very fast. I was coordinating the whole show. The crucial decision, for which I was already tensing though I had a few minutes yet, was when to lift the straight-line, overhead fire of the tanks and TDs. Artillery was also laying down an intense barrage on the hilltop, but its shells arced in with plenty of clearance of the ground troops and could be lifted later.

The tough decision was when to lift the 75s and 90s. If I stopped the firing too soon, the Germans would rush out of their bunkers and blast our men when they were exposed on the open slope. If I waited too long, I might wipe out my men from the rear. I was sweating, but at least I could clearly see the men and the shell bursts of our 75s and 90s. I watched closely through my binoculars as the advance continued, and I knew the men were scared to death hearing their own shells whip a few feet over their heads while waiting for the enemy to open up.

All I could do was watch and worry. It was the first time I'd directed that kind of fire, and I could only hope this was not the first time the armor had done it. I also knew that short rounds cropped up occasionally, and I gave a fleeting worried thought to the workers back in the States who had packed the shell cases. Now and then I put down my field glasses and checked the men directly because I didn't want the magnification to make me think they were closer to the top than they actually were.

When I finally gave the command to fire, the barrage was extremely intense and accurate, giving us exactly what we wanted. The Krauts could not come out in that awful blasting; they must have been terrified, strained to the limit of their nerves. Our men continued to walk rapidly up the slope, and I knew they were not getting any return fire because none of them hit the ground.

My moment was almost at hand, and I watched closely through my field glasses. When they seemed to be only a hundred yards from the edge of the woods I couldn't hold out any longer, and I signaled the tanks and TDs to cease firing. The artillery FO then raised his range slightly to clear our men as they reached the edge of the woods.

As they got near the bunkers the infantry was firing from the hip. Most of the Germans were so shaken that they stayed in their shelters. They offered almost no resistance as our men moved in and captured them. Their SS commander tried to get them to fight but was unsuccessful.

I made my way quickly up the hill, and when I arrived a few minutes later everything was completely in our hands and our boys were jubilant. German prisoners were being led out, along with an arrogant SS officer in full dress uniform and long coat. He was mad as hell, and I only wished I could understand his German sputtering.

Captain Newcomb was busy setting up our new defense,

so I took over the care of the wounded, of which there were only two. Both were given some first aid. They were then able to walk back to the aid station on their own. Remarkably enough, only a few of the Germans were wounded, a testament to the quality of their bunkers.

The sides of those dugouts went down about four feet into the ground and stuck up another two feet, with the dirt from the excavation being piled against the front and on the roof. The walls were logs about fifteen inches thick, and they could take anything but a direct hit. The entrance was in the back, and in front were machine gun trenches and communication trenches. Inside, the walls were lined with bunk beds, enough to accommodate eight men comfortably, twelve in a pinch.

The attack had been an absolute classic, worthy of any textbook on tactics. The advance had been almost a thousand yards uphill across a wide-open slope, with close overhead fire support, against a strongly entrenched defender. It was my first experience in this kind of precision attack, and I'm not so sure I would have thought of the correct solution all on my own. I hated to think of the losses we might have had if a green company commander had had the job. I marveled at the savvy of Captain Newcomb, and while I was as disgusted as he with his demotion, I had to admit it probably had saved a good many lives.

All the gratification of this triumph was taken away by one of our discoveries. It seems that after the Germans had retaken the hill with their vicious counterattack earlier in the day, they had taken a small number of prisoners and tied them up with telephone wire, probably for safekeeping. At the outset of our tremendous shelling the Germans had apparently rushed to their bunkers and abandoned the prisoners. It probably would have been too much to expect a German to risk his life to save a prisoner, and thus some more Americans were killed by their own shells. It was small comfort that only a few were found there.

The defense was all set up for the night, and we had just finished our K-ration supper when Captain Newcomb received word from Colonel Kenan to report to Batallion for a company commanders' meeting. Much to my surprise, and some consternation, the captain asked me to go in his place. He should have been flushed and excited from the afternoon's great achievement, but instead he was just quiet and reserved. Never before had I known him to beg off anything at all. But I didn't ask questions.

The company runner and I walked back down the hill to Sellericher-hohe and battalion headquarters. The moon was bright and the countryside so serene and peaceful that we almost forgot why we were there. We turned right at the road and soon were close to the scattering of buildings that was the hamlet.

Several men seemed to be loitering in front of one of the buildings, and they didn't bother to challenge us; this slackness irritated me. As I came closer, all set to bawl them out, I realized they were Krauts and quickly turned my rifle on them and yelled at them to put their hands up. They did at once, being as surprised as I. I found out later they had been on patrol; they were lost in the darkness and had been too busy talking to recognize us. We took them prisoner.

Then, to further ruin my disposition, the guard at battalion headquarters only fifty yards away also failed to challenge. I grumbled to Colonel Kenan. He was pretty upset, because almost anyone could have captured his headquarters. One of his staff went right out to check, and I'm sure someone caught hell.

The Colonel asked briefly about Captain Newcomb and

then got right down to business. The next day, February 8, F Company was to wait until it was relieved by another company and then swing down the northeast slope into Obermehlen, now controlled by G Company. F and G then were both to attack eastward across the swollen river to the high ground beyond while another battalion would attack abreast of us on the south side of Hill 553 and go on to take Niedermehlen.

Captain Newcomb, still somber and very quiet, gave the briefest of routine instructions to the platoon leaders. He then led the forward elements in a wide semicircle to the rear and cut right around to the long, wide slope into Obermehlen. Enemy artillery began to pick them up as they reached the edge of town, but most of the men found safe shelter in or behind the buildings. It was my turn with the rear elements of the company, and I pushed them ahead as rapidly as possible over the exposed hillside. The shells soon started to drop in, forcing us to take cover. After each salvo, we got up and moved quickly forward, and we always managed to stay ahead of the next volley.

Suddenly the great good luck, the almost sensational good fortune that had blessed me for eight months, abruptly left me there on the open road to Obermehlen. I clearly heard the whistle of the shell and could tell by its sound that it was falling on me; I threw myself flat on the frozen ground so hard that my chin strap broke and my helmet flew off.

At that, I had a little luck left, for the shell hit about twenty feet directly in front with a blast that seemed to split my head. In an instant I heard the shrapnel whipping past and also got a sledgehammer blow on my left foot. I shuddered with the impact as I lay there stunned by the concussion.

The top of my snowpak had a jagged hole with blood

showing, and I wondered if my toes were gone. The whole foot was numb, for which I was thankful.

Everyone else seemed okay, so I yelled at the men to keep going and to tell Captain Newcomb I had a slight wound in my foot and would call him from the aid station. Some of them looked a little surprised, but they kept on toward town as I began to limp back to the battalion aid station.

I was interestedly watching the medic cut off my boot and expose the wound when I heard Lieutenant Lee Lloyd announce over Colonel Kenan's radio that Lieutenant Wilson had been wounded and Captain Newcomb had been killed. I lay there in tears. I had no idea what the medic was doing to my foot, and I only vaguely heard the colonel fill in Lieutenant Lloyd on the attack plan. Nothing really registered with me.

During my months of front-line combat death was something that came and went. I had lost some very good friends and had had to keep going, but never had the loss been so close and personal. Arthur O. Newcomb was my best friend in the Army, and I'll never forget February 8, 1945.

Captain Newcomb was by far the best company commander in combat that I ever knew, though he really didn't look the part. He was short and of slight build, with a sober, unprepossessing personality, but with a quick, dry wit and an exceptionally sharp mind. He took everything in stride, thinking ahead all the time and never giving way to panic. His men and officers grew to love him because, for one thing, they knew that if anyone ever could get them through, it would be Captain Newcomb.

Lieutenant Colonel Kenan, who was also terribly unsettled by the tragedy, later observed that Captain Newcomb was of that rare breed that can act and can inspire others to act courageously on a battlefield. He was an exceptionally able, brave, and gallant soldier. It was difficult to imagine any harm coming to him.

He was, I believe, an ROTC officer, and he used to talk a lot about the good times he'd had at the University of Wyoming and in the West. He also mentioned quite a bit about his family and their sheep ranch in the hills.

Some time later friends at F Company told me that shelling forced them to take cover in buildings as soon as they had reached Obermehlen. Captain Newcomb had been entering a building when a shell hit the doorway. A battle-wise veteran, Captain Newcomb should have taken any cover available, yet witnesses said he had made no effort to protect himself.

The Twenty-second Infantry Regiment went on a few days later to take the important rail center of Prum, the main mission of that campaign, but of this I am not able to give a firsthand account.

XVI

EVACUATION

As I sat flat on the floor of the battalion aid station my mind was on Captain Newcomb, and I was only dimly conscious of the medic sprinkling sulfa powder on my foot and dressing it. I returned to reality when a jeep took me to the rear battalion aid station, although I was still deep in shock. A medical technician used some surgical forceps to remove the piece of shrapnel from my big toe, telling me that the toe was broken and that I'd be going back for a nice long rest.

At the next stop down the line, regimental aid station, a doctor looked at my foot and decided to leave it alone. He ordered a medic to put a tag on me with a brief description of the wound. A short time later I was loaded into an ambulance with three other wounded men, then the driver headed for the field hospital fifty miles farther back. The trip was very bumpy over torn-up roads. The medic riding with us had to spend the entire time sitting or kneeling beside a casualty in an attempt to keep plasma flowing into him.

He was typical of all the medics I saw. They did their best willingly and unhesitatingly. We infantrymen knew that if we got hit, a medic would run out and drag us back in if at all possible. They were so dedicated, it seemed they simply ignored bullets. Actually, they were just as scared as we were.

It was almost dark when we reached the field hospital, and our stretchers were lined up on the floor of a large receiving room that must have been a gym. The place was unheated, and someone threw a blanket over each of us. Medics walked up and down the lines of stretchers weeding out the most urgent surgery cases, and my turn came after about a two-hour wait. As I looked out across the gym at row after row of stretchers the scene reminded me of one in *Gone with the Wind*. It is always the infantryman who suffers worst in war.

I was stripped of all my clothes and personal belongings by an orderly. Nothing was ever returned. Perhaps it was a bit of poetic justice—the most valuable object I had was a gold watch with a diamond marking each hour. I had taken it from a fifty-year-old German who had been sent to the German infantry as a replacement when we first attacked the Siegfried Line in September, 1944. He had formerly been stationed as an interpreter in Paris, where *he* had taken it from a shop. Though offered as much as $300 for the watch, I had decided to keep it. I wonder if the orderly ever got home with it. I also lost a very good Luger pistol.

Surgery was a small room with a few gas lanterns and the usual table. The young surgeon who worked alone there looked extremely tired. He gave me a local and quickly began to clean out the wound. Then he began to cut along each side of my toe to get at the ends of the severed tendon and tie them together. He told me there was nothing he could do about the bone, which was cut almost through.

I tried to sit up to watch him in action, but he firmly pushed me back and said, "Sorry, but you can help me more lying down."

He finished tying the tendon, sewed up the wound, and then taped a protective wire cage over the foot.

Early next morning we were moved by train to a nice, large hospital not far from Paris. There my wire cage was replaced by a walking cast. We stayed about two days and then were put on a train to Cherbourg, where we were loaded on a hospital ship for the crossing to England.

While on the English Channel headed for Plymouth, England, my stomach got very upset, and I vomited. At first the doctors thought I had the usual seasickness, but when it persisted after my arrival at the 101st General Hospital near Bristol the doctors became quite interested. Three were assigned to work on my problem. After experimenting for three or four days with the usual tests and remedies for stomach ailments, with no cooperation at all from the patient's stomach, they gave it all up and decided to start from scratch.

They went into my medical history right back to childhood, particularly about digestive problems, of which I had had none. Then they came up to the recent past and asked about my eating habits in the Army. They probed and found out I had been almost entirely on K rations since June, 1944. That they couldn't believe, so I explained that I'd been on the front continuously for eight months and that we received normal food from our kitchen trucks only when it was safe to bring them close to the front. That had not happened very often. I said it was a safe bet that about ninety percent of my total meals had been Ks and that there were stretches of several weeks at a time when we never saw our kitchens.

The doctors explained that they had had a great many

combat veterans come through, but never anyone who had been in combat so long. I felt they were being polite, that they really didn't believe me, so I told them to check my records.

They finally took my word for it and decided the long siege on K rations had gradually changed my stomach so much that it couldn't readjust to regular food. Then they put me on pap, and my digestion cleared up right away, though not my disposition. I was starving, and they wouldn't help me. The other men in the ward got deliciously loaded trays, and all I received was a little dab somewhere in the center of my plate. After about a month they relented and put me on a regular diet. I never thought hospital food could taste so great!

While my toe wound was legitimate enough, about twenty other men were in the ward, and every one was in worse shape than I, which made me feel somewhat out of place. A couple of them had been riding in jeeps that were blown up by mines, and their bodies had been shattered. Worst of all was a soldier who had nineteen fractures in his arms and legs. He was strung up in traction with several pins through each leg. His condition was so bad the doctors couldn't even move him into the operating room for the setting of still more fractures, so a team of doctors and nurses worked on him in the ward. I watched in fascination as they knocked him out with a shot and then used a bone drill and put more pins in his legs. We could hear the bones grate as they were being set.

That night this poor fellow, who never complained, had a bad dream. He screamed and thrashed around in the bed and yelled at his men as he fought a battle all over again.

I rang for a nurse, who was elsewhere, and then hobbled over to his bed and tried to rouse him out of the nightmare by talking to him and very gingerly shaking him. He didn't respond, so I slapped his face quite gently, which brought him around. I hated to do that, but the nurse later told me he was probably doing himself a lot of damage tossing around.

The doctors worked on him for several more hours the following day then kept him under heavy sedation for the next few days.

After the war, I met our ward nurse near home, much to our mutual surprise. She told me the poor fellow was in her ward for over a year but finally did recover.

About a week after my cast was removed, I was transferred to a rehabilitation hospital near Barnstable. There we went through a program of exercise, some pretty darned severe, but it did have the salutary effect of getting us back in shape. For recreation we played volleyball and ping pong, and after a while we were given passes to Birmingham, eighteen miles away.

While there I also managed a short orientation course under the exchange program at Birmingham University, and I even wound up living in a very posh private boys' school adjacent to the university. There, despite the war, everything was most formal.

As part of the course, we also visited some public schools, a government slaughterhouse, and the city's water system. This last was a major problem because the water for that city of over two million came over open viaducts from rivers in the hills seventy-five miles away. The Germans had sabotaged the system for a while, and the people suffered shortages. Water had to be trucked in.

Most interesting of all was our trip to the very old city of Coventry, the site of the immortal King Arthur and his legendary Round Table. Less than one hundred yards from the King Arthur collection was a church dating back to A.D. 500 that had been hit by German bombs. About seventy-

five percent of the church was in ruins, but the local people
had pledged to rebuild it.

In mid-April I must have been in a most peculiar state of
mind because I actually passed up a chance for a brief
vacation in Ireland. It seemed I was silly enough to want
to get back to the Twenty-second Infantry before the
war ended. Soon I found myself in a replacement center
—"Repple-Depots," we called them—near Birmingham;
because my records showed I'd been a company commander in combat, I was given command of a company of two
hundred black troops and was told to get them equipped
and delivered to France.

For a staff I had five white officers and one black, and I
should mention that at this time in history there was no
such thing in the Army as integration. All the officers had
been wounded and were returning to duty. Of the two
hundred enlisted men, only three had been wounded in
battle; the rest were mostly V.D. casualties.

It was something of an adventure to keep the men
equipped. What was issued one day might be gone the
next. Every day thefts were reported to me. Some of the
men sold, traded, or gave away their personal equipment. I
soon learned that some of the local Englishwomen were
available for cash or goods.

Most of the men had had very little schooling, and their
ringleaders, most of whom had decent educations, seemed
devoted to keeping them stirred up. The black first sergeant
was very good, however, and he soon had the ringleaders
picked out. Our job then was to try to keep them so busy
they didn't have time to bother anyone. Nonetheless, I did
have to break up one knife fight, and I also had to stop dice
games, which usually led to combat, though not the kind
we were in Europe to fight.

At last we were ordered to stand final inspection before embarkation, and some of these actors went all out to louse up the inspection and delay returning to their units. One character even lipped off to the inspecting major when ordered to turn in his personal luggage to the sergeant for shipment home. This black soldier, a really huge man, deliberately addressed the major as "captain" and told him he'd have to come and get the luggage himself if he wanted it so damned bad.

Without an instant's hesitation, the major jerked the luggage from the man's hand and tossed it to the sergeant. The big soldier just sulked as his cardboard suitcase was taken away. Later the major confided to me that he thought the soldier wanted to be thrown into the brig, and that the best punishment for such men was to return them to the front.

Next the doctors lined the men up for "short arm" inspection, and, of course, that also had its antics. Some of them still had V.D., and when these souls were pulled off the list for shipment out they laughed and clapped their hands with glee and sometimes did a little jig.

A few days later, our group did indeed reach Le Havre, France. To my immense personal relief, the unit was broken up, and the men were shipped out to their own units, mostly service or truck companies. My stint as their commander had lasted only ten days, and I very much doubted I could have coped much longer. Keeping the men in the proper equipment was a constant worry. Lack of cooperation can be immensely more frustrating than some days of actual combat.

I was immediately assigned to a replacement pool. Next day we began a series of moves back to our outfits. If this had been the time of the Bulge, we could have been shot back to the front by express, but now we had no great priority, and the Army seemed in no hurry to return us to our units.

Our first stop was a French military base behind the Maginot Line, and we stayed there for three or four days in nice brick officers quarters much like the permanent buildings on the main post at Fort Benning, Georgia.

One day we toured the Maginot, entering this massive underground defensive line through huge doors in the rear. The French captain guiding us admitted that the Germans had taken that sector of the impregnable line simply by going through a gap and approaching from the rear, which was not defended.

The fortifications of the Maginot Line were four stories of concrete, with two stories below ground and with the excavated dirt being piled on the sides and on top so that it looked like a long, low ridge. There were apertures for small arms fire, for machine guns, and for cannon. Large gun turrets facing the front were retractible and had periscope sights so the crew could operate entirely behind the cement walls. What amazed me, though, was that the largest guns behind all these elaborate, expensive turrets were only the old 75s of World War I.

Other features that impressed me were the conveyor systems for feeding ammunition to the guns, the comfortable living quarters for the crew, and larders with enough supplies to withstand any sort of siege for at least three months. Overall it was a tremendous engineering feat, of which the natives still seemed quite proud. It was an even more outstanding example of military futility. The old French generals had still been planning on static trench warfare. Even if they'd been able to stop the Germans from breaking through a gap, it would have been easy for the Germans to drop paratroops and take the undefended rear.

And yet the Germans—the inventors of the modern

warfare that obsoleted the Maginot—themselves built a Siegfried Wall, which we were able to break through in only one day.

In addition to touring the Maginot, we were also allowed to visit a nearby town of some five hundred folks. One thing that should be said about France, and probably much of the Continent, is that they openly accept as matter-of-fact and part of normal life some institutions that more strait-laced nations endure, if at all, more discreetly. Thus the local sin emporium was flourishing, in no small way supported by Army personnel, and the base commander recognized it to the extent of sending in Army doctors to examine the girls.

Then all of a sudden some higher Army commander ordered those spas closed at once, and it became the job of the current guard—led by me—to execute the orders and evict the madam and about twenty girls. Our orders did not require us to follow through, however, so the girls were soon out on the streets enterprising.

Finally, after so many long, bleak years for the natives and pain and suffering for all of us, Victory in Europe—VE day—arrived! May 8, 1945: The population exploded into the streets and danced and drank the night away amid fireworks and everything else they could cut loose with. Some of us got a little homesick. All of us celebrated on this happy occasion.

The balance of our trip to Nuremberg was interminable, slow, and unpleasant, for we no longer rated anything but the infamous 40 & 8 boxcars—forty men or eight horses—and I wouldn't treat a horse that way. Occasionally we were sidetracked for supply trains headed east into Germany and for long trainloads of pitiful Frenchmen who had been slave labor for four years and who were headed home to France. Their faces were thin, and their eyes were set in deep, dark sockets. They were jammed in worse than we, with barely enough room to stand. Though dirty and helpless, they still were going in the right direction, and they waved in wild excitement as their boxcars crawled past.

I couldn't help thinking of the awful shock some of them might be facing—houses in ruins, wives who had fraternized, children fathered by the enemy, no money, no jobs, no prospects, and nothing but the shakiest government.

Nuremburg, which we went through on trucks, was my first view of a major city bombed by the Allies. Besides being an important railhead, it was also a highly emotional target as the sacrosanct heartland of the Nazi cult, the wellspring of Hitlermania, the breeding ground of the Third Reich plague.

British and American bombers had attacked day and night, hitting it with everything from incendiaries to blockbusters. Fires had raged out of control, and we heard that casualties on one night's raid reached 75,000. Blocks and blocks were level acres of rubble. Now and then we would see a building with some outer walls gone, the inner floors still suspended in midair with furniture, rugs, and bedding standing intact, looking like a huge dollhouse.

The old walled inner city was completely demolished. Nothing was standing, nothing moved. It was all broken bricks and dust.

The rail yards were a mess of shattered boxcars, steam engines, and roundhouses. Heavy rails were bent like wires, some being twisted into giant corkscrew spirals thirty or forty feet in the air. Wooden ties were splintered or burned, and even the heavy steel supports under boxcars were melted so they sagged to the ground.

At one point we passed the massive, deserted stadium

Hitler had built for his mass rallies, and I remembered the newsreel shots of the sea of rabid, uniformed, chanting disciples responding to his posturing and ranting.

Our trucks continued out of town toward Bamberg, present home of the Fourth Division, and I couldn't get used to the sight of former German soldiers still in uniform, for that's all they had to wear, straggling homeward. They were walking; even the few who had bicycles just walked beside them as though afraid to ride on the highways with all the American trucks. They didn't eye us directly, and their appearance was most ragged and dejected. Nevertheless I had the feeling they were deeply relieved that it was all over.

The other civilians we happened to see were mostly women, and their expressions were uniformly stiff and unsmiling. In addition to the usual fear of conquering invaders, still an unknown quantity, they must have had their worries about whether any of the stragglers would turn out to be sons or husbands.

I reached Bamberg, headquarters of the Fourth Division, about May 10, and soon I was in a jeep headed for Rothenberg and the Twenty-second Infantry Regiment. Colonel Ruggles, our new regimental commander, greeted me warmly and told me Colonel Buck Lanham had been promoted to brigadier general and transferred.

We had a pleasant chat about all the changes in the Twenty-second and in my Second Battalion during my absense. Then I asked if he knew what had happened to my promised promotion to captain. He told me that all promotions for the Second Battalion had been scrapped. I gathered that for some reason Colonel Lanham had gotten mad at the entire Second Battalion, had discarded the suggested promotions, and had even replaced Lieutenant Colonel

Kenan. I was never able to learn why.

I told Colonel Ruggles that it didn't seem fair to penalize those who had earned and deserved promotions, and I asked him to recommend me for a captaincy based on his personal knowledge of my record. This may seem pretty pushy, but I knew I deserved a captaincy and was gradually learning to speak up for myself.

Without hesitation, Colonel Ruggles said he would be happy to put my name on the list but that he couldn't promise anything now that the war in Europe was over. As it turned out, the Army had frozen all promotions. He tried again once he reached the States, but that, too, was denied, so I remained a first lieutenant.

A jeep now took me to Dinkelsbühl, headquarters of Second Battalion, where I reported to our new commanding officer, Major Clifford "Swede" Henley. I had heard of the big Swede and had seen him a time or two but never had met him. His welcome was warm and pleasant, and he introduced me to several of the new officers. I also shook hands with some of the veterans, including Captain George Kerr and Captain McClain.

Major Henley was extremely decent to me, and I could tell by his somewhat uncomfortable manner that he was most reluctant to have to tell me he had no company commander positions left in the battalion, that the best he could do was offer me a job as company exec. What I replied, in effect, was, "From all I can see, sir, my experience alone makes me senior to almost any company commander in this battalion. I want a company here or in another battalion. If you really can't make enough changes to give me a company, then I'll go back to Colonel Ruggles and ask for a transfer."

I can't imagine myself having said anything remotely like that a few short months earlier, and it's a wonder he didn't throw me out. Instead he just said, "Well, give me a couple of days to see what I can do. Hang around battalion headquarters and maybe we can work things out."

So I was given a room in the small hotel that served as battalion headquarters, and a few days later Major Henley sent for me and asked if I would agree to take command of H Company. That's about the way he phrased it. I told him a heavy weapons company (water-cooled machine guns and 80mm mortars) would be new to me, but I was sure I could handle the job.

So it was arranged. Charles Pillard, H Company's commander, went to battalion headquarters as an Assistant S-3, and I became commander of H Company.

In H Company's area of operations was a German military hospital filled with wounded German soldiers, and this had to be guarded. I assigned Sergeant Flipowitz and two squads of men to the job. They had no trouble at all keeping things under control.

Also nearby, though not my company's responsibility, was a large prisoner-of-war stockade filled with German soldiers. As might be imagined, German officers and noncoms kept the strictest discipline within the stockade. These Germans were still official prisoners, and it must have been odd to them to see former comrades-in-arms who had lain down their arms at the end of the fighting walking about freely on the outside as they straggled homeward. As a matter of fact, there was some irony in this, for we American conquerors were still indentured to the military while our vanquished paraded around as instant civilians. Of course, we had another war going on halfway around the world in the Pacific, and some of us worried that MacArthur might be aware of the fine combat record of the Fourth Infantry Division. He was, we learned later.

Another thing we kept a wary eye on was an old camp for a few hundred displaced persons just released from slave labor. These poor people had existed in long Quonset huts where they were packed in like animals, being forced to sleep on the floor in rows. They had been imprisoned in filth, and the first steps in their emancipation were hot showers and delousing, a clean set of clothes, and burning of the old rags. After a few days, they were sent on their way home, which for most was in the Balkans.

As for our relations with local civilians, there weren't supposed to be any. The Army had set up a strict ban against what it called fraternization, which was emphasized with a 9:00 P.M. curfew. That seemed the safest rule, considering the number of irrepressible mischief makers among our ranks and the newness of the peace.

One of my men soon proved the value of the rule. He finagled a jeep and driver from the motor pool after the curfew and, with the generous help of a Lithuanian refugee, located a friendly place where he could load up on local moonshine. After a while, delightfully drunk, the man pushed the driver into the passenger seat and took over the wheel. Soon he had up enough speed on the gravel road to miss a turn, totally wreck the jeep, send the driver to the hospital with a back injury, and kill the refugee. Apparently totally relaxed, the cause of it all walked away with a few bumps and bruises.

His luck didn't end there, either, for the battalion commander let him off with a severe reprimand and even classified the jeep as our final combat loss to make it expendable. A few weeks later, and the fellow would have had to pay for the jeep. Given Army pay in 1945, that might have stretched out a while.

Another disturbance in our routine was the arrival of some replacements directly from the States. The group had been lucky enough to hit the end of the war, but one of their number at once ran into combat with our first sergeant. The veteran top sergeant, a virtuoso in the art of chewing out GIs, had been getting a little out of practice due to our humdrum duties, and he pounced lovingly on one of the new men. This unfortunate had been a "saltwater" corporal, one appointed unofficially and very temporarily for the duration of the journey. He had decided unilaterally to keep the rank and sew on real corporal's stripes. He also had some whoppers on his service record, and when this form finally reached the first sergeant there was something of a verbal explosion. After the sergeant had run out of words, he scratched a six-foot-by-six-foot square on the ground, presented the new private with a pick and shovel, and had him dig down six feet. Many, many hours later, when the excavation was completed, the sergeant was quite pleased with it, and as a reward he let the man fill it up again.

As for living quarters, we were practically in garrison. One big school building housed the whole company. Our only continuing problem was the electricity, for we never knew whether we were plugging into A.C. or D.C., 110 volts or 220. Several of our people blew up radios before we figured out the system.

The geography there was reminiscent of Michigan farmland, with its rolling hills, wide fields, and patches of woods. Another link to home was the type of storage bins in common use, which were very similar to what we called fruit cellars when I was a boy in Michigan: mounds of earth lined with straw to hold potatoes, carrots, turnips, cabbage, etc. The vegetables kept well all winter and could be dug up as needed.

Peacetime duty in Dinkelsbühl was most pleasant; our most serious overall business was recreation. Some of us became pretty good at pitching horseshoes. At first we were handicapped by having to use what was available, and this meant the huge old iron shoes of local farm horses. After a while we acquired the regulation shoes used in competition and soon were holding tournaments.

Although we had to be mindful of fraternizing, we didn't think this applied to the local trout; some of us picked up some of the best trout fishing ever in the small river that ran right through town. The Burgermeister managed to come up with old cane poles, lines, and a few hooks. We then dug up some worms and headed for a bend in the river about a mile out of town, where he had suggested the fishing was exceptionally good. Lee Lloyd and our driver went along, and after about three hours we came back with almost a hundred nice ten- to fifteen-inch trout for the cooks.

This simple, pastoral life couldn't go on forever, and in June, 1945, we entrucked for the first leg of our move home. Soon we bivouacked near Furth. Our entire company stayed in tents on the edge of a big hayfield, and without much else to do we watched interestedly as the German farmer, his robust wife, and his strong-armed daughter cut the entire field by hand using cradle scythes. Then they used huge rakes with wooden tines to get the hay in rows to dry. The farmer in me noticed the hay had to be turned a couple of times in the next few days.

When the hay was finally dry, they loaded it onto a wagon drawn by a big draft horse and a milk cow hooked up side by side. The farmer stayed on the wagon, and the two women pitched all the hay up to him.

It was a crude, old-fashioned way of farming, but it worked. I supposed that Hitler could not spare the metal for farm machinery and that many of the workhorses had become military casualties.

After a few more restless weeks with plenty of horseshoe pitching, we were happy to board the trucks again for the final overland leg as we followed the autobahn to Metz and then traveled clear across the rest of France to reach the English Channel at Le Havre.

Our ships were not yet in the harbor, and this meant a few more days to kill in a tent camp nearby. Practically all my time went into tedious paperwork, for Customs required a declaration to be made out for each nonmilitary item a man wanted to bring home, and the company commander had to examine every piece of paper and then sign it. Later, when we reached the States, the Customs people didn't look at a single thing, and all that paperwork had been for nothing.

Finally, on July 3, we boarded the famous Liberty Ship, the U.S.A.T. *Excelsior*, and sailed for the good old USA.

For several days the seas were high, and the ship pitched and rolled and vibrated severely when the stern came up and the propeller was out of the water. Our speed was cut to about five knots, and we didn't think we'd ever get out of the Atlantic. I didn't feel too well most of the time, and once I was knocked flat on the deck by a sudden pitch. Many of the men were very seasick and spent most of their time below deck and away from the mess hall. Then, ten days out of Le Havre, we landed at Hampton Roads, Virginia, along with M Company, while the rest of the regiment was landing in New York.

We were given thirty days off, but that wasn't too much for all the things on my schedule. From Le Havre I had written Florine, my bride-to-be, that she should go ahead with the wedding arrangements. I estimated my arrival home at about July 15. As it happened, I missed it by two hours, arriving home in Grand Ledge, Michigan, at 2:00 A.M. on July 16. No one was at the station to meet me. I had wired, but they never received the message. So I phoned from the station in Lansing and that brought everyone to attention. Soon they all arrived to drive me the last twelve miles home.

I had been gone fifteen months, over half of it in combat, and there is no describing the delicious feeling of being home again. The feeling doesn't last long, and it has to be earned, but during its fleeting moments it is absolute bliss. I couldn't believe it; I was *home*!

On July 21 we had a nice church wedding and a big reception, which was what Florine wanted. My dad loaned me his 1937 Hudson Terraplane, and a friend at a Shell station got me some gas coupons for the short honeymoon trip to Grand Rapids and Half Moon Lake, near Stanton. We rented a lakefront cottage, and our honeymoon was beautiful.

News of the first atomic bomb dropped on Japan came while I was still on leave, and a few days later came the tremendous news of Japan's complete surrender. At that moment I happened to be in Grand Ledge, and I could not control nor was I ashamed of the tears that suddenly flooded my face. I now was a married man, and the Fourth Division would not, as rumors had insisted, be part of the invasion of Japan. I was flooded with relief.

Just as I was beginning to adjust to the incredibly pleasant civilian life my thirty days' leave ran out, and I had to report back to the Fourth Division, now at Camp Buckner, outside Durham, North Carolina. Florine soon joined me, and we came upon a small two-room apartment in Durham for $40 a month. It had a kitchen equipped with a kerosene stove, a portable tin oven, and an ice box. I also picked up a 1942 Hudson and shared rides with other officers back and forth.

The peacetime Army wasn't too bad at that point. We managed to keep ourselves occupied with much routine and a halfhearted training schedule. I couldn't help but notice that some of the men marching out to remote training areas seemed to have extra bulges inside their shirts and that some of their rifles looked an awful lot like softball bats.

Finally the Army faced the inevitable and set up a system of priorities for releasing its guests. They awarded points for time in service, with extra points for overseas duty and five points for each major campaign and every medal. I was one of the lucky ones to get an early release, rolling up over a hundred points with my three years' service, fifteen months overseas, five major campaigns, three Purple Hearts, two Bronze Stars, and one Silver Star.

On September 30, 1945, one day after my twenty-fourth birthday, I became a full-time civilian. Three years and eleven days had passed since my first encounter with the United States Army.

Jobs were scarce, and many people were out of work now that war production was over. I could have returned to my old job on the railroad, but I just didn't want to; I was a different person. I found I liked to deal with people face to face, person to person, and it seemed the best place for that was in sales. I started off with vacuum sweepers, which I sold fairly easily until the company went on strike. I went into other lines until I wound up in insurance. There seems to be further irony in my life in the fact that I, who as a young man saw so much death and destruction that carried with it no compensation whatsoever—except perhaps the honor of having fought with courage and distinction—should go into a business that attempts to put a price on a loss.

Out of all this damned useless war I hope I am entitled to a few simple observations.

The cost in grief and devastation, if it's on the scene, is so immeasurably expensive that no one really wins. No human being disputes this fact of life, so why can't human beings think of this *before* a war?

If war there must be, then above all it must be kept

away from our shores. If I and all of my fellows learned one thing, it was that. Keeping war at arm's length may not be possible with modern long-range weapons, and so there must be no war in the first place. Such prevention seems possible, with human beings, only if there is strength overwhelming enough, and obvious enough, that no one would dare take the first step toward war.

The war we fought in Europe was uneven enough when calculated in terms of puny men in the face of incredible firepower and colossal war equipment, unfair enough when seen in terms of the futility of strategy in the face of brute strength. It was surely the last war in which strategy could still be employed and make a difference in outcome. Nuclear weapons are bound to render this time-honored convention of war null and void.

One of the most visible religious leaders of the world, the Pope, stood at the memorial to the dead at Hiroshima and proclaimed that mankind must take a step forward in wisdom and emotional maturity so that this sort of catastrophe will never happen again. I hope we are up to it.

Let there be peace!

INDEX